PRAYERS
that *Heal*
the
HEART

ENDORSEMENTS

"In their book, **Prayers that Heal the Heart,** *Mark and Patti Virkler give us valuable practical tools for applying the teachings so many of us have pioneered in inner healing and deliverance. Much has been discovered. What has been lacking is how the common man can apply inner healing revelations to his own life. Some have wanted healing to happen sovereignly, by God's intervention, or through the prayers of others (requiring little personal effort), and sometimes it does occur those ways. But we who are in the inner healing ministry have long wanted tools to help those who know that healing often requires diligent personally disciplined efforts. Mark and Patti's book goes a long way towards filling that 'how-to' gap. Their book is really a workbook, an invaluable hand-out for counselors to assign to their counselees. Much healing and transformation can result from its use."*

John Sandford
Co-founder of Elijah House

"A person who is sick and doesn't know it will never go to a doctor. A Christian who is crippled on the inside but who

thinks his life is normal will never ask for help! Many Christians struggle with major issues in their life but are ignorant of the fact that the victory Jesus won for them on the cross does not only assure them of eternal salvation, but also provides the keys to healing.

"Mark Virkler's new book is a very practical guide to how the keys to healing that are contained within Scripture can be applied with great effect in the life of a believer. His own testimony illustrates how God brought deep healing into his own life as he looked again at the consequences of things that had happened in earlier days and was willing to let God have His way. The road to healing is not however a road without choices. Some of the choices are like crossroads with different ways to go—do I go this way or that way? Am I willing to forgive or not forgive? Am I willing to own mistakes I have made or am I going to sweep them under the carpet? Am I going to admit to the consequences of wrong relationships or pretend they never happened? Have I really understood that in life there is a law of sowing and reaping? These and many other issues are tackled with sensitivity and genuine insight and in such a practical way that the teaching can be readily applied.

"An excellent book which will encourage pastors and people alike to begin a journey towards wholeness and realize that discipleship and healing are two facets of the same precious diamond of truth."

Peter Horrobin

International Director of Ellel Ministries

Ellel Grange, England

"Mark and Patti have creatively and concisely expressed the Lord's revelations to them, to us, and to others. We are

delighted that the revelation, understanding, and necessity for the Integrated Approach to Ministry will be shared even more broadly throughout the Body of Christ. The Virklers have expressed these revelations in a very user-friendly and practical way. With the exercises and worksheets, anyone that desires can use these tools to receive more healing and freedom from the Lord. This is His Heart, that our hearts be healed."

Chester and Betsy Kylstra,

Founders and Overseers of Proclaiming His Word Ministries.

"Dr. Mark Virkler's **Prayers that Heal the Heart** *deals in a comprehensive way with the prisons we find in our minds and hearts—prisons of repetitive sin, self-hatred, traumas and pain that seem never to go away, and demonic oppression and attacks. Many Christian leaders are still carrying wounds that only Jesus can heal, and these wounds become destructive time-bombs that Satan sets off to destroy leaders at the peak of their fruitfulness for God's Kingdom.* **Prayers that Heal the Heart** *effectively helps to defuse these silent time-bombs by letting the Holy Spirit pin-point the lies that need to be exposed and the memories that need to be healed. This book will show you how Jesus still heals the broken-hearted and sets the captive free."*

Dr. Gary S. Greig

Educational Advisor

Wagner Leadership Institute

"While much of what you have written relating to the issues (generation, vows, judgments, etc.,) and the consequent

prayers that can bring healing is not new, the inclusion of your material on listening to God, on the visual, dreams, experiences and related content, gives this book a unique place among those resources directed toward healing the heart. One of the key things we find in our prayer counseling ministry that significantly helps in a person receiving his healing is his understanding and ability to hear God speak to him. This is an area we often find ourselves having to teach the person who has come for counseling. So we bless you in this venture and look forward to being able to recommend this book to those who come for ministry."

Will and Madeleine Walker

Pastors: Prayer and Care

Toronto Airport Christian Fellowship

"I have recently finished reading Mark's book, **Prayers That Heal the Heart,** *and have found it a very insightful book. As you read through the pages of this book it becomes clear how a mental stronghold is developed in one's life and how that same stronghold can be pulled down. Mark points out that as the Holy Spirit is given the opportunity to reveal the many strongholds in our lives and also given the liberty to replace them with the truth of God's Word, a person begins to experience the abundant life in increasing ways. I would heartily recommend this book to all who would seek to experience the reality of Jesus' words where He said, 'If the Son sets you free, you will be free indeed.'"*

Rev. John J. Koch

Pastor: First United Mehodist Church

Cape May Court House, NJ

"The new book by Dr. Mark Virkler, **Prayers That Heal The Heart,** *is an outstanding work worthy of reading by every believer. Contained within the pages of this highly readable manuscript are keen insights born from the Word of God and the authors experience as wounded healer.*

"The need for clearly established patterns in prayer to bring about deliverance and inner healing has been needed for many years. This book provides to the struggler and the counselor tools for effective and professional ministry.

"As a counselor for the past 25 years, I can highly recommend this work for personal study, Bible College teaching or for usage as a tool with clients."

Stan E. DeKoven, Ph.D.

Licensed Marriage and Family Therapist

President, Vision International University and

The American Society for Christian Therapists

"As I read the draft of **Prayers That Heal the Heart,** *I realized that this book was going to be to me—and to many, many others also—what Mark Virkler's* **Communion With God** *was. In 1985, there was a overwhelming hunger in my heart to be able to hear from God on a continuous basis. At that time, I heard about Mark's course and went to his retreat in Aurora, N.Y. My life would never be the same.*

"In recent years I have become increasingly aware that there were blockages, bondages and strongholds in my life. These things were inhibiting my spiritual growth and were preventing the life of Jesus from freely passing through me to others. Some of these things were of long-standing. Other things appeared to be things I had 'picked up' through my responses to life that was happening to me.

"Mark's book, **Prayers That Heal the Heart,** *has come along, again, at just the right time. If the Church is going to be the people of God He intends them to be, we are going to have to be healed of the things that have kept us in virtual prisons. The walls we have built around ourselves so that we won't be hurt, or fail, or be rejected again have become dungeons, locked from the outside, from which we need Jesus Christ to set us free.* **Prayers That Heal the Heart** *will be uniquely used by God to help the Body of Christ so that they can be the people that will usher in a new century in which "the knowledge of the LORD will cover the earth as the waters cover the sea."*

Rev. Maurice Fuller

Queens Park Full Gospel Church

Calgary, Canada

PRAYERS that *Heal* the HEART

PRAYERS that *Heal* the HEART

Mark & Patti Virkler

Bridge-Logos

Newberry, Florida 32669

Bridge-Logos

Newberry, Florida 32669 USA

Prayers That Heal the Heart
by Mark and Patti Virkler

Library of Congress Catalog Card Number: 2007924468
International Standard Book Number 978-0-88270-852-2

VP 06-17-19

TABLE OF CONTENTS

DEDICATION

Special thanks to Ellel of Canada, Peter Horrobin, Steve and Kay Cox, Chester and Betsy Kylstra, John and Paula Sandford, and Bill and Sue Banks, whose ministries have provided the stimulus for my healing and for the writing of this book.

Special thanks to Gale Chapple and her counselees who allowed us to test out these principles and worksheets in their counseling sessions. One third of the book came as a result of these real life counseling sessions. In them the process and worksheets were perfected considerably.

INTRODUCTION

This book is the result of the united efforts of both
authors. The concepts and ideas are a culmina-
tion of cooperative study and revelation. The experiences described are common to both. The pro-
noun "I" is used to demonstrate the unity of our
thoughts.

Who needs *prayers that heal the heart?* Everyone! Everyone should be led through these prayers at the point of salvation, at certain, specific times throughout their lives, and
whenever led to do so by the Spirit. Marriages would be
built on stronger foundations if both partners experienced
these purifying, healing prayers during pre-marital counseling. All believers would be more joyful, more powerful, more
effective in every area of their lives if they would use these
prayers to follow the examples of John Wesley and the Jesu-
its in annual self-examination, cleansing, and re-dedication.
Each January, Wesley required his followers to take stock of
their lives to find out where they were with the Lord, and
Jesuit priests were required to do a nine-day retreat every
year to examine their lives.

The pre-requisite for healing the heart is that one has made
Jesus Christ his or her Lord and Savior. It is also important
for the counselee and the counselor to be able to hear the

voice of God. It is only God's voice, vision, and anointing which heal the heart.

This book is not designed to be an exhaustive study of all the topics covered. Instead, it is designed to be a working manual for individuals and counselors to use in healing hearts.

The bibliography lists books with more exhaustive documentation of the scriptural basis for the various prayer ministries recommended in this book. I will lay a brief biblical foundation for each prayer approach. However, the reader who wants a more extensive biblical foundation will find it in the books in the bibliography.

Twenty years ago I ministered a lot of deliverance. I prayed for hundreds of Christians and ejected thousands of demons from their lives. However, I became discouraged with the ministry because sometimes the battle to get the demon out was intense, and I hated sitting there for thirty minutes commanding a demon to leave while it refused to budge. I didn't know why it wouldn't go, and I wished I had a road map for the heart so I could navigate it with more certainty. However, I didn't.

I did add inner healing to the process, and that proved to be a great complement to deliverance. However, I still did not have a guide to the heart, so I was glad to train others in what I knew and delegate the inner healing and deliverance ministry to them. I could press on to other things.

God has finally given me a map for the heart of man, which is an understanding of the truths which underlie the seven prayers of this book. These prayers, when used together as a group, and in a sequential way, have proven to be powerfully effective in healing the hearts of man, and in releasing demons quickly and easily. Chester and Betsy Kylstra have been instrumental in showing me and others many aspects of an integrated prophetic counseling approach. I am very thankful to them for their pioneering work in this field.

The deliverance prayer takes place after five other prayers have accomplished their work. The first five prayers dismantle the demon's home and remove any possible areas which the demon could use to anchor himself into the person's life. With the anchors dislodged and the house dismantled, the demon must leave with very little hassle. Deliverance has again become an exciting ministry for me, for I have insight on to how to effectively root the demons out.

The Foundational Prayer that Heals the Heart - The Prayer to Make Jesus your Personal Lord and Savior

The absolute first step to healing the heart is asking Jesus to give you a new heart and a new spirit (Ezekiel 36:26-27). This occurs at the point of salvation when you ask Jesus Christ into your heart to be your Lord and Savior.

You see, man was created hollow at his core. We are vessels (2 Corinthians 4:7) needing to be filled with something. We are temples (2 Corinthians 6:19) needing to be inhabited by (a) God. The God of this universe, Yahweh, desires to fill and control you from within. He desires to commune with you and to have fellowship with you from within your heart and spirit.

This He will do if you invite Him into your life, your heart and your soul. He enters when you give over the reins of your life to Him, when you acknowledge His rightful place as Lord and Savior of your life. Then He takes His place upon the throne of your life, washes away your sin, and restores fellowship with you through His Holy Spirit which He joins to your spirit. He actually joins Himself to you (2 Corinthians 6:17) and begins to flow effortlessly out from deep within your heart.

So, you need to ask yourself, "Who rules my life? Have I given it over to the Lord, the Creator of the universe, or do I rule it?" (Isaiah 53:6). If you have not given your life to the lordship of Jesus Christ, then you need to do so now in a prayer of repentance. Pray the following from your heart:

"Dear Lord God, I acknowledge You as my Lord and my Savior. I repent and turn from going my own sinful way, and I acknowledge that You have the right to the reins of my life. I place my life back under Your control where it should have been from day one.

"I acknowledge my sinfulness and self will and stubbornness, and I turn from these sins and from the many other sins which come from my independent living. I acknowledge You as the One to Whom I will come for direction for my life from this day on. I ask that the blood of Your Son, Jesus Christ, which was shed on Calvary, be applied to my sins and wash them away as far as the East is from the West. Let them be remembered no more.

"Teach me Your ways. Instruct me in the way that I should go. From this day on, I look to You as my Lord and my Savior. Thank You for Your gift of eternal life, of life both now and in eternity. I worship You, Lord. In Jesus' Name, Amen."

This prayer, prayed from your heart, makes you a child of God and grants you eternal life in heaven with Him (Romans 10:9-10, John 3:16). It also re-connects you to the river of God within your being, so that your life here on earth will become much more full and rewarding. Welcome into the kingdom of God.

Lordship of God

If you hold out on God and don't make him your Lord, then your life will continue to have many problems, and your ability to be healed by the prayers in this book will be greatly hindered. He is the Lord of all. Let Him be the Lord of your life so your life can be blessed and so your healing can be swift and complete.

1

My Healing in Australia

Touchdown

Our plane landed at 6:00 A.M. in Sydney, Australia. It was the last day of August and the weather was still warm. The entire city was under construction, as in just twelve months the 2000 Olympics would be held here. My wife Patti and I spent the day sightseeing, taking in a bus tour of the city and a two-and-a-half hour boat tour of the beautiful Sydney Harbor. We hoped that if we stayed up all day we would be able to sleep in the evening and get our body clocks readjusted from Buffalo, NY, time, which was a full 14 hours different than Sydney time.

It worked. We slept the entire night and were ready the next day for a two-hour drive to Newcastle, where I would begin the first of five ten-hour Communion with God training seminars in five different cities in Australia.

This was my fifth trip to Australia in twelve years. Peacemakers Ministries had published our book *Communion with God* as well as other titles in Australia, and had been responsible for scheduling four of the five tours in Australia, including this one.

As I prepared for the first seminar at Church at the Bay, I

was aware of the inner tension in my heart, which had seemed to grow stronger in recent years. I struggled with fear and doubt and anger when I prepared to speak. I fought against them and sought to prepare my heart so I could speak and teach in the anointing of the Holy Spirit.

I *could* teach in the anointing of the Holy Spirit—that is what everyone always said. They would tell me that the teaching was so life-giving and so transforming that everyone came out of the seminars hearing God's voice and journaling and seeing vision. They were such exciting times, watching the transformation take place in people's lives. I loved it. And I loved the fact that God had allowed me the privilege of committing my life's ministry to seeing this happen over and over with audiences all over the world. What a wonderful opportunity to minister unto God in such a marvelous way! I truly felt I was blessed to be called by God to carry such a message to the world as communion with Him.

However, I was increasingly disturbed by the fact that it took longer and longer to fight through the issues in my heart so that I would be ready to minister. Over the last year especially, I had struggled with a fear that people would reject the message I generally spoke on Sunday mornings entitled, "Experiencing Covenant Blessings." During the worship time before I preached, I would battle with this fear of rejection and bind it and command it to go. Eventually faith would triumph and, sure enough, as soon as I began to preach, I was fine. The message was anointed, people were challenged and transformed by it, and everything was okay.

However, it was not okay with me that the battle seemed to have become more and more intense within my heart as I prepared to preach this message. Somehow I knew I did not have the faith and confidence that I had had in my younger years, when I was in my twenties—not that I'm old now, or anything like that! I'm *only* 47, you see.

2

In my twenties, I would attack and battle anything with no fear—probably because I had no common sense! Now that I had "matured," I had learned that there were things to fear. "Things to be cautious about," was the way I put it. My caution, however, was actually a constant inner battle against fear and anger and rejection.

It seemed like everything made me angry. When things didn't go right, I felt anger. When I "goofed up," I felt anger. When I heard about the antics of the government, I felt anger. When I viewed the phariseeism in the Church, I felt extreme anger. The fear of the New Age Movement (and anything and everything else) that the Church manifests made me angry. Was the Church called to live in fear or in faith? Faith, obviously, and so I stormed against their fear as I preached in city after city.

I was not too happy, however, with the inner anguish I was experiencing. I sensed I was "damaged goods," that life had dealt me some fairly heavy blows and my heart was not open and free as it had been in my younger years. Well, perhaps that was just the way life was. Perhaps as you grew older and wiser, you realized that life was not the utopia you had hoped it would be when you were young. Perhaps maturity was acknowledging the pain and the disappointments, and learning to live in an imperfect world, holding on as best you could. Perhaps I was just finally growing up.

Well, perhaps, but perhaps not, for you see the Lord was preparing me for big change. Just before leaving for Australia, I had finished writing a book that capsulized the lessons God had taught me during my 32 years as a Christian. One of the things I had reviewed in Chapter Four of this book, *Wading Deeper in the River of God*, was the ways God heals the heart. I had reviewed what I had learned over the years concerning inner healing, deliverance, renouncing negative expectations and inner vows, and breaking generational sins and curses. In addition, just a week before leaving for Australia, I had discovered from my mom that her father, my grandfather, was a Mason.

I was coming to the conclusion that perhaps I needed prayer ministry to heal some of these things in my heart. God's grace and leading always astound and amaze me! Not only was there a brand new book on Peacemakers' book table detailing how to become free from the generational power of Free Masonry, but at the first church I preached at in Australia, I met a surgeon, Stephen Cox, who told me how he and his wife work together in ministering to his patients. His wife, Kay, is extremely skilled in ministering inner healing, deliverance, and the breaking of generational sins and curses. He told me of one of his patients who had gone through two or three surgeries for abdominal pain, yet no one had been able to find the root cause. He asked this patient if she would like Kay to pray with her. She agreed, so Kay asked her, "When did the pain begin?" She answered, "About five years ago." Kay's next question was, "What did you do five years ago?" She replied, "I had my tarot cards read." A quick renunciation and prayer of deliverance brought this patient to health and canceled her need for future surgery.

Stephen said that he is careful not to give all his patients to his wife for prayer ministry, or he wouldn't have a job anymore!

That was enough for me. With my inner battle against anger, fear, and doubt, and eighteen days of constant teaching set before me, I asked what I should have asked for a few years earlier: "Is there any chance you and your wife could get together and pray for me?" The answer was immediate and affirmative. I was thrilled. The following day, Sunday afternoon after I had preached, we got together and Steve and Kay prayed for two-and-a-half hours with me.

Kay was the most anointed, effective, Spirit-led minister from whom I have ever had the privilege of receiving ministry. With an adeptness and skill that took my breath away, she identified various demons, negative expectations, and inner vows, along with generational sins, which we broke and of which I repented.

That day I was set free from various generational sins and curses, several inner vows and negative expectations, and about half a dozen demons. The change was powerful and instantaneous. I preached that night with a new freedom, a freedom I had never had in my entire 30 years of ministry, since some of these inner spiritual forces had been with me since birth. And some, of course, I had picked up in more recent years.

My new-found freedom lasted the entire 18-day ministry tour in Australia, and continues today, which is four months after returning to the United States and conducting seminars in Toronto, Buffalo, and New Jersey.

I was astounded! I am astounded—over several things. One is that I have experienced such a wonderful new freedom in my heart in the areas in which I received deliverance. These were problems I had battled for years and just assumed they were a part of who I was. I figured they were a part of the battle of life. And now I found that they were negative spiritual forces operating within me and seeking to bring me down.

How could I, as a Spirit-filled pastor and teacher in the body of Christ, make such a horrific mistake? How could I assume that these things were *me*, when in actuality they were demons within me? How could I be so blind to the reality of spiritual forces within me, especially since I had ministered deliverance and inner healing to hundreds, if not thousands, myself? How could I have battled these things, using ineffective prayers that did not solve the problems but only put a Band-Aid on them for a short time? How could I have been so blind?

I was elated over my healing, but aghast at the spiritual blindness which had allowed me to walk for so many years under the influence of negative spiritual energies within my heart and my soul. I knew I must search out and discover what I had failed to see. I realized I needed to experience an even deeper revelation of a truth I had written about years earlier, the truth that I am a vessel who contains another. Most of what goes on inside me is not me but the one I contain. The negative energies within me are driven by the sin energies of the curse and/or demons. The positive energies are empowered by the blessing and Holy Spirit of God. (See *Naturally Supernatural* by the same author).

Since I am a teacher, I wanted to share with others the story of my healing and my new understandings, so they would not need to walk in bondage as I had.

I began by rereading the books on my shelves on inner healing, deliverance, breaking generational sins, and renouncing inner vows and negative expectations, for I was sure these all worked together to destroy a life, and that the counselor who would heal must use them all together in order to be mightily effective.

I re-read *The Transformation of the Inner Man* by John and Paula Sandford, *Restoring the Foundations* by Chester and Betsy Kylstra, *Healing Through Deliverance* by Peter Horrobin, *Healing from the Inside Out* by Tom Marshall, and others.

I meditated and prayed, dialogued with these authors, and then wrote my story of what God was showing me so I would not be easily caught in this trap again, and so I could help others who were likewise in bondage to find the release and healing I had found. That is what this book is about. It is what I have discovered about how to determine one's need for such prayer ministries, what these ministries are, and how to progress through them. The design is practical, and has examples to help you throughout the material. As I come to the sections that discuss the different kinds of healing prayer, I will describe in more detail my own personal healing as it relates to the area being discussed.

I will try to be extremely practical, so an individual or a small group can pray through these different kinds of prayers and receive ministry themselves. Obviously, if one can receive ministry from a skilled counselor who knows all these types of prayer ministries and can minister them under the anointing and guidance of the Holy Spirit, that is by far the best. However, if that kind of person cannot be accessed for one reason or another, then this book becomes a place to start in praying these prayers for yourself and for others in your small group.

Available Ministry Centers

Centers which train in and offer most, if not all, of the prayer approaches discussed in this book include:

Chester and Betsy Kylstra's regional "Healing Houses," where you (and your spouse) can go for a week of intensive healing prayer counsel. You may contact them at Proclaiming His Word Inc., P.O. Box 2339, Santa Rosa Beach, FL 32459-2339; phone 850-835-4060; e-mail: office@phw.org; web site: http://www.phw.org; additional web site: http://www.healinghouse.org.

"Ellel" (the organization that trained Kay and Stephen Cox) offers many of the prayer ministries mentioned in this book. They provide training seminars and a place to go for healing. Their Toronto contact information is Ellel Canada, RR

#1, Orangeville, Ontario, Canada; phone: 519-941-0929; e-mail: info@ellelministries.org.

Ellel's main headquarters is in England. Their contact information is Ellel Grange, Ellel, Lancaster, LA2OHN, UK; phone: (0) 1524 751651; e-mail: info@grange.ellel.org.uk.

John and Paula Sandford have established "Elijah House, Inc." in Idaho where you can go for a week of counseling. They can be contacted at Elijah House, 1000 S. Richards Rd., Post Falls, ID 83854-8211; phone 208-773-1645; fax 208-773-1647; email: ehinfo@elijahhouse.org; Web site: http://www.elijahhouse.org.

The Idaho office can inform one how to contact the other Elijah Houses in Australia, New Zealand, Finland, Austria, and Canada, and trained prayer counselors in many places throughout Canada, the USA and the world.

I have received ministry over the years from Ellel and the Sandfords, and have sent several to Kylstra's "Healing House" in Florida. All offer an excellent ministry. Each has its own emphasis.

Pride and receiving ministry from a stranger

Was it easier for me to receive ministry from a complete stranger in Australia than it was from someone I know? Perhaps. I suppose we always like to think we have it all together and to project that image. To admit that we are not seems hard for some reason. Perhaps it is because we want to be more than sinners saved by grace. Perhaps we want to be able to say we have reached some outstanding spiritual level in our Christian walk, and to admit that we still have such negative energies harassing us just seems to be unspiritual.

Well, I have decided that it is best if I simply accept the fact that I am a saint who still sometimes sins. Without a daily dose of God's almighty grace to sustain me, I am nothing. I am content with that. If you need me to be more than that, then I will have to disappoint you. If I need me to be more than that, then I will just have to disappoint myself. Perhaps, however, being a vessel filled and sustained daily with the grace of God is a sufficient function for people. Perhaps I should be more than content that this miracle can happen on a daily basis. Perhaps I should be glad to simply celebrate this wonderful miracle and let it go at that.

Healing prayers we will learn about in future chapters

1. Breaking generational sins and curses from the third and fourth generation by putting the cross of Jesus between the generations (Exodux 20:4-6).

2. Identifying and renouncing ungodly soul ties.

3. Identifying and renouncing negative expectations.

4. Identifying and renouncing inner vows (underlying promises you have made because of the hurts you have experienced).

5. Experiencing inner healing, allowing Jesus to walk through the art gallery of your heart, removing pictures which do not have Him in them and replacing them with pictures which do have Him in them.

6. Experiencing deliverance, becoming free of demons in the name of Jesus Christ. Once the demons' home is dismantled by the preceding five steps, demons come out quite easily.

7. Breaking the enslavement to sin, by applying the law of the Spirit of life in Christ Jesus (Romans 8:1-2).

Personal Application

1. Are there any areas of your heart or mind that are under constant attack by the enemy? Do you fight with negatives in any area of your life? Is this a continual battle? If so, it is likely an area that could be helped with some prayer ministry.

2. Have you ever experienced inner healing, deliverance, or any of the other prayer ministries mentioned in this chapter? If so, can you recall and describe the situation and the release it brought to your life?

3. Are there any areas in your life today that might be improved if you experienced more prayer ministry?

Group Application

1. Invite people to share their answers to the above questions as they feel comfortable doing so. Do not force anyone to share what they do not feel ready to.

2. Pray at least a general prayer for God's sustaining grace to minister to the needs of those who share. If you have someone skilled in the prayer ministries discussed in this book, that person may feel led to pray more specifically for an individual in the group. If there is an individual in the group who desires such prayer ministry even this first week, invite him or her to volunteer and, as long as you have one in the group trained in at least one of these prayer approaches, that one, along with the group, may minister to the volunteer.

3. Close in worship for what God has done.

2

FOLLOW-UP MEDITATIONS
AND PERSONAL DISCOVERIES

*If we say that we have no sin, we deceive our-
selves, and the truth is not in us. (1 John 1:8)*

The release I felt in Australia and that continued afterward was wonderful and absolutely astounding. It reminded
me of my younger days when I felt whole and full of faith,
hope, and love.

And the release from workaholism was totally unexpected.
I didn't really believe that was a problem in my life. I loved
my work. I loved to do it. I enjoyed the drive I had. Someone
had once told me I was driven and I had responded, "No, I
have drive." Now I found, however, that the "driving" in
my personality had been removed. It even took me longer to
teach the "Communion with God" seminar. I would run about
15 minutes overtime each night because I was not pushing
so hard to get through the material. I was more relaxed. My
personality had changed as a result of my deliverance.

And fear was gone. When in a tense situation, I used to feel a spirit of fear grip my heart and mind. It would just sweep over me and take control of my responses. I would bind it and fight it off, but it was always ready to come back at a moment's notice, and I sensed it was never far away. Now that I was released from the spirit of fear, I no longer felt fear come upon me in threatening situations. My heart was relaxed and at peace and I could seek out a biblical and spiritual solution to the need before me.

The problem of doubt had been growing steadily worse for years. I doubted most things. I doubted the integrity of the government, the Church, individuals, institutions—you name it, I probably looked askance at it. I rationalized that it was because I was growing up, maturing, and seeing that things were not the utopia I had hoped and believed they were when I was younger. My real problem, however, was a spirit of doubt from which I needed to be set free. When it left, I was free to believe in people and events and even in the government—to believe that God does indeed work through all these things and accomplish His will in and through them.

It is not that I didn't believe theologically that God worked through governments even before I was delivered. I did. What my head believed, however, and what I could preach as true when under the anointing, was not what the emotions of my heart believed when the anointing to preach left. So I was one living in a dilemma: having a mind that believed one thing—faith, and a heart that experienced something else—doubt. After my deliverance, my heart also felt faith, it felt hope, it felt release from the anger and doubt and unbelief. It was so exciting and refreshing and wonderful. It was like being saved all over again.

My journaling in the days immediately following my deliverance went like this. You will note my intense frustration at having lived so long under these spiritual forces without recognizing my need for deliverance and inner healing.

September 5, 1999

My experience of deliverance yesterday afternoon:

Yesterday I received two-and-a-half hours of deliverance and prayer counseling ministry which was tremendous and healed my heart and my life.

I have never experienced this kind of ministry before, as far as it being so complete and powerful and healing and releasing. The woman who ministered to me was the most skilled, anointed, Spirit-led counselor I have ever received ministry from. It was a joy to be ministered to by someone so competent and skilled in her job.

I was freed from:

1. *Performance orientation (workaholism)*

2. *Distrust, fear, doubt and unbelief*

3. *Anger, wrath, hatred*

4. *Being judgmental*

Mark, I have healed you. Walk in My peace and in My power and in My deliverance and in My healing. Walk in Me and you shall stay healed.

Exhibit love, mercy, and forgiveness not judgment. Believe, trust, have faith, and hope.

Thank You, Jesus, for healing me.

You are welcome, My son.

September 7, 1999

I feel so free and healed and clean inside. All trauma and tension and anger and malice and being judgmental are gone. Thank You, Lord. Lord, I want to stay free.

You will, My son, if you stay in Me.

Lord, what does that mean?

That means to find your life in Me and not in yourself; to stay tuned to My Spirit, and not to your own heart and mind.

Lord, why didn't I get healed when I prayed myself?

Because you did not use the right approach to healing. You did not follow My laws. You did not repent of inner judgments and inner vows. You did not use deliverance prayer. You did not break generational sins and curses, and complete the other prayer ministry approaches that were necessary. Whatever you sow you will reap. You had sown many judgments and you were reaping the whirlwind.

I understand, Lord.

Processing judgment

Mark, do not judge lest ye be judged. The measure which you use to judge will be the same measure by which you are judged.

Walk in love and harmony and mercy toward others and you will receive the same.

You may judge truths but you may not judge people. You may decide to disagree with a truth a person holds, but you must not judge the person. Judging people is up to Me. They are My servants, not yours. According to their Master they rise and fall. According to their Master are they judged. Not according to you. You may judge truths and decide which are for you at any particular time in your life and share that. But do not become disdainful toward people. Hold My children up in respect and their gifts will flow toward you.

If you honor and respect the person, you still have an open door to them, to give and receive. If you dishonor and disrespect a person, you cut off the flow of My Spirit between you two. Never disrespect a person, even when disagreeing with his theology. Make it clear to him that you hold him in high esteem and value him and his positions, even if you happen to at this particular point in your life disagree with them. You change and he will change, so let's stay friends and continue to share ideas. He is not a "jerk," any more than you are a jerk, when you hold a position I disagree with. I still love you and honor you and respect you as I gently suggest alternatives, when you ask for them. I wait until you ask before I teach you. Then there is no opposition, because your heart is hungry.

Wait until people ask before you give answers. They are not hungry enough to hear and to listen and to see and to obey until they have asked.

Thank You, Lord.

You are welcome, My son.

Rest in Me and trust in Me and your life will be whole and complete.

My frustration (anger) at staying unhealed for so long

Lord, I do not want to be angry with You, but I am angry that it has taken me so long to discover the inner vows and negative expectations that have dominated my life. I need Your help in understanding the process, as well as why it has taken me so long to uncover this in my life.

Mark, truth is revealed in layers. You are to accept that as a fact in life. I am revealing layers of My truth to My Church and they are becoming healed as the layers are revealed.

As one seeks Me deeply concerning an area of life, I reveal that which he can handle at that time. Remember, I am a God who hides Himself and I only reveal Myself to those who seek Me with all their hearts.

15

Have you sought Me with all your heart for the healing of your heart? I think not. That is why you have not seen. Seek Me and you will find Me, saith the Lord of Hosts. However, do not attack or judge Me.

Lord, I repent. Please forgive me.

I will, My son. I will. Now seek Me and you shall find Me, saith the Lord of Hosts.

Note: To "seek God deeply in an area" means to me that I spend an extended period of time (usually about a year) immersing myself in the area, reading, researching, meditating, praying, experimenting and discussing the area with leaders in the field.

Some steps toward forgiving deeply, and processing anger

Lord, I thank You for Your wonderful power and grace in healing my heart. May the forgiveness run ever deeper, I pray.

It will, My son, as you allow it to. Go through the years of your life and forgive everyone and everything that has hurt you. Thus, you shall find healing.

I forgive fundamentalism for its legalism and phariseeism, and for the hurt it has brought against me and my life and so many others. I confess its sin and my participation in that sin as I have judged with narrow-mindedness and legalism.

I forgive and release them for passing on to me this sin and for the resulting curses in my life of anger, being judgmental, legalism, narrow-mindedness, hatred, and exclusivity. What I have judged has come upon me. I have become that which I have judged.

Lord, please forgive me of these sins and for the resulting curses I have brought upon my life. I repent of these sins.

I forgive myself for participating in these sins.

I renounce the sins of being judgmental, anger, legalism, narrow-mindedness, hatred, and exclusivity, and I break their power in me and all resulting curses through the redemptive work of Christ on the cross and His shed blood.

I receive God's freedom from the sin and from the resulting curses.

A revelation concerning what was creating doubt in my life

I have been battling to increase my faith for several years now. The excellent teaching of the church I have attended for the last four years has been a great help. I have also just meditated upon every verse in the Bible on faith, and memorized several of them. Recently, I also meditated upon every verse in the Bible on reason, since it was my reason that attacked my faith so violently.

I discovered that nowhere does the Bible ever command me to reason. The only time I am ever encouraged to reason is when I do it together with God (Isaiah 1:18). See the appendices for a discussion on "study versus meditation" and on the proper use of the mind (which is to allow God to use it through anointed reason).

As a result of my meditations, in recent months I had made some great strides in understanding what had been attacking my faith and how to overcome these attacks.

However, the battle with doubt was still there, because it was being amplified by a demon of doubt. When the demons of doubt and unbelief left, I could feel a definite difference within me. The constant force that drove me to doubt was broken and I was free to believe without a battle to overcome negative spiritual energies within me.

Then my concern was to understand what I had done wrong in the first place that had allowed the demon of doubt in me. What process was I using that was producing doubt? The answer became clear as I pondered it in the following weeks: I had not been properly relating to negative experiences in my life. The following are three key insights which will help me properly relate to negative experiences in the future.

1. God uses experiences to test our hearts to see if there is faith there. Abraham was asked to put his son on an altar and raise a knife to kill him in obedience to God (Genesis 22:1-18).

2. One must apply a proper understanding of the principle of sowing and reaping which is that, after you sow biblical truth and practices in your life, you will need to wait awhile for a harvest of biblical blessings (Galatians 6:7-9). The harvest will not be immediate. There is a growing period between sowing and reaping which may take many years, even generations. For example, the sin of not letting the land lie fallow every seventh year was finally reaped in Habakkuk's lifetime when the Israelites were taken into Babylonian captivity for 70 years. For a while after you plant new seeds of righteousness, you are still reaping the old crops of unrighteousness. It takes time to change the process around—to move from an ungodly harvest to a godly one.

3. If the experiences of life require us to die in faith, we are to do so, still believing in God! That is what the heroes of faith in Hebrews chapter eleven did.

Previously, I had not had a revelation of any of these three truths concerning negative experiences in my life, and thus I was wrongly interpreting experiences and assuming God was not watching over me as He had promised. An extended teaching on the revelation I received concerning the Bible and experiences may be found in Appendix C.

Reflecting on other curses in my family line

As I reflect on things which have been passed down to me through the family line, I remembered renouncing and breaking a curse a number of years ago. I had fought with colds for much of the year, every year. When a prophet prayed about my condition, the Lord told him that it was a curse that had been passed down through the family line that was causing the respiratory problems. I considered the fact that my mom had throat problems while I was growing up, and my brothers and sisters have a variety of lung, chest and throat problems. So I prayed for the Cross of Christ to stand between me and this generational curse. I felt something immediately release within my chest, and I have literally gone for years since then without catching a single cold.

I also discovered that there was masonry in my family line, so I have prayed for any curses from that to be halted at the Cross of Christ.

An awareness was growing within me that I needed to meditate on how God heals the heart, and understand it much more completely than I had in the past. Future chapters will show you what I discovered.

Instantaneous versus process healing

I mentioned in Chapter One that there were some instantaneous changes within me. That is true, but there were also some things that were healed through a process that continued over the next few months. In the areas where demons were cast out or where negative spiritual powers were broken through repentance, breaking off generational sins and curses, breaking soul ties, or inner healing, there was an **in-**

stantaneous reduction in negative pressure.

However, I also found that there was some mopping up work to do. God gave me a dream two nights after the counseling session, showing some soul ties that needed to be broken in an area of my life. I prayed and broke them in the middle of the night after I had journaled out the dream and its interpretation. You should expect and seek God's revelation through dreams. You must learn to interpret your dreams, and act, of course, upon the messages you receive.

Some areas of negative pressure were greatly reduced after that first counseling session, but not totally gone. I found that going back and asking God to show me areas of incomplete repentance helped, for then I was able to repent more extensively and thoroughly and obtain an even greater level of freedom.

I felt God impressing me to do intensive biblical meditation and journaling in various areas so I could understand how I had become caught up in these traps in the first place, and what biblical guidelines I needed to obey to keep me from falling back into these sin patterns. Therefore I studied my Bible and wrote out summaries of what God was showing me. I also journaled about these areas, asking God to show me the mistakes which I had made that had allowed me to enter into bondage.

As I have counseled with others, I have found several additional procedures which need to be used from time to time to help overcome stubborn sin areas. These include confessing sins to one's spiritual counselor, enacting fences to protect yourself from temptation, creating an "Impassioned Repentance Worksheet," and others. I have written about these procedures in later chapters.

To complete my healing I used several skills which the Lord had taught me through the years. I believe you will need these skills, also, for your healing to be complete. They include: doing a complete, Spirit-anointed, Bible meditation in an area of need in your life; hearing God's voice; journaling (i.e. writing down what He says to you); seeing divine vision; receiving and interpreting dreams from God; applying the "Law of the Spirit of life in Christ Jesus" (Romans 8:2—turning inward and drawing upon the indwelling power of the Holy Spirit when tempted); being willing to thoroughly and completely repent of sins, dead works (things I do on my own, without calling upon God's strength), negative judgments and inner vows; and finally, taking a definite stand against sin in one's own life. These are skills which the Bible teaches release God's grace to us, and they will be taught throughout this book.

I have discovered that people who have these biblical skills, and use them in overcoming life-controlling problems, can receive long-term spiritual and emotional healing as described in this book. Those who don't have these biblical skills, and don't take the time to develop them, find that their healing does not spring forth, or does not last. Healing comes as we receive and apply the spiritual grace of our Lord and Savior Jesus Christ. The tools mentioned above are the key biblical approaches God has given us to receive His grace. If we will approach Him in the way He has shown us to in His Word, we will receive His grace and divine power which overcomes our weakness.

Don't assume everything will be instantaneous. Some of your healing may be immediate as negative spiritual powers are instantly severed in your life, and some may be a process, as you take the appropriate steps to apply God's grace on a daily basis. Be prepared to work through whatever processes are necessary until you reach your goal of full and complete freedom.

Personal Application

1. List the things you have learned from this chapter.

2. Ask God to help you search your heart, showing you negative inner energies and negative inner processes which you are using that are producing negatives in your life rather than positives.

3. Ask God to begin to show you how to heal these negative processes or energies within you.

Group Application

1. Let the group share their answers to the questions above as they are free to do so. Discuss together what they have discovered.

2. Pray for individuals as needs arise and the Spirit leads.

3

THE ROOTS OF NEGATIVE ENERGIES WITHIN THE HEART

Becoming aware of the power of God and Satan within the heart

Man's heart contains a spirit. For the Christian, this spirit has been joined to the Holy Spirit, so in reality, his innermost being is joined to Almighty God through a wonderful miracle of grace.

> But the one who joins himself to the Lord is one spirit with Him. (1 Corinthians 6:17, NASB)

> And for this purpose also I labor, striving according to His power, which mightily works within me. (Colossians 1:29, NASB)

Thus the power of God's Spirit begins working within the heart of the individual at the point of salvation. As one works out his soul's salvation, this power from God's Holy Spirit permeates more and more of his heart and soul, and even his body (Philippians 2:12). As the light of God fills more of an individual, Satan's darkness is progressively driven out. This process of sanctification is ongoing, probably until the day we die. So even though we deal with an issue on one level, years later we may come back and deal with it on an even deeper level. We are healed in layers.

The power of the Holy Spirit ministers the abiding realities of God into our beings, things like faith, hope, love, joy, peace, power, purpose, dream, vision, anointing, and everything else that God is. This is driving out demonic forces from the person, forces which are best characterized by Satan's names and activities. These negative sin energies (pressures) include: doubt, fear, anger, guilt, depression, madness, death, and anything that lines up with a name of Satan. His names include: the accuser (Revelation 12:10); the father of lies (John 8:44); the adversary (1 Peter 5:8); the condemner (Romans 8:1—implied); and a thief who comes to steal, kill and destroy (John. 10:10).

Therefore, one can fairly easily take a barometric reading of his heart to see how well he is doing and if the presence of negative demonic energies is thriving or if godly positive power saturates his heart and mind.

When can a command change the heart?

If anyone has been caught up in spiritually negative forces, he has no doubt discovered that to command himself to "Get over it!" has not worked at all. For example, to say, "Get over it" to a person who has a spirit of anger will create a fight in his heart and life that will be terrible. He will try as a good Christian to still the anger within but to no avail, unless he understands the true spiritual roots of the anger and how to properly undermine and remove it from his heart. That is what this chapter is about. If one who knows his authority in God attacks precisely the root of anger (or other negative force), then the command can change the heart and release the anger.

What laws and principles create the bondage of negative spiritual energies within the individual? What laws set men free? What laws fill them with positive spiritual energies of the Holy Spirit?

The words "power" and "sin energy"

I have two reasons for using the expression "sin energy." One is that "energy" is exactly what it feels like to me when these negative (or positive) influences are operating within and upon me, putting pressure on me to move in a particular direction.

Secondly, one of the Greek words translated "power" in the New Testament is *energes*, and it literally means "active energy." ***Strong's Concordance*** defines *energes* (#1756) as "active, operative, effectual, powerful." ***Strong's Concordance*** goes on to define another form of *energes*, (*energeia* - #1753) as "efficiency, energy, operation, strong, effectual working."

More New Testament Greek support for the word "Energy"

Young's Concordance defines *energes* as "energetic, efficacious."

Colon Brown defines *energes* as "adopted to accomplish a thing, to communicate energy, to come into activity, energetic in-working."

The ***Analytical Greek Lexicon*** by Zondervan defines *energes* as "active, energetic, effectual." It defines *energeia* as "energy, efficacy, power, active energy, operation." It defines *energew* as "to effect, to put into operation, to be active, to communicate energy and efficiency, to come into activity, to be an active power of principle instinct with activity, operative."

25

Energeia can quite legitimately be translated as energy wherever it occurs.

Energeia is used in 2 Thessalonians 2:9 and 2:11 to describe the "working" of Satan and the "working" of error or delusion.

The verb form of this word group, *energew*, is used in Romans 7:5 for the "impulses of sins that are, through the law, at work (*energew*) in our members to bear fruit leading to death" (this death is present in us inhibiting the life of Christ from flowing in us).

Second Corinthians 4:12 also speaks of "death working (*energew*) in us." And in 2 Thessalonians 2:7, the "mystery of iniquity already works (*energew*)." So *energeia* and *energew* both demonstrate the Greek basis for the expression "negative energy."

Ephesians 2:2 speaks of living according to the prince of the power of the air, the spirit that is now "working" within the children of disobedience. "Working" is a form of the Greek word "energes," which means that this indwelling evil spirit is "energizing" the individual.

These words are also used for God's positive energy. In fact, the *Theological Dictionary of the New Testament* (Vol. 2, page 652) says, "In the O.T. and N.T., *energeia* and *energew*, are used almost exclusively for the work of divine or demonic powers."

A distinction: While *energes* is the root from which *energeia* and *energew* were derived, they had, by New Testament times, diverged in meaning so that *energeia* and *energew* began to be used in a negative sense as well as a positive sense. *Energes*, however, retained its original positive meaning only and was never used for demonic or carnal energy.

In summary: the three primary words in the New Testament translated power are *exousia* (108 times) which means "right or prerogative," *dunamis* (108 times) which means "might, power, force," and *energes* (and its forms - 31 times) which means "active energy, energetic in-working."(See our book *Divine Authority, Divine Power, Divine Energy* for a complete listing and discussion of the verses in which all three of these words occur in the New Testament.)

"Sin Energy" and the "Law of Sin" in Romans Seven

There are two words used in Romans 7 that help us understand this sin energy within us: "law" and "dwell."

The word "law" in Romans 7:23 ("the law of sin") has the meaning of a law or principle that cannot be evaded because of the presence, power, or force of that which energizes it and thus controls our conduct.

In Romans 7:17-18, 20, the word "dwell" is used. This word in the Greek is *sikew*, which has the meaning here of "to be operative in one's being" (not merely passively "dwelling"). Here it is "sin" that "dwells" or is "operative in one's being." Being under sin's power is being controlled by the energy of sin that, in effect, enacts an actual "law" within us, which, Paul found, could not be overcome by mere willpower (Romans 7:17-24).

Since will-power cannot overcome this sin energy, Paul declares that the solution is appropriating the power of the Holy Spirit. In Romans 8:2, Paul states that it is the law of the Spirit of life in Christ Jesus that sets us free from the law of sin and death. So the power (or energy) of the Holy Spirit, breaks the power (or energy) of sin in our lives.

Isn't the word "energy" a New Age word?

Words take on different meanings at different times in various cultures. In other words, cultural context can change their connotation. Take the word "gay," which meant "happy" fifty years ago, but means something entirely different today. It seems the same has happened with the word "energy," as lately it has been linked with the New Age. (I personally do not think the New Age or the homosexuals or any other unrighteous group has the right to claim any word or symbol, such as the rainbow.) So for the sake of all our readers, we will clarify our intent in using the word "energy" as follows.

The Church currently thinks of "power" as coming from God and "energy" as being more of a New Age concept. I think we would all agree that the New Ager is involved more in the demonic than in the power of God.

Since the junk in our hearts that we are trying to heal is essentially demonic garbage, perhaps "sin energy" and "demonic energy" are fully acceptable phrases to describe it. The Christian wants to replace this negative demonic sin energy, which pressures him toward acts of sin, with the power and anointing of the Spirit of Almighty God, which moves him toward acts of righteousness.

Thus, the Christian being delivered is being set free from "negative demonic sin energies" and becoming increasingly more filled with the power and anointing of Almighty God.

My personal feeling on the use of the word "energy" is as follows: I recommend that we not give the New Age anything. God created everything for Himself. It is all designed to bring glory to Him. So let's plan on maintaining the words "energy" and "energetic" for the Christian. "Energetic" is derived (via Latin and French intermediaries) from the Greek word "energeia." Even though the goal of this book is not to fight for the use of the word "energy," I resist any suggestion that these words be given to the New Age.

In an absolutely real sense, we are dealing with divine

power and spiritual energies within our hearts, souls, minds and bodies. These energies respond to certain biblical laws and certain specific prayer approaches. Demonic sin energies are connected with the curse, Satan, and the work of demons. Positive energies are connected to the anointing, blessing, and power of the Spirit of Almighty God.

In this section, we will discuss possible roots of the sin energies within your heart, soul, or mind. In the next chapter we will discuss the proper kind of prayer application for dealing with each of these root problems.

Special thanks

I want to especially thank John and Paula Sandford, Peter Horriban, Bill and Sue Banks and my close friends, Chester and Betsy Kylstra, for their writings that have provided the enlightenment for the ideas that follow in this chapter. They have been a blessing to the body of Christ.

Possible roots of sin energies or demonic energies within

1. Generational sins and curses pass sin energy down through the family line

Some sin energies and godly anointings within you did not begin with you. They began in your ancestral line and have been passed down to you from previous generations. You were actually born with a sin energy or an anointing that is producing either a curse or a blessing in your life.

The Bible says that curses can be passed down to the third and fourth generations (Exodus 20:4-6). Sin energy from sexual sins has an effect to the tenth generation (Deuteronomy 23:2). And the blessing of obedience to God is passed down a thousand generations (Deuteronomy 7:9).

Obviously, then, one of the first questions you want to ask when you are struggling with an energy or pressure toward sin within you is, "Is this problem also evident in my ancestral line?" If so, you will want to begin your attack on the problem by cutting off the forces which are being passed down through the family tree. The method for doing this will be discussed in the next chapter.

Actually, the more appropriate question might be, "Who in my ancestral line manifested this same trait?" In four generations, you have thirty ancestors, and in ten generations you have 2,046. The chance that almost any sin, especially sexual sin, is present in the thirty or the 2,046 is almost a certainty.

What can be passed through the family line? Anything and everything. The list includes: alcoholism and all other kinds of addictions; all kinds of physical ailments and sicknesses; all kinds of emotional and mental problems; besetting sins; as well as all types of spiritual blessings, anointings and giftings.

One question we could ask is, "When a person is confronted with a strong negative force in his life, what are the chances that it is rooted in some way in energies passed down through his family line from the last four (30 people) or ten (2,046 people) generations?" My guess is 100%. Therefore, praying to break generational sins and curses is an automatic response when dealing with anything, for surely there are some roots to it in the family line. Practically speaking, I don't need to wonder if I should break generational sins and curses. I should.

It is wise to begin my healing by praying to break any specific generational sins and curses I am aware of, and then a general prayer for any and all remaining generational sins and curses to be cut off.

As I get into more specific healing prayer later on, and I am seeking to deal with a specific issue in my heart, I would again pray and break any generational sins and curses from the family line as they relate to that specific issue. I would rather be sure I don't miss anything than simply say, "Oh, I believe I dealt with that awhile back." Let's nail it down for certain.

2. Ungodly soul ties stemming from covenant or contractual relationships pass sin energy down through the family line

Soul ties are the result of covenant relationships. Covenants are contracts which may be written, verbal, or understood. Today, we may use the terms "a close or committed relationship," or "a soul mate," or "a bosom buddy." When you enter into a covenant with another person or with God, a soul tie develops which allows the life, energies, and provisions of the two to be shared. Jonathan and David had such a soul tie.

> *And it came to pass, when he had made an end of speaking unto Saul, that the soul of Jonathan was knit with the soul of David, and Jonathan loved him as his own soul. (I Samuel 18:1)*

Covenants and soul ties are a common part of life. They are to be godly, and to be a sharing of giftedness one to the other. Examples of covenant relationships include: husband and wife; parent and child; pastor and parishioner; teacher and student; employer and employee; and a Christian to all others in the body of Christ, by virtue of the fact that we have all been baptized into Christ's body (1 Corinthians 12:13) and are joined to His Spirit (1 Corinthians 6:17). Blood pacts (and possibly even blood transfusions) create soul ties which may be either godly or ungodly. A biblical covenant was sealed with blood, as between Abraham and God in Genesis 15, which is an example of a godly soul tie.

Any of the above soul ties can turn ungodly and release sin energies. Ungodly soul ties exist when one partner seeks to dominate, manipulate, or control another. If violence, fear, or abuse becomes part of the soul tie, it is ungodly.

The Bible says that sexual intercourse results in the two becoming one flesh (and creating a soul tie, for sure). This is true in marriage (Genesis 2:24) as well as in fornication or adultery.

> *Know ye not that he which is joined to an harlot*
> *is one body? for two, saith he, shall be one flesh.*
> *(1 Corinthians 6:16)*

In marriage, when one joins himself to his partner in sexual intercourse, the life and energies of his partner become joined with him. Likewise, in adultery or fornication there is a joining of the life and energies of the two bodies. And it is even more serious than that. If you have joined yourself to a harlot and that harlot has already joined herself to a thousand other people, then logic dictates you become joined to those thousand other people as well. The energies flowing through her now have access to flow into you, causing all sorts of sins, sexual pressures, sicknesses and problems.

The solution to this horrible state of affairs is the breaking of all ungodly soul ties, and especially those between you and anyone with whom you had a sexual encounter. Even if the sexual encounter did not end in intercourse, it is still wise to break off any soul ties. Jesus said that if you look at a woman to lust after her, you have committed adultery with her in your heart (Matthew 5:27-28). It is therefore important that the prayer for the breaking of soul ties be utilized to break all relationships that have been formed in lust, pornography, infatuation, sexual activity short of intercourse, and intercourse. If you do this, you will feel an amazing release and freedom from negative sexual energies that have been hounding you.

I personally doubt that this joining is limited to the transmission of sexual energies one to another. The Bible doesn't indicate that the joining is only sexual. The Bible says the two have become one. So I suspect that any and all energies are passing from one to the other, from the thousand to you. Now that should be enough to do anyone in!

To heal this problem, I begin by answering the questions in the following chapter and listing all people the Lord brings to my mind to whom I have had any kind of erotic joining or ungodly covenantal relationship. I specifically pray through the prayers for release from this joining.

Then, later, when I am working with healing specific issues in my heart, I again pray for a specific severing of sin energy which is contributing to this specific problem being prayed for that is coming from any soul ties.

Greek insights concerning fornication and soul ties (drawn from a study by Rev. Maurice Fuller)

This section regards the specific results of soul ties in our body when one is joined to a harlot, or involved in any illegitimate sexual encounter, including the use of pornography. Here, I Corinthians 6:18 is important: "Flee sexual immorality. Every sin that a man does is outside the body, but he who commits sexual immorality sins against his own body."

First, the word translated "sexual immorality" is *porneia*, from which the word pornography is derived. *Porneia* includes "every kind of unlawful sexual activity." "He who commits sexual immorality" is *ho porneuon* in the Greek, a present participle indicating one who chooses sexual immorality as a lifestyle and indulges in it on a relatively continuous basis.

The word translated "against" in the above verse more literally means "entry into." So Paul says that every sin which a man commits has its immediate effect outside of the body. (They could affect relationships and have many other consequences but all of which would be external to our inner being.) Sexual activity, on the other hand, affects a person internally, in the core of his being. So the idea of the deep spiritual effect of sexual activity of any sort has its solid basis in Scripture. (End of section by Maurice Fuller)

Since the life is in the blood (Leviticus 17:14), we are commanded not to consume another's blood, for in so doing we would be receiving his life, which could be a semblance of a soul tie. It is possible, therefore, that the giving and receiving of blood (through blood banks) may also create soul ties which should be broken. If you have received a blood transfusion, renounce any ungodly life you may have received through that blood and send it back to the giver of the blood. If you have given blood, ask God to restore and bring back to you any life which has been lost.

3. Negative expectations are negative belief systems that generate sin energies which pressure one toward acts of sin

A negative expectation is a negative belief system which has been established in your heart somewhere along the road of life. Negative expectations can be against yourself, others, authorities, institutions, or God. Most of these are established on the unconscious level, so we are generally not even aware that we are holding them. Yet all must be repented of.

They can come from word curses spoken over you or word curses you speak over yourself. Someone may tell you that you are stupid or you may tell yourself you are stupid. Both these word curses will likely produce a negative expectation that you should act as if you are stupid. I used to speak word curses over myself. I said things like, "I am a 'B' level student. The alphabet and I don't get along well together. I can't spell." Obviously, each of these produces negative expectations and sets negative forces alive within me.

Negative expectations can also come from someone preaching unscriptural truths, which you then accept as true and seek to live out. Negative expectations may come from your heart digesting a negative experience and then creating a negative belief from the experience. For example, if you open your mouth to share and are ridiculed for it, you could begin to believe the lie that, "If I ever open my mouth, I will be put down."

The list of negative beliefs is endless. For example: "I will probably fail. I will probably end up in divorce. Nobody likes me. All politicians are evil. The government is out to get me. A godly man can't succeed in business. Women don't like making love. All men want is sex."

Negative expectations activate the Law of Faith

Often these expectations are self-reinforcing, for whatever you expect and believe will happen, most likely will happen. The Bible is clear to say that whatever one believes for he will receive.

According to your faith be it unto you. (Matthew 9:29)

All things are possible to him that believeth. (Mark 9:23)

One's faith makes even what appears impossible, possible. So even if it were unlikely that I would fail in life, if I believe I will, I will. Because I have sown a judgment or a belief system in my spirit saying I am going to fail, several biblical laws are activated in my life.

Negative expectations activate the Law of Judgment

The first is the law of judgment which says, "Judge not, that ye be not judged. For with what judgment ye judge, ye shall be judged" (Matthew 7:1-2).

Therefore, there is now an opposite force that is activated in the universe that comes back against me and performs the judgment on me which I have made about others.

If you judge (or expect) people to be unfriendly, they will be unfriendly toward you. If you judge (or expect) them to be friendly, they will be friendly toward you. Obviously, it may take some extremely unfriendly people awhile to warm up to your friendliness. This is where the law of sowing and reaping comes in. You sow into a person's life for awhile and eventually you reap a harvest.

Negative expectations activate the Law of Honoring, Loving, Fearing

Rather than a negative judging of others, the Bible tells us what our attitude is to be: "Honor all men. Love the brotherhood. Fear God. Honor the king" (1 Peter 2:17).

Remember, we will receive back the judgment we send out. Wouldn't it be nice to receive back honor and love from others and blessing from God, because we reverence and obey Him?

When we disdain others, we cut ourselves off from any gifts or blessings God may have planned for that person to give us. Honor obviously begins with our parents, as that is one of the Ten Commandments. God even has a promise for keeping this particular commandment: "Honor thy father and thy mother: that thy days may be long upon the land which the LORD thy God giveth thee" (Exodus 20:12).

In any area we judge our parents, our lives will not go well. To generalize this principle, in any area we judge anyone, our lives will not go well for us.

Negative expectations activate the Law of Sowing and Reaping

According to the law of sowing and reaping, I must reap a harvest in light of what I have sown.

> *Be not deceived; God is not mocked: for whatsoever a man soweth, that shall he also reap. (Galatians 6:7)*

> *Sow to yourselves in righteousness, reap in mercy. (Hosea 10:12)*

> *Even as I have seen, they that plow iniquity, and sow wickedness, reap the same. (Job 4:8)*

This would mean that I should expect judgments to come back to me in the same areas I have made them. For example, if I have made a judgment against people who are overweight, then I may find that I have put spiritual laws in motion which end up in myself becoming overweight. Or I might find that I draw an overweight spouse to myself. Even if she is slender when we marry, my gale-wind judgment being constantly sent forth from my spirit that I don't like people who are overweight, and that I won't approve of her if she becomes heavy, will cause a constant belittling of her self-worth as I criticize any and every activity that I see her doing that could cause her to gain weight. Eventually she succumbs to the constant criticism and the negative expectation that she will become heavy and, sure enough, I have received back exactly what I have judged. I now have an overweight spouse.

Negative expectations activate the Law of Multiplication

For they sow the wind and reap the whirlwind. (Hosea 8:7)

When sowing a negative expectation, I have sown to the wind and now I must reap the whirlwind. You may only sow a small seed of anger, but you will reap an entire crop of wrath, because one little seed sown can produce hundreds of seeds in return.

The Law of Delay—don't be deceived, give the law of the harvest time to work

It may take awhile for the harvest to grow, so your initial sins may not bring you back a negative recompense immediately. This deceives some people into believing that "God doesn't care that I am sinning; nothing bad is happening to me." But the Bible says, "Be not deceived; God is not mocked: for whatsoever a man soweth, that shall he also reap (Galatians 6:7)." Don't let the fact that there is a delay between the sowing and reaping processes make you think things are not happening in the spiritual world. They are— either good things or bad things, depending on what seeds you have sown.

Summary: The seed of judgment or negative expectation sown in my spirit obediently sends out a message to all within its reach. My spirit might say, "I am programmed to fail;

please respond to me in that light." In this case, everyone else's spirits hear and receive that message and respond in kind. Their spirits say, "Let's do everything we can to ensure that this message is fulfilled." And so I continue to attract events, people, and situations to my life which ensure my failure over and over again. I draw to myself that which I believe to be true. I create my own lifestyle based on the beliefs I hold within.

Hebrews 12:15 (NASB) says, "See to it . . . that no root of bitterness springing up causes trouble, and by it many be defiled."

Clearly, the fruit I am harvesting in my life can become an important clue which can guide me as I search for possible expectations I have made, whether good or bad. One can discover unconscious negative expectations by observing the fruit his life is producing, and then tracing back to possible roots which might be causing these fruit.

I will want to examine the conscious and unconscious beliefs and judgments I hold, and ensure that they all line up with the Bible. Those that don't will need to be repented of and renounced and replaced with a more biblical belief system.

4. Inner vows galvanize one's purpose in life, and release sin energies and pressures in light of the vow

Inner vows are the promises or statements you make as a result of the negative expectations that you hold. Inner vows follow and correspond to the negative expectations you have. Inner vows generally are made on the unconscious level also. For example:

The negative expectation "I believe/expect…"	The resulting inner vow "Therefore…"
I'll probably fail.	I won't try.
Most marriages fail.	I won't give myself totally to my spouse.
Nobody likes me.	I will be unfriendly first.
I'm ugly.	I will hide myself.
I'm dumb.	I won't do my best.
I'm fat.	I will just be a couch potato.
I'm no good.	I will act out my evil impulses.
I don't deserve a good life.	I won't try to improve my life.
I don't expect financial freedom.	I won't try to excel financially.
I don't deserve God's blessing.	I will make it on my own.
My sin in unforgivable.	I will hide from God.
I expect my children to rebel.	I will control them.
Life is unfair.	I distrust and withdraw.

Satan is powerful.	I will try not to attract his attention.
People don't accept me.	I will put up a protective wall.
I must be perfect.	I will try hard.
Men don't cry.	I will stuff my emotions.
If I'm transparent I'll get killed.	I will hide my weaknesses.
Prophets get carried away.	I won't trust prophecy.
Christians are hypocrites.	I won't trust a Christian.
Pastors are authoritarian.	I won't come under a pastor.
All politicians are evil.	I will never trust a politician.
The government is out to get me.	I will prepare for siege.
Godly businessmen can't succeed.	I will compromise my integrity.
Women don't like making love.	I will have an affair.
All men want is sex.	I will use sex as a weapon.

Your corresponding inner vow ensures that all the spiritual energies being developed in your heart by your negative expectation have a focused avenue of release into the outer world. The message is sent out loud and clear through the inner vow.

> "Do this to me, for I am expecting with all my heart and all my energies for this to happen, so please come alongside me and help me accomplish this goal."

Whatever you have expected and vowed to get, you will receive. It is that simple. You receive exactly what you believe for and exactly what you have promised yourself. If you promise yourself failure, you will fail. If you promise yourself destruction at the hands of an evil government, you will be destroyed at the hands of an evil government.

> *How long shall I bear with this evil congregation, which murmur against me? I have heard the murmurings of the children of Israel, which they murmur against me. Say unto them, "As truly as I live," saith the LORD, "as ye have spoken in mine ears, so will I do to you." (Numbers 14:27-28)*

The Israelites had confessed over and over that they were going to die in the wilderness. They expected to die. They said they would die, and sure enough, God said, "I am going to give you exactly what you have been believing for and confessing. You will die in the wilderness." This actually countered God's plan for their lives, for God had intended to give them the Promised Land. But their negative expectations and inner vows and negative confession brought them destruction rather than God's plan of promised land blessings. What a sobering truth for our own lives. We can miss God's choice blessings for our lives by believing for and confessing demonic negatives rather than Holy Spirit positives.

Of course, you realize immediately that this works just as well, if not better, in the positive. If you expect God's promises of blessing and provision and His watchful care over you, you will receive them, also. According to your faith be it unto you, and what you say, you get.

5. Traumas leave negative pictures that produce sin energy or demonic energy, which pressures us to do evil

Our culture says, "A picture is worth a thousand words." Is that true? I believe it is. Life is made up of individual scenes. Some scenes are positive and some are negative. Pictures carry great power with them. A picture is as strong as a thousand confessions. If a picture were combined with a thousand confessions, think how strong that would be!

Let us say a woman has a negative picture of men in her mind because a man raped her. She may know that she is supposed to forgive everything against everyone (Mark 11:25), and that she is not to let the sun go down on her wrath (Ephesians 4:26). So she may say a thousand times, "I forgive him." But if she still maintains a picture in her mind of the man raping her, then that picture will create more energy within than her confession of forgiveness, and she will find that in her heart she still hates the man (if not all men).

What this woman needs is a new picture to replace the old one. She needs a picture of how Jesus was responding to the situation, because surely Jesus was there. David said, "Even if I go to Hades, you are there" (Psalm 139:8). So what was Jesus doing in that hellish situation? What did Jesus do when He was in a similar hellish situation, when men had mocked

Him and tore off His clothes, and spit on Him, and plucked out His beard and smashed thorns into His head and hung Him up to die the most painful of all deaths?

He looked down upon his tormentors and said, "Father, forgive them, for they know not what they do" (Luke 23:34).

Can this woman who was raped invite Jesus to come and stand beside her and show how He was responding to the situation she was in and what He is asking her to do? If she can, she will then have a new picture of herself with Jesus in the scene, doing with Jesus the supernatural, the impossible, ministering deep forgiveness in a situation which in the natural would be totally unforgivable. If she can, she will be healed of the negative spiritual energies polluting her heart and soul which were birthed by this traumatic event and fed by her holding these negative pictures in her heart for months or years. She will have a new energy rooted in forgiveness which now permeates her inner being.

You may suspect that in this scenario the woman not only has a negative picture she must get rid of, but she most likely also has a negative expectation and inner vow which also must be renounced and removed. The negative expectation is probably something like, "All men are pigs." The inner vow may be, "I will never trust a man again." So now we have three things producing sin energies within the woman. In addition, she is determining her future fate because her spirit is sending out a strong message of expectation to every man who can hear, saying, "I expect you to treat me badly, and I don't trust you." The man's spirit hears the two messages which are saying to him, "I am supposed to act like an unfeeling animal around her. I am not to be trusted when in her presence." Therefore, she will be drawing more molestation and abuse toward herself.

This woman will need healing on several levels. If generational curses are part of this, she will also need to break them. If demons of fear and mistrust have entered, she will need to get rid of them, not to mention all the demons of sexual perversion which will likely need to be dealt with.

6. Demons add their demonic energy to the sin energy already present within us, compounding the problem

Demons are spirit entities which seek to enter people and manifest their evil energy out through the human personalities.

Footholds which allow demons to enter include: continuous sin, addictions, emotional trauma, faulty belief systems, involvement in false religions, fears/phobias, immorality, pornography, occult involvement, self-pronounced curses, unforgiveness, and ungodly soul ties (John 14:30, 1 Corinthians 2:10-11, Ephesians 4:25-27).

If a demon can find a way to attach itself to a person's being, it will do so. If this happens, the New Testament calls the person "demonized" (*daimonizomai* in the Greek), and it literally means "to be under the influence of a demon" (i.e., not "demon possessed," as the King James Version inaccurately translates it). You see, Christians' spirits are joined to the Holy Spirit. It is God who possesses the Christian's spirit. The demonization is not a possession; it is an infiltration of the enemy armies into one's castle. These enemy spirits must be thrown out again so that the Lordship of Christ can reign supreme throughout each and every area of one's being, body and soul and spirit. That is what the deliverance ministry is all about—casting out the invaders.

About twelve of Jesus' forty-one recorded prayers for healing were prayers of deliverance in which He cast out demons. That may give you some idea of how often we should be praying deliverance prayers—approximately one-quarter to one-third of the time.

Demons cause many abnormalities in the categories of physical ailments, emotional ailments, mental ailments, and even spiritual darkness and bondages. Demons appear able to cause almost any physical, emotional or mental sickness known to man. Any sin problem can also invite a demon to come in and compound it, so now one has both a sin problem and demonization. For example, if you need to repent of the sins of anger, fear, and doubt, you likely also need to have demons of anger, fear and doubt cast out of you. Do you see the pattern?

Following are some of the disturbances caused by demons in the New Testament: deafness (Mark 9:25); blindness, muteness (Matthew 12:22); infirmity (Luke 13:11,12); madness, anti-social behavior (Mark 5:1-20); and epilepsy (Matthew 17:14-18).

The commission to cast out demons is given in Matthew 10:8; Mark 3:15; 6:7, 13; 16:17-18; and Luke 9:1-2.

7. Enslavement to sin—habitual failure to repent of sin—generates sin energy and pressure toward acts of sin within the individual

The Law of Sin

> *Now if I do that I would not, it is no more I that do it, but sin that dwelleth in me. I find then a law, that, when I would do good, evil is present with me. For I delight in the law of God after the inward man: But I see another law in my members, warring against the law of my mind, and bringing me into captivity to **the law of sin** which is in my members. (Romans 7:20-23)*

Sin has a power and an energy, also. Paul describes the law of sin as an inner energy in his body which has the power to enslave him to its demands. This is the power that sin and the flesh can have over a person. There is a way of stepping from this enslavement to a new life in Christ Jesus. The detailed steps for doing this are found in the next chapter when we discuss the Law of the Spirit of Life in Christ Jesus (Romans 8:2).

Failure to repent of sin is our problem. "All have sinned and come short of the glory of God" (Romans 3:23). Sin is not the problem in our lives. Failure to repent of sin is. God gave the Law to prove that none of us could keep it (Galatians 3:21-22). Then He provided mercy and grace through repentance and the application of the shed blood of Jesus on the Cross as the answer to the sin in our lives (Galatians 2:23-27).

God understands better than we do that temptation will be a part of our lives. What God expects, invites, and requires us to do when we sin is to come to Him in repentance, seek His forgiveness, and receive the application of the shed blood of Jesus to wash away our sins.

> *If we confess our sins, He is faithful and just to forgive us our sins, and to cleanse us from all unrighteousness. If we say that we have not sinned, we make Him a liar, and His word is not in us. (1 John 1:9-10)*

The one who does not do this, but instead continues in willful sin, cuts a groove in his heart that leads him to continually sin. The more this sin is committed, the easier it becomes to keep committing it, until finally he is living habitually in the sin, and is totally overcome by its power in his life. Of course, as he has continued in the sin, he has probably added the sin energy of several of the other categories mentioned above to the problem in his heart, and now he has major house-cleaning to perform to become whole again.

Remember, sin is not the problem. The problem is when one doesn't confess his sin to God quickly and ask for His forgiveness and cleansing. Learn to keep short accounts with God. Get everything cleaned up on a daily basis.

A summary review of seven possible roots to sin or demonic energy within our beings

1. Generational sins and curses
2. Ungodly soul ties
3. Negative expectations
4. Inner vows
5. Traumatic/negative pictures
6. Demonization (under the influence of a demon)
7. Enslavement to sin (habitual failure to repent of sin)

Now we need to discover seven ways of praying for healing for these seven situations. That is what the next chapter is about.

Personal Application

1. Review the above categories of things which generate spiritual energies within one's being, and begin asking God to make you aware of some of the ways these are operating in your own life.
2. To help you become aware of negative expectations and inner vows, make a list of at least 30 negative expectations and the corresponding vows which a person might make.
3. Begin seeking God for healing concerning any negative spiritual energies you discover within yourself.

Group Application

1. Let students share their answers to the personal application questions as they desire.

2. As a group, seek to list as many negative expectations and corresponding inner vows as you can.

3. Pray together with any students who are seeking healing in any of the ways discussed in this chapter. (This assumes that a group leader has read through to the end of this book and is aware of ways to pray and minister effectively to the needs demonstrated by members within the group.)

4

Prayers That Heal the Heart

In Chapter Three we discussed seven roots to inner energies

1. Generational sins and curses
2. Ungodly soul ties
3. Negative expectations
4. Inner vows
5. Traumatic/negative pictures
6. Demonization
7. Enslavement to sin

In this chapter we will discuss seven ways of praying that heal those seven roots

1. Breaking generational sins and curses
2. Severing ungodly soul ties
3. Replacing negative expectations
4. Renouncing inner vows
5. Receiving divine pictures/visions

6. Casting out demons

7. Experiencing the Law of the Spirit of life in Christ Jesus

The place and value of checklists

For airline pilots, surgeons, astronauts and many others, complete detailed checklists are a standard part of their procedures to ensure everything is in place as they proceed. So it is for us as we pray to heal the heart.

The lists below will jog your memory and ensure that you work in cooperation with all the spiritual laws that are part of the seven prayer approaches. We do not worship these lists. They are simply reminders of the ways our hearts have been invited to reach out and avail themselves of the wonderful healing grace of God. When prayed in faith from the heart, they release God's grace. When turned into rote mechanical formulas and prayed from the head, they are ineffective.

Prayers from the heart

Prayers from the heart will experience the Holy Spirit ministering faith, flow, pictures, visions, and divine emotion. Prayers from the mind involve rational, analytical thought. Therefore, as you pray the prayers below, switch from analytical thought to faith, flow, pictures, visions, and emotions. Picture in your mind the things and people and situations that you are praying about. Feel the emotions connected with the picture, and ask for and follow the Holy Spirit's "flow" as you pray. If the Holy Spirit is encouraging you to repeat the prayer several times so it sinks deeply into the heart, then do so. Honor the Holy Spirit's flow, pictures, and emotions as you pray.

Your prayers will have a thousand times the impact if you

have entered the picture of the event you are praying about,
are seeing it, feeling the emotion of it, interacting with Christ
about it, and tuned to Holy Spirit flow, letting Jesus appear
in the scene and speak to you from the midst of it.*

Using the discovery questions

You will note some questions near the beginning of each
of the following several prayer approaches. These questions
are designed to help you discern your need for prayer. The
proper use of these questions is to first quiet yourself before
the Lord, ask Him the question in prayer, and then wait for a
few moments with your heart tuned to "flow" (i.e., the river
of God within the heart of the believer—John 7:37-39). See
what flows into your mind. It will be answers you may have
long forgotten.

Don't make this a mental racking of your brain. Let it be
the seeking and waiting of a quiet heart before God. This
posture makes all the difference. We are trying to heal the
heart not the head, so let your heart do the searching, not
your brain.

The authors acknowledge with appreciation the contributions to the prayer steps that follow. Most are drawn from
Ministry Tools for Restoring the Foundations, Proclaiming
His Word, Santa Rosa Beach, FL, 1996 and 1999. All ministry steps used by permission of their authors.

1. The prayer steps for breaking generational sins and curses

The goal is to cut off sin energies which are flowing down
through the generational line. Pray for each specific generational sin and curse that you are aware of. Then pray a general prayer for all remaining generational sins and curses
that you may not be specifically aware of.

Question for discovering the need to break generational sins and curses:

- Lord, is this trait or issue present in my family line?

    1. I **confess** and repent of the sin of my ancestors, my parents, and my own sin of _____, and of my anger and resentment against You, God, for allowing this to happen in my life.

    2. I **forgive and release** my ancestors for passing on to me this sin and for the resulting curses of _____ (be specific). I ask You to forgive me, and I receive Your forgiveness. I forgive myself for participating in this sin.

    3. I place the Cross of Christ between my ancestors and myself, as a baby in my mother's womb. I command the sin of _____ and all accompanying curses to be halted at the Cross of Jesus Christ, and for freedom and release to flow down from the Cross of Christ to that baby in the womb.

        - Curses are stopped at the Cross of Christ (Galatians 3:13).

        - It is most powerful to apply the grace of God at the point of need (i.e., when the child received the curses in his or her mother's womb). God lives in timelessness, so this is no problem for Him.

2. The prayer steps for severing ungodly soul ties

The goal is to cut off any ungodly soul tie with another. These may have been created through sexual activities, or close relationships like teacher/student, parents/children, employer/employee, and best friends. These allow sin energies to pass among the people in the soul tie. Ungodly soul ties must be severed. Repeat these six prayer steps specifically for **each and every** person with whom you have had an ungodly soul tie. Cast out familiar spirits after severing soul ties.

Questions for discovering the need to sever ungodly soul ties:

- With whom have I had a close committed relationship that was unhealthy, dominating, controlling, or manipulative?

- Lord, please remind me of everyone with whom I have had a sexual encounter of any kind.

- Lord, were there any sexual encounters in my early childhood that I was too young to remember?

- When have I given or received blood or eaten blood?

    1. I **confess** and repent of my sin of an ungodly soul tie with _____, and of my anger and resentment against You, God, for allowing this to happen in my life.

    2. I **forgive** _____ for their involvement in this sin. I ask You to forgive me, and I receive Your forgiveness. I forgive myself for participating in this sin.

    3. Lord, sever the ungodly soul tie between _____ and me and restore the broken or torn portions of my soul. Lord, destroy anything that has come into me through this soul tie and, Lord, bring back anything godly that has been stolen from me.

3. The prayer steps for replacing negative expectations

The goal is to remove all negative judgments and expectations about the world, life, people, institutions, and God that attract destruction to you, and to replace them with positive Biblical expectations that release God's grace and life out through and to you. Most of these negative expectations have been made on an unconscious level. You need the Lord to show you by the Holy Spirit and from the Bible the positive Holy Spirit expectation which is to replace the negative expectation.

These prayer steps should be taken for each negative expectation discovered within you. Whenever you become aware of additional negative expectations (negative belief systems) within yourself, you should pray through these steps.

Questions for discovering the need to replace negative expectations:

- Lord, what negative confessions come out of my mouth?
- Lord, what negative expectations are in my heart?
- Lord, what things do I believe that do not line up with what the Bible and Spirit are revealing to me?
- Lord, what expectations rob me of love, joy, and peace?
- What expectations keep me from giving thanks for all things and in all things (Ephesians 5:20, 1 Thessalonians 5:18)?
    1. I **confess** and repent of my sin (and if appropriate my ancestors' sin) of believing the lie that _____ and for the ways I have judged others and/or institutions based upon this negative belief.

2. I **forgive** _____ for contributing to my forming this negative expectation/belief. I ask You to forgive me, and I receive Your forgiveness. I forgive myself for believing this lie.

3. I confess the countering divine truth that _____.

The reverse of negative expectations—Spirit-anointed expectations

You will immediately note that motivational speakers teach the corresponding positive side of this truth when they say that their students can receive what they believe for. The reason their principles work is that they are based on the biblical laws of faith, sowing and reaping, judging and honoring others.

I will receive whatever I believe because my faith ensures that I receive it. My faith draws it to me. My negative faith (fear) develops demonic energies within me which will not be halted unless I repent of the negative belief system and replace it with a positive belief system. My positive faith develops Holy Spirit power within me which will not be halted until its purposes are fulfilled. A later chapter of this book will more completely develop the concept of blessed root expectations.

Spirit-anointed expectations (i.e., godly beliefs) are birthed in the revelation one receives from God

To replace my negative beliefs, I need more than a "one-liner" from the Bible that states an opposite to my old belief system. It is not enough for my brain to memorize a new verse which counters the negative belief I was holding. I need more than a new verse; I need a new faith. Faith is born in revelation, when God speaks into my heart enlightening me to new insights from the Holy Scripture.

*So then faith cometh by hearing, and hearing by
the word* [rhema] *of God. (Romans 10:17)*

This verse clearly states where faith comes from. Memorizing a new verse can assist in the birthing of a new faith within my heart, but, technically speaking, faith doesn't come from my memorizing a verse of Scripture. Nor does faith come through the persuasive words of wisdom given me by my counselor (1 Corinthians 2:4-5). Faith comes by hearing the *word* of God. In the original Greek, *word* is *rhema*, and it means *spoken word.* Faith comes from the spoken word.

Specifically, I believe, faith comes when the Holy Spirit speaks a word into my spirit, or when the Holy Spirit illumines a verse of Scripture, making that verse leap off the page and hit me between the eyes. Then I know in my spirit that God is giving that verse to me for the situation I am facing. God's faith is a result of receiving God's revelation.

I have heard counselees confess by rote a verse that I have told them to confess, and yet I am fully aware that they do not believe *in their heart* the verse they are confessing. They have not mixed faith with the words they have heard (Hebrews 4:2). Instead, they are still believing the contradictory negative thought which brought them into my office in the first place. Saying a verse does not mean you have revelation concerning that verse in your heart. People often say one thing while believing another. It is the revelation of God in your heart that changes your heart, not the words you parrot with your mouth.

How exactly does one receive divine revelation?

Remember how the disciples experienced revelation on the Emmaus road: "Did not our heart burn within us, while He talked with us by the way, and while He opened to us the Scriptures?" (Luke. 24:32).

This is what we need! We need the Holy Spirit opening Scriptures to our hearts and minds. We need this burning sensation in our hearts that is a result of faith springing up and saying, "YES, YES, YES. NOW I SEE!"

Divine revelation can occur when I get together with the Holy Spirit and I invite Him to show me things which He sees and I have not yet seen. This can come in the form of illumined verses jumping off the pages of Scripture, or, as with Adam and Eve, these insights can come from simply conversing with Him in our prayer times and the Holy Spirit speaking a word into our hearts.

How does one hear God's voice?

Divine revelation obviously requires that one be able to hear God's voice and see divine vision, for revelation comes from God. Thus, one must be able to receive from God through the spirit. This is easier for some to do than for others. We teach four keys to hearing God's voice in our books *Communion With God* and *Dialogue With God*. These four keys are: 1) becoming still, 2) tuning to vision, 3) tuning to spontaneity, and 4) journaling or writing out what the Holy Spirit causes to flow within you. These four keys are expanded in Appendix A.

In addition, we describe the process of biblical meditation (Joshua 1:8) in Appendix H. Biblical meditation is much more than simple "Bible study." Bible study may simply be an academic exercise. Biblical meditation, on the other hand, involves the mind and the heart, and the receiving of revelation from the Holy Spirit, who is illumining the Scripture to your heart and mind (Ephesians 1:17-18).

Please prayerfully read Appendix A and Appendix H *now*, asking God to give you a spirit of revelation concerning them. Then prayerfully read Appendix G, "The Mind and the

Heart," asking God for a revelation of how to live comfortably in the flow of His Spirit within your heart, rather than living in the reasoning of your mind.

It is **imperative** that the counselee be able to receive revelation from God through the Holy Spirit. It is the Holy Spirit Who is the Wonderful Counselor. Your number one job as a counselor is to insure that your client is connected to the Wonderful Counselor. The Holy Spirit will anoint Scripture within one's heart so that he has a positive heart faith. This replaces negative heart faith. You do not replace negative expectations (i.e., negative heart faith) with a new mental understanding of a verse of Scripture. You must allow God to reveal this new verse to your heart so it burns with revelation knowledge and faith springs up and grows. Don't use the mind to try to overcome the heart. Negative expectations in your heart must be overcome by revelation from God through the indwelling Holy Spirit who resides within your heart. GET THIS!!!

You must learn how to receive this revelation through the process of biblical meditation and through hearing the voice of God within your heart as you pray. Only in this way can you replace negative expectations with positive faith—with a faith that has been birthed by the revelation of the Holy Spirit within you!

If the counselee has trouble clearly hearing the voice of God and receiving divine revelation within his heart, have him read the book *Dialogue With God* or *Communion With God*. Instruct him to practice journaling and share his journaling with his spiritual counselor until he feels confident that he is hearing God's voice clearly within his heart. Without the revelation of God within the human heart, the human heart will not be healed. You will be spinning your wheels if the counselee is not himself hearing from God in his heart and responding to His leading, His revelation, and His Spirit, the one who is called "Wonderful Counselor."

Faulty processes often create negative expectations within us

I need God to shed His light on the process which brought me to the negative expectation I have been holding. Most likely, my negative belief is actually the result of an unbiblical process which I am using.

Once God shows me the unbiblical process I am using, I then need Him to show me the biblical process which is to replace it. Of course, the biblical process stimulates healing within me, just as an unbiblical process stimulates death.

I may need to ponder and meditate for several days or even weeks upon what the processes are that I have been using and/or should be using, asking God to give me a clear insight into the issues involved. This is where the insight and counsel of Spirit-anointed friends can be a great catalyst to one's healing.

One example of a faulty process at work is when reason and sense knowledge are allowed to override your faith in a wonderful promise God has spoken into your spirit. This promise could be about your life, ministry, finances, spouse, children, or anything. This is a faulty process, for the Bible says, "We walk by faith and not by sight (2 Corinthians 5:7)." To allow ourselves to be controlled by what the eyes see rather than by what our spiritual senses are telling us will bring us to death rather than to life. **It is a wrong process!**

The biblically correct process demands that I am to stand in faith, and says that through faith and patience I will inherit the promises (Hebrews 6:12). I am to believe God's promise spoken to me by His Holy Spirit in spite of all odds.

I am to believe that God is faithful and God's purposes will be fulfilled. I am not to murmur and grumble as the Israelites did when they found themselves in tight situations. I am to say, "God will keep His word to me and that settles it! Glory be to God!"

This is just one example of many false processes people may find themselves using which brings shipwreck to their faith, their heart and their lives.

Summary: Healing negative expectations involves repenting of negative beliefs and of faulty processes and replacing them with divine beliefs and biblical processes which the counselee receives through the revelation of the Holy Spirit. This process involves hearing God's voice, practicing biblical meditation, and a complete willingness to conform to what the Spirit of God is revealing to them.

Once God gives you a clear understanding of the revised process you must use to heal your heart and mind, you should write this new process down *next* to the wrong process you formerly used. This way you can remind yourself daily to step from the wrong process to the right process, until living the right process becomes natural and normal. Then you can stow your notes away.

4. The prayer steps for renouncing inner vows

The goal is to renounce all vows you have made on a heart level (often unconsciously), and to cut off the sin energies released when your heart issued the inner vow (command) to your entire being. Your being is now in slavish obedience to that vow and must be released to the empowering of the Holy Spirit.

Questions for discovering the need to renounce inner vows:

- Lord, what do I promise I will do?
- Lord, what do I promise I won't do?
- Lord, what do I promise about myself?
- Lord, what do I promise about others?

    1. I **confess** and repent of my sin of vowing that

       _____.

    2. I **forgive** _____ for contributing to my forming this vow and myself for making this vow.

    3. Instead, I now purpose by the power of the Holy Spirit to _____.

Concerning vows: "Let your `Yes' be `Yes,' and your `No,' `No'"

But I say unto you, "Swear not at all; neither by heaven; for it is God's throne: Nor by the earth; for it is his footstool: neither by Jerusalem; for it is the city of the great King. Neither shalt thou swear by thy head, because thou canst not make one hair white or black. But let your communication be, `Yea, yea; Nay, nay:' for whatsoever is more than these cometh of evil." (Matthew 5:34-37)

Paul purposed in the spirit to go to Jerusalem. (Acts 19:21)

We are not to make any vows. We do not know the future. We do not know what resources we will have available to complete the vow. Therefore, when one repents of his negative expectations and replaces them with "Spirit-anointed expectations," he should not also replace the negative vow with a positive vow. Rather, he should establish a positive purpose in his life. Let us say, like Paul, "I have **purposed** by God's grace to do this in my life."

When I was young, I made a judgment (a decision) that I wanted to be like the Apostle Paul. My vow was that I would have the same results as Paul did: every city I went to would experience either a revival or a riot. After experiencing numerous "riots" in my life, I repented of that judgment and made a new one: "I want to be like the Apostle John who said, `Little children, love one another.'" My new inner purpose was, "By the grace of God, I will love at all costs and in all situations." I had had enough riots. I wanted some peace in my life for a change. The new judgment and vow brought an end to "riots," and much longer-lasting relationships.

As you look, you will discover that your life may be full of judgments in many areas.

5. The prayer steps for receiving divine pictures/ visions

The goal is to remove the sin energies attached to negative pictures which stem from traumatic events in your life, by inviting Jesus to show you what He was doing in the situation and how His love and mercy and grace were there sustaining you. This prayer can be prayed whenever you become aware of negative pictures in your heart or mind. We do not make the pictures move, rather we invite the Holy Spirit to show us what Jesus was doing. Then we tune to the flow of the Holy Spirit within and watch to see what unfolds.

Questions for discovering the need to heal traumatic/ negative pictures:
- Lord, what negative pictures are in my mind?
- Lord, what traumatic pictures have I tried to block out?
- Lord, what negative pictures come up in my dreams?
  1. I **confess** and repent of any anger and bitterness I have against You, God, for allowing this event to happen in my life. I ask You to forgive me, and I receive Your forgiveness.
  2. Lord, please take me back to the appropriate memory that is underlying this issue in my heart. (See the scene. If a rape or other extremely traumatic scene, you may go back to just after it is over.)
  3. Lord, show me where You were in this scene. (Look and see where Jesus is/was.) Holy Spirit, take over this scene and give me a vision, showing me what Jesus was doing. (Respond to what the Lord is showing and doing.)

The transforming power of seeing divine pictures/ visions

Walking through hellish situations can produce inner gifts and strengths rather than destroy us, if we don't fix our gaze on the horrible situation, but rather look into the spiritual world.

*For our light affliction, which is but for a moment, worketh for us a far more exceeding and eternal weight of glory; **While we look not at the things which are seen, but at the things which are not seen:** for the things which are seen are temporal; but the things which are not seen are eternal. (2 Corinthians 4:17-18)*

What are we to look at in the spiritual world when we are walking through difficult situations?

> **Looking unto Jesus** *the author and finisher of our faith; who for the joy that was set before him endured the cross, despising the shame, and is set down at the right hand of the throne of God. (Hebrews 12:2)*

If we will fix our eyes on Jesus in the midst of life's trying circumstances, we will see how He is responding to the hurt, and how He is wanting us to respond. This vision of Jesus in action at our side will bring healing to our hearts. Therefore, stay tuned to vision as you walk through life as Jesus did (John 5:19-20, 30), and the vision you receive of Jesus in action at your side will be worth more than a thousand words of counseling and comfort.

If you didn't see Jesus as you walked through the hurt initially, then you need to go back to the hurt (in your mind's eye) and invite Jesus to show you a vision of what He was doing in that situation. Since He is an omnipresent God, He obviously was there and was doing something. However, in your spiritual blindness you failed to see Him. Now you are asking for the blinders to be removed from your eyes so that you can see clearly what is transpiring in the spiritual realm. You are becoming like Jesus (John 5:19-20, 30; 8:26, 38).

You are allowing God to replace the pictures in the art gallery of your mind, removing pictures which do not have Jesus in them and replacing them with pictures that do have Jesus in them. You are moving from a picture which contains a lie (i.e., Jesus isn't present watching over and protecting His children) to the truth (Jesus is always there watching over and protecting His children).

You can look for Jesus to appear in the midst of the negative scene in your mind. Then, if you invite the Holy Spirit to guide the flow of pictures, you can watch Jesus do some remarkable things in the midst of that situation. You can read some astounding examples of these kinds of healing prayers in Chapter Four of our book, ***Wading Deeper in the River of God***.

As the Holy Spirit takes over the vision, the picture in your mind will come alive and will begin to "flow" with a life of its own, or actually, the life of the Holy Spirit. For when Jesus described the experience of the Holy Spirit within our hearts, He described it as flow (John 7:37-39):

> *From his innermost being shall flow rivers of living water. But this He spoke of the Spirit. (John 7:38,39)*

Flow is simple and very childlike. It simply demands faith like a child to believe that there really is a river within the heart of the believer and that that river really does flow, and that that flow is the Holy Spirit. Will you believe as a child and be healed? I pray you will! If you have a negative expectation that God doesn't do this anymore or that He wouldn't do it for you, then I suggest you renounce that negative belief system and adopt instead Acts 2:17 as your new belief.

> *"And it shall come to pass in the last days," saith God, "I will pour out of my Spirit upon all flesh: and your sons and your daughters shall prophesy, and your young men shall see visions, and your old men shall dream dreams." (Acts 2:17)*

Caution! Warning! Don't make up the scenes yourself!

I don't have to make Jesus do what I think He should do in the pictures in my mind. I don't need to paint the picture myself. I can simply ask the Holy Spirit to take over the picture of the negative scene and show me where Jesus was and what He was doing, and the Holy Spirit will. I will experience a divine vision which is very healing to my heart and soul.

An example of receiving divine pictures

Let me share one experience I had when praying for a rape victim. The woman I was praying for (let's call her Sally—not her real name) had been raped as an eight-year-old by her uncle, who was supposed to be baby-sitting her. Sally had hated and feared men ever since that day. We went back and picked up the scene just after it had happened. Sally was cowering naked where he had thrown her in the corner of the bedroom, and he was lying on the bed. Sally tuned to "flow" and invited Jesus to appear. As He did, here's what Sally saw and heard.

Sally saw a picture appear in her heart/mind of Jesus entering the room and coming over to her. He was holding out a white sheet which He wrapped and clothed her in. He then offered her His hand, which she took, and He walked with her outside. Jesus took Sally to their backyard where there was a swing and a sandbox. He played with her in the sandbox and then pushed her on the swing for a while. After about 20 minutes (in the vision, but only two or three minutes in the counseling room) Sally was calmed down and Jesus offered to take her for a walk along a path behind their home. She went with Him and when they returned, Jesus indicated He wanted to take her back in the house.

> (Sally is sharing the story with me as she is watching and experiencing it. Sally is tuned to spontaneous pictures allowing her to see Jesus, and spontaneous thoughts allowing her to hear what Jesus is speaking to her. I am just sitting next to her, holding her hand and encouraging her over and over to keep looking at Jesus and watching what

He is doing, and keep listening to what He is saying to her, and to share with me the experience
she is having. When she tells me Jesus wants to
take her back into the house, I have a red light of
caution go on within me. That's where the perpe-
trator is. However, since I have learned to honor
and follow the flow of God's Spirit, I tell her to
go ahead and go in with Jesus. I assume that if
things do get out of control, I can step in and tell
her we need to stop the scene.)

Sally goes into the house holding Jesus' hand. Then she
says, "Jesus wants me to go with Him back into the bedroom." Now I have lots of red flags swirling in my mind, but
I tell her, "Let's follow Jesus."

Once in the bedroom, Jesus takes her over to the bed and,
as they look down at the sleeping man, Jesus says, "See, he
can't hurt you anymore."

And in that one step, Jesus removed her lifetime fear of
men. How astounding! If I were painting the scene or imag-
ining what I thought Jesus should do, I would have never in
a thousand years suggested that. But that is what He did.

6. The prayer steps for casting out demons

The goal is to remove the sin energies connected with demons who have attached themselves in some way to wounded
areas within your personality. Begin by dismantling the demons' home by going through the above five healing prayers.
Once the home is dismantled, demons come out quite easily. Deal with one demon at a time, or one grouping of demons at a time (a grouping includes related spirits such as
doubt, fear, and unbelief). If the demon is not coming out
when commanded, or is returning after leaving, go back
through the above healing prayers to dislodge it fully, and to
seal up any doors which are allowing it back.

Questions for discovering the need for deliverance:

- Lord, what compulsive pressures are within me?
- Lord, what sins can I not defeat?
- Lord, what stumbling blocks occur over and over?
  1. Make sure the demon's house is thoroughly dismantled and his anchors completely pulled up by praying through the above five prayers. If the demon does not come out, go back to the above five prayers—something has been missed. Ask God what has been missed and honor what flows back in response.
  2. In the Name of the Lord Jesus Christ, I renounce and break all agreements with the demons (strongholds) of _____, _____, etc.
  3. I take authority over the demons (strongholds) of _____ and I bind you and command you to leave me now in the Name of the Lord Jesus Christ.

Demons compound one's problems

Now you may find yourself fighting negative energies from a combination of all of the following: 1) generational curses, 2) soul ties, 3) negative expectations, 4) inner vows, 5) traumatizing pictures of "reality," and 6) demons. And you may be fighting these all **with your own self-effort,** rather than appropriate biblical prayers. You will not win. You will be defeated and in despair if you are coming against these sin energies using the strength of your will.

How prevalent should deliverance prayer be?

Twelve of Jesus'41 recorded prayers for healing were prayers of deliverance in which He cast out demons. That's about ¼ to ⅓ of His prayers for healing being deliverance prayers. LET'S MAINTAIN THE BALANCE OF JESUS as we pray for people's needs. If we don't use His balance, whose will we use?

7. The prayer steps for experiencing the Spirit of Life in Christ Jesus

The goal is to overcome the power of the flesh and sin within you by turning your focus from laws and self-effort to the Holy Spirit and His power within you. The power of the Holy Spirit in your heart breaks the power of sin in your flesh. Your flesh cannot break the power of your flesh, only the indwelling Holy Spirit can.

Use this prayer whenever you find sin invading any area of your life. Pray through the previous six areas first to make sure the sin is not being fed by any of those forces.

Questions for discovering the need for freedom from enslavement to sin:

- Lord, what sins am I attacking with my will?
- Lord, what sins continue to trouble me?

    1. God, the power to overcome the sin of _____ is in You, the One Who lives in me.

    2. I turn away from my self-effort to overcome this sin, and embrace the power of the Holy Spirit Who flows within me.

    3. Jesus, I release the flow of the power of the Holy Spirit out through me, to overcome completely the sin of _____. (May use vision, seeing this happen.)

Overcoming sin by the power of the indwelling Holy Spirit

There are two ways to attempt to overcome sin. One works, the other doesn't. The approach that doesn't work is to come against it ourselves, attacking and fighting against it and seeking to subdue it. Even if through the strength of our wills we were able to overcome the sin, it would have been done through our own strength, rather than by the power of the indwelling Holy Spirit. The Bible says,

> *If by the Spirit you are putting to death the deeds of the body, you will live. (Romans 8:13)*

You see, I can try to overcome sin, or I can turn to the Holy Spirit within me and ask Him to overcome the sin. If I do it, it is self-effort and religion and a dead work (Hebrews 6:1-2). If the indwelling Holy Spirit does it, it is Christianity.

The law of the Spirit of life in Christ Jesus

> *For the law of the Spirit of life in Christ Jesus hath made me free from the law of sin and death. (Romans 8:2)*

Simply stated, this law says that:

> By looking to and drawing upon the power of the Holy Spirit within me, His power will overcome the power of sin in my life.

Rather than attacking sin myself and trying to overcome it with my strength, I turn my attention to the Holy Spirit Who lives within me and speak forth the release of His power out through me, destroying the power of sin in my life. Thus, it is God in action rather than me in action. I have chosen to come to the power of God to overcome my flesh, rather than trying to overcome it through the power of my flesh (which only ends up being a struggle). This theme is developed extensively in the book *Naturally Supernatural* by the same authors.

Impassioned Repentance

If you have prayed through the seven prayers and you are still falling back into the same sin, then you need to impassion your repentance with some detailed pictures of the end result of both sinfulness and righteousness as it relates to the issue you are struggling with.

Complete the following questions on paper or on computer. Use as much detail and vividness as you possibly can. The more graphic and lifelike the picture, the more power and passion it will generate within you. Your desire to sin in any specific area should be dealt a death-blow by your completing the exercise on the following pages.

Impassioned Repentance Worksheet (Page 1)

A detailed picture of the devastation and destruction of the sin of _____.

"Lord, show me the destruction it will bring into my life if I continue in the sin of _____."

Tune to Holy Spirit flow and pictures as you write:

Biblical (and other) principles which relate to this sin.

A detailed picture of the sin and the way it grows in one's life.

A detailed picture of what it will do to my physical health.

A detailed picture of what it will do to my soul's health.

A detailed picture of what it will do to my spiritual health.

A detailed picture of what it will do to my relationship with God.

A detailed picture of what it will do to my acquaintances.

A detailed picture of what it will do to my spouse.

A detailed picture of what it will do to my children.

A detailed picture of what it will do to my ministry.

A detailed picture of what it will do to my job/finances.

A detailed picture of what it will do to my eternal life.

"As a result of this meditation, here is my confession of what I will do: _____." (Speak this aloud several times.)

Impassioned Repentance Worksheet (Page 2)

A detailed picture of the blessing of the righteous act of
_____.

"Lord, show me the blessing it will bring into my life if I continue in the righteousness of _____."

Tune to Holy Spirit flow and pictures as you write:

Biblical (and other) principles which relate to this act.

A detailed picture of this act of righteousness and the way it grows in one's life.

A detailed picture of what it will do to my physical health.

A detailed picture of what it will do to my soul's health.

A detailed picture of what it will do to my spiritual health.

A detailed picture of what it will do to my relationship with God.

A detailed picture of what it will do to my acquaintances.

A detailed picture of what it will do to my spouse.

A detailed picture of what it will do to my children.

A detailed picture of what it will do to my ministry.

A detailed picture of what it will do to my job/finances.

A detailed picture of what it will do to my eternal life.

"As a result of this meditation, here is my confession of what I will do: _____." (Speak this aloud several times.)

Concluding instructions: Meditate upon this completed "Impassioned Repentance Worksheet" for the next two weeks in your daily devotional time, asking God to deepen, broaden, and internalize these truths in your life. Read it aloud, for speaking is part of meditating and speaking it aloud deepens the truths within you.

See Appendix J for an example of a completed "Impassioned Repentance Worksheet" on the topic of lust, pornography, and adultery.

Personal Application

1. Which of the seven prayer approaches have you used? Which haven't you used? Are the steps in the prayer approaches listed in this chapter different than the steps you have used in the past? If so, how are they different?

2. Which of the above prayer approaches do you feel could benefit you and ought to be tried? Feel free to begin trying them.

3. Are there any other prayer approaches which you have tried and found successful? Record them.

4. If you are facing a stubborn sin, work through the steps described in "impassioned repentance," and if necessary, use the final step of confessing sins to your elders and establishing accountability relationships.

Group Application

1. Invite group members to share the answers to the questions above as they feel free.

2. Pray for one another as needs arise and it seems appropriate, using the prayers taught in this chapter.

5

KEYS TO USING THE SEVEN HEART PRAYERS

Your life in Christ gives you authority to pray these prayers of release for yourself and others.

If the Son therefore shall make you free, ye shall be free indeed. (John 8:36)

Jesus . . . spoke . . . saying, "All authority has been given to Me in heaven and on earth. Go therefore and make disciples of all the nations." (Matthew 28:18-19, NASB)

For in Him all the fulness of the Deity dwells in bodily form, and in Him you have been made complete, and He is the head over all rule and authority. (Colossians 2:9-10, NASB)

And raised us up with Him, and seated us with Him in the heavenly places, in Christ Jesus, in order that in the ages to come He might show the surpassing riches of His grace in kindness toward us in Christ Jesus. (Ephesians 2:6-7, NASB)

And as you go, preach, saying, "The Kingdom of heaven is at hand," heal the sick, raise the dead, cleanse the lepers, cast out demons, freely you have received, freely give. (Matthew 10:7-8, NASB)

And I will give unto thee the keys of the kingdom of heaven: and whatsoever thou shalt bind on earth shall be bound in heaven: and whatsoever thou shalt loose on earth shall be loosed in heaven. (Matthew 16:19)

God has given you the spiritual authority you need to pray prayers of release from bondage. You may pray these prayers for yourself as well as for others. However, if you can find other people skilled in these types of prayers, it is often helpful to have a couple of others praying with you and for you. Their added prayers and insight from the Holy Spirit often speed the process and help you see things you may not otherwise see.

Defining a Healed Heart

A healed heart is one that is permeated with faith, hope and love. (1 Corinthians 13:13)

Faith, hope and love are also the spiritual attitudes which protect the heart and the mind. (1 Thessalonians 5:8)

What grants access into the throne room? The same three spiritual attitudes (Hebrews 10:22): true heart (love), faith, clear conscience (i.e., which results in hope).

What is the goal of our instruction? To nurture the same three spiritual attitudes (1 Timothy 1:5): faith, love, good conscience (i.e., hope).

For what does Paul commend believers? For their faith, hope, and love (Ephesians 1:12, 15; Colossians 1:4-5).

Are there any areas of life which disturb or remove your faith, hope, and love when you think about them? Are there any situations you cannot face with a heart full of faith, hope and love? If so, these need healing.

Defining the Language of the Heart

Will an eloquent Englishman be of much assistance to a French speaking person? Why not?

Just as English and French are two different languages, the heart speaks in a language that is different from that of the mind. The language of the mind is logical ideas. The language of the heart is pictures, emotions, flow and faith.

The hearts' healing occurs in the heart, not in the mind. To heal the heart *we must use the language of the heart.*

The heart speaks using a language that is different from that of the mind.

(The KJV is used in all references in the next six paragraphs.)

Analytical reason is the language of the mind (Matthew 16:7).

Mental reasoning takes place when one reasons alone and does not merge reason with faith and revelation from the Holy Spirit. (Note in the following verses the ineffectiveness of using reason: Matthew 16:5-12; Mark 2:5-12; Mark 8:15-18; Luke 5:21-22). The result of using reason alone is vanity or meaninglessness (Ecclesiastics 12:8).

In today's society, analytical reason would be considered the language of the mind. From the above KJV references, it is clear that man's analytical reason is NOT AN EFFEC-TIVE LANGUAGE of the heart.

"Flow" is the language of the heart (John 7:38-39).

When our heart and our eyes are fixed on Jesus (Hebrews 12:1-2), this flow can become the pure revelation of God to the heart (prophecy - 1 Corinthians 12:10).

"Imagination/pictures" is considered the language of the heart (KJV Bible - 1 Chronicles 29:18; Genesis 8:21; Psalms 140:2; Proverbs 6:18; Jeremiah 7:24; 23:16).

When God fills our heart's capacity to imagine, what do we receive? (Numbers 12:6; Acts 2:17; John 5:19-20, 30; 8:26, 38). God-inspired dreams and visions.

"Emotions" are considered the language of the heart (Genesis 6:6).

When God fills the emotions of the heart, what do we experience (Galatians 5:22)? Love, joy, peace, patience...

"Pondering" is considered the language of the heart (Psalms 77:6).

When God fills our ability to ponder, it becomes "anointed reason" (Isaiah 1:18; Luke 1:1-3) in which the Holy Spirit's "flow" (John 7:37-39) guides the reasoning process, turning it into Godly meditation (Psalms 19:14). Illumination (Ephesians 1:17-18) perception (Psalms 73:16-17) and revelation (Ephesians 1:17,18) can then take place.

What the wounded heart looks like:

Examples of possible emotions in one's spirit.

Troubled (Genesis 41:7b-8; Daniel 2:1-3; John 13:21); anguished or oppressed (1 Samuel 1:15); angry (Ecclesiastics 10:4); discouraged (Isaiah 19:3); forsaken or grieved (Isaiah 54:6); enraged (Ezekiel 3:14); distressed (Daniel 7:15); hardened (Deuteronomy 2:30); doubting (Mark 11:23; Luke 24:25); haughty (Proverbs 16:18); defiled (2 Corinthians 7:1).

Take the time necessary for your healing to be complete.

Do not rush through the prayer sections in the previous chapter. You may want to use your devotional times for the next few weeks (or months) to fully apply the healing prayers. If you hurry through this step, you have missed the entire value of this book. So slow down and take your time. In the next chapter we will give you some clues to help you discover areas in your life which need healing.

The importance of using the right prayer

You may recall that I was flabbergasted that I could have lived for forty years with workaholism in my system and not seen it as a problem. In addition, I had lived for a good many years with other problems like doubt and anger and fear.

My deceptions went like this.

I assumed the doubt was just part of the process one goes through as he seeks knowledge, and that maturity was learning to live with doubt. Wrong! I needed a revised process for seeking knowledge, which I found. (This is recorded in Chapter Two, and the appendix, "The Bible and Experience.") Then doubt stayed away permanently.

I assumed the workaholism was just part of my personality and part of my love for serving the Lord. Wrong! I needed to apply the prayers of "replacing negative expectations" and "repenting of inner vows." Then my workaholism (which was rooted in a very early working relationship) vanished.

I assumed the onslaughts of fear I experienced were just demonic attacks, so I would bind Satan and command him to leave. However, fear never went very far away and would always return at the first sign of a threat of any kind. This was because the fear was being fed by a spirit of doubt, and the spirit of doubt was being fed by my faulty epistemology (system for knowing). I was wrongly interpreting the experiences of my life and thus not fully believing in God's protective hand over me, and therefore the spirits of doubt and fear were continuously fed in my life. I needed to change my interpretation of the experiences of life if I was going to permanently cut off the demons of doubt and fear in my life.

I assumed the anger I felt was simply righteous indignation and it really wasn't a problem at all. However, I was noticing that I was angry more and more of the time, until eventually it was most of the time. Everything seemed to make me angry. I was beginning to feel that anger was getting out of control. I was angry at institutions such as phariseeism, legalism, western education, the government, and stupidity wherever I found it.

When I was finally healed of my anger, I recognized a step in prayer which I had completely missed. I had not repented of my negative judgment (and thus anger) against institutions which I felt were in error. So I held a grudge against phariseeism, for example. Every time I thought about phariseeism, I became angry, for I had a negative judgment against it.

Therefore, my prayers for healing my negative expectations needed to include repenting of my negative judgments against institutions which I deemed were faulty. The institution could be alcoholism (i.e. the whole industry which creates and markets liquor), phariseeism, government, legalism, western education, the abortion industry, you name it. I am not to live in a negative judgment concerning an institution. I am to give my judgments to God so that I can minister life to those individuals who are caught in these institutions. If I harbor a judgment against the institution, I will have a negative spirit when I communicate with people in that institution. This negative spirit will cut off my ability to minister effectively to them, and will leave me with floating hostility.

My earlier prayers (before Australia) would bring a temporary relief to my system, but I could feel that these things were not too far away and that just about anything could trigger them. So in reality they weren't gone, they were *just kept in abeyance.* Perhaps that is one of the keys we can look for. Are our hearts really healed of the problem or is the problem just kept "under control"? Let's nail this down as one sure-fire way of determining the need for prayer ministry.

You will observe that the reason my prayers had not been working before I received ministry in Australia was because I was using the wrong prayer to try to solve the problem, or because I was leaving out key elements when I was using the right prayer. (i.e., I didn't repent of my judgment against institutions I didn't respect.) The purpose of this chapter is twofold. The first is to get you using the right prayers to solve the problem. The second purpose is to make sure you don't forget any of the parts of the prayer, so that the prayer can do its full and complete work in you.

I have prayed with others, some of whom have struggled with sensuality. Many assume that they will just have to learn to live with the situation. Their prayers to bind or rebuke their sensuality do not work to release its controlling power, possibly because they are praying the wrong prayers. They should be breaking generational sins and curses, and praying to break ungodly soul ties from the earlier days of their lives, and then casting out demons. When they do finally pray the right prayers, a great release from sexual pressure generally sweeps over them. However, never forget that we are by nature sexual, so do not assume that all sexual desires are going to disappear.

Use the right healing prayer approach, not the wrong one!

When in Australia, I came to the shocking realization that I had been using the wrong healing prayer approach with several issues I had been struggling with for years. Therefore, I was not healed. The problems remained, and I fought and fought against them. *You should not have to endlessly fight internal battles. If you are doing so, then you probably have not applied the right prayer approach.* Stop what you are doing, and pray and meditate in the Lord's presence, asking, "Lord, which prayer is the right approach for healing this problem I am struggling with?" As you feel His leading to use one or the other of the prayers, do so and see if indeed it has set you free. If not, repeat the process again and again until you are totally free.

If you cannot get your heart free by praying on your own, then go to a counseling team who is skilled in these kinds of prayers and receive prayer from them. Life is too short to live it in misery. Get yourself free so you can enjoy and celebrate life.

The various strands of forgiveness—apply them ALL!

> *If we confess our sins, he is faithful and just to forgive us our sins, and to cleanse us from all unrighteousness. (1 John 1:9)*

"Forgive, and ye shall be forgiven" (Luke 6:37). God will forgive you as you forgive those who have hurt you. Thus, a key to your healing is to forgive deeply, thoroughly, and completely. This includes: confessing the sins of your ancestors (Leviticus 26:40; Daniel 9:2-20); forgiving them for what they passed on to you, as well as forgiving others who have hurt you; forgiving yourself for living in the sin you find yourself in; and asking God to forgive you for any resentment you have toward Him for allowing this problem in your life in the first place. Without thorough, deep, and complete forgiveness, your healing will be incomplete.

Why forgive a person when I hate him for what he did to me?

One value of forgiveness is that it releases you from being a slave to the person you hate. If you don't forgive him, every time you think of him and what he did to you, you will be filled with anger and rage, and you will be whipped and beaten emotionally. This emotional slavery can go on for years and years, even until the end of your life, if you don't forgive him. He may be free and living a joyful life, but you are a slave to him, as well as to anger, wrath and bitterness.

This anger, wrath and bitterness you feel will destroy your health. Not only will you be an emotional slave to him, but your physical health will be drained, also.

Forgiving a person frees you emotionally and physically from the control and domination of the one who has hurt you. Of course, forgiving others does much more than that. It opens up God's forgiveness, blessing, and anointing upon your life. It also keeps you from sending out the wrong message from your spirit to others, which would cause you to reap a harvest of unpleasant realities.

Things which go along with the confession of sins

Establishing fences. Ask, "Lord, what fences do You want me to construct around myself so that my susceptibility to ongoing temptation in this area is reduced?" List these fences and see that they are constructed. God may tell you to avoid certain situations which pose an extreme temptation to you. For example, the Bible does tell us to flee youthful lusts (2 Timothy 2:22). That would mean that one would put up a fence which instructed him to run away from situations which produced sensual lust. One might even list those particular situations that he is going to make it a point to avoid.

Hosea prayed for a hedge of thorns to be constructed around Gomer, his wayward wife, so that she could no longer find her way toward evil (Hosea 2:6-7).

Making recompense. The Lord may ask you to approach certain people and ask their forgiveness and make recompense to them. Do as He says.

> *Then they shall confess their sin which they have done: and he shall recompense his trespass with the principal thereof, and add unto it the fifth part thereof, and give it unto him against whom he hath trespassed. (Numbers 5:7)*

If I keep falling back into the sin, then what? Perhaps...

1. I am in bondage to spiritual forces which I have not yet fully broken.
2. I don't really want to overcome the sin—I am enjoying it too much.
3. I need to confess the sin to a close spiritual friend and make myself accountable to him.

If there are spiritual forces operating within me, then praying through the seven prayers taught in this manual will release me from them. If I am enjoying the sin too much to really want to overcome it, then I need to discover how to add passion to my repentance. This is discussed below, as well as the idea of adding the accountability of a close spiritual friend's oversight to my life in this particular area of weakness.

Impassioned repentance

Connect enough pain to an activity and it becomes repulsive. Connect enough pleasure to an activity and it becomes desirable.

Since pain and pleasure are both emotional responses, and emotions are the by-products of pictures, hold clear, detailed pictures of the effects of both sinfulness and righteousness in your mind as you walk through life.

Create a detailed picture of pain. To acquire a profound motivating repulsion against a specific sin in your life, see all the ways this sin damages, devastates and destroys your life, both now and in eternity. Try Deuteronomy 28:14-68 for a picture of pain. Principle: The more detailed you make your picture, the more power it has to move you.

Create a detailed picture of blessing. To acquire a profound motivating passion toward righteousness in your life, see all the ways righteousness enriches, enhances and anoints your life, both now and in eternity. Try Deuteronomy 28:1-14 for a picture of blessing. Principle: The more detailed you make your picture, the more power it has to move you.

Asaph's loss of passion to live righteously (Psalm 73)

Asaph lost his pure fervent heart and stumbled when he took his eyes off the Lord and gazed longingly upon evil (Psalms 73:1-2). He developed a detailed picture of the pleasures of sin. He became envious of the proud, saw their prosperity, their pain-free life, their fat bodies, their mockery of others including God, and he decided it was vain for him to maintain personal purity (verses 3-15).

Then he went into the presence of God, and through revelation, received a detailed picture of the devastation at the end of their lives. They were on slippery places, and would eventually fall and, in a moment, experience destruction and sudden terror, and God would despise them (verses 16-20).

Asaph's first picture enticed him toward evil. His second picture enticed him toward righteous living. Watch over the pictures in your mind. Are they enticing you toward evil or toward righteousness?

Are you picturing things of the flesh or things of the Spirit?

For those who are according to the flesh set their minds on the things of the flesh, but those who are according to the Spirit, the things of the Spirit, for the mind set on the flesh is death, but the mind set on the Spirit is life and peace. (Romans 8:5-6, NASB)

Overcome the flesh by the Spirit, not by the flesh

Therefore, brethren, we are debtors, not to the flesh, to live after the flesh. For if ye live after the flesh, ye shall die: but if ye through the Spirit do mortify the deeds of the body, ye shall live. For as many as are led by the Spirit of God, they are the sons of God. (Romans 8:12-14)

The ultimate step—confessing the sin to a close spiritual friend and making yourself accountable to him.

Confession of sin to a close spiritual friend and personal accountability in a particular sin area is a step reserved for stubborn sin areas in your life.

Repentance begins by praying through the seven prayers to break spiritual forces in your life. Then, if the sin problem is still persisting, you would impassion your repentance by creating a detailed picture of the devastation this sin will ultimately cause in your life if allowed to continue and grow, as well as a detailed picture of the blessings of righteousness.

If the sin problem still persists, then you need to add this final step of confessing the sin to a close spiritual friend and making yourself accountable to him.

> *Is anyone among you sick? Let him call for the elders of the church, and let them pray over him, anointing him with oil in the name of the Lord; and the prayer offered in faith will restore the one who is sick, and the Lord will raise him up, and if he has committed sins, they will be forgiven him. Therefore, confess your sins to one another, and pray for one another, so that you may be healed. The effective prayer of a righteous man can accomplish much. (James 5:14-16, NASB).*

Obviously, the above command to confess our sins to one another and to pray for one another is in the context of being healed of a physical sickness. One point to make here is that if a sin is allowed to continue and grow in our lives, it will eventually turn into a sickness. This is clearly exemplified in Job 33:13-22, as Elihu explains that God does tell us what is going on in our lives. God starts first by speaking to us through dreams:

> *Indeed God speaks once, or twice, yet no one notices it. In a dream, a vision of the night, when sound sleep falls on man, while they slumber in their beds, then he opens the ears of men, and seals their instruction. (Job 33:14-16, NASB)*

The purpose or reason for this counsel from God in our dreams at night is also clearly stated:

> *That He may turn man aside from his conduct, and keep man from pride; He keeps back his soul from the pit, and his life from passing over into Sheol. (Job 33:17-18, NASB)*

So God is attempting to steer us away from sin through the dreams He gives us at night. Now, if we do not listen to our dreams and interpret them properly and respond to them with prayers of repentance, then God speaks to us in a second way, that is, through pain and sickness.

> *Man is also chastened with pain on his bed, and with unceasing complaint in his bones; so that his life loathes bread, and his soul favorite food. His flesh wastes away from sight, and his bones which were not seen stick out. (Job 33:19-21, NASB)*

How often does God use this process?

> *Behold, God does all these oftentimes with men. (Job 33:29)*

What is God's ultimate goal?

> *To bring back his soul from the pit, that he may be enlightened with the light of life. (Job 33:30)*

Several things clearly emerge here. God is trying to help us overcome our sin by speaking to us about it at night. If we let the sin continue, then God allows the pain and sickness the sin produces in our bodies to be another voice, saying, "Turn away from this sin."

So now back to James 5:14-16. If your sin has been the persistent, continuous kind, and has resulted in a sickness in your body, then you are to take the ultimate step of confessing your sin to your elders and being prayed for by them, and you will be healed.

My observations are as follows:

1) All sins do not need to be confessed to my close spiritual friends, only those which are severe and persistent or have resulted in pain and sickness in my body. If we all confessed every sin we have to one another, we would spend most of our time groveling around in one another's sins, which would not be very uplifting.

I might add this suggestion. Why would I want to wait and persist in my sin until my health breaks down? Why not deal with it while I still have my health? If I have a severe and persistent sin which I have not been able to overcome through praying the seven prayers of this book or impassioning my repentance with detailed pictures, then I should go to my close spiritual friend and confess my sin and be prayed for by him.

2) The values of confessing my sin before another are that: a) When I bring my darkness to the light, it weakens and removes the power of that darkness. Confessing my sin to my close spiritual friend brings an increased amount of light upon the sin and thus contributes to its dissipation; b) My friend will probably have counsel he can give me of effective ways to overcome the sin; c) Having two or three others standing with me in prayer multiplies the power available to overcome it. One can put a thousand to flight, and two, ten thousand. A cord of three is not easily broken (Ecclesiastics 4:9-12).

3) Let God guide you in a careful choice of the close spiritual friend(s) to whom you confess your sins and become accountable. Make sure they are your friends and that they will join in supporting you in overcoming this sin, and that they will not publicize it widely to the Church or the world, or come against you and attack you for it. If they are pharisees or legalists, steer clear of them, for such people will attack you for your weakness, rather than coming alongside you and strengthening you in your time of need (as God does).

One horror story a person told me just yesterday was that he had gone to his pastor and confessed his sin of sexual impurity with his girlfriend. He had repented and cut off his relationship with this girl. However, the pastor held him up as an example of a sinner in the following Sunday's sermon when she preached against sexual sin. Two weeks later, since the man did not leave the church of his own accord, the pastor called a church meeting and excommunicated him.

This obviously is not the kind of support I am looking for in the people I confess my sin to! Clearly this pastor was a pharisee and a legalist and not responding biblically to this repentant sinner.

So ask God to show you a person to whom you can confess who will be a friend, a counselor, and a strengthener to you. God can show you who this person (or persons) is to be. Then approach that person, asking if he or she willing to pray with you in the manner described in James 5:14-16. If so, then proceed. Note: The person or persons may or may not be part of the eldership team in your local assembly. Follow God's leading in this.

4) Accountability relationships. In addition to confessing your sin(s) to these close spiritual friends and receiving their prayers, you may want to ask if they would become partners who would hold you accountable. In other words, you are

asking if they would ask you regularly how you are doing in this area. This will keep you on your toes, because you know that you will have to give an account to them whenever they ask. This added awareness will be one more impetus to assist you in putting off this sin.

I stand convinced that these three steps in deepening repentance will work even against the most stubborn of sins. 1) Start by praying through the seven prayers. 2) Then, if necessary, impassion your repentance with detailed pictures of the consequences of both sin and righteousness. 3) Finally, if the sin is still persisting, confess it to your close spiritual friend(s) and establish an accountability relationship with that person or persons.

Do it. Don't let your sin continue, for if you do, it will lead you into pain and sickness and eventually death.

The soul that sinneth, it shall die. (Ezekiel 18:4)

Personal Application

1. What is the language of the mind? What is the language of the heart? Have you ever tried to heal the heart using the language of the mind? Have you ever tried to heal the heart using the language of the heart? Describe your experiences.

2. Have you had persistent areas in your life which have not responded to the prayer approach you are using? If so, what other prayer approach might the Lord be encouraging you to use? Use it (or them) and describe the results.

3. If you are facing a stubborn sin, work through the steps described in "impassioned repentance," and if necessary, use the final step of confessing sins to your elders and establishing accountability relationships.

Group Application

1. Invite group members to share the answers to the questions above as they feel free.

2. Pray for one another as needs arise and it seems appropriate, using the prayers taught in this chapter.

6

An Example of the Healing Process at Work

Seven initial clues that indicate prayer ministry is needed

1. Pressures within you that are being held at abeyance, and are not truly gone.
2. Issues which come back regularly.
3. Any habitual or stubborn sin pattern.
4. Habitual weaknesses - mental, emotional, spiritual, physical.
5. Anything within that is contrary to peace, faith, hope and love.
6. Anything within that lines up with any activity of Satan.
7. Addictions or out-of-control areas.

Seven steps to healing a hurt in your heart

1. Discover heart needs with "What Is in My Heart? Worksheet."

2. Assume all seven healing prayer approaches are needed.

3. Complete a "Contributing Strands Worksheet."

4. Pray through the "Prayers That Heal the Heart."

5. Seal the truths with a "New Truth Bible Meditation."

6. Create "Memorial Stones" for remembrance and testimony.

7. Complete the circle of life: Minister life out of death.

These seven steps are expanded and delineated below

Examples of corresponding worksheets (empty and completed) may be found at the end of this chapter. Refer to them as you read through the seven points below so can you see what the instructions are telling you to do.

1. Discover basic heart needs by asking "What is in my heart?"

Start by simply asking the Holy Spirit Who lives within your heart, "What is in there?" Then, tune to the Holy Spirit's "flow" and capture the spontaneous thoughts, feelings and pictures which float up to your consciousness (John 7:37-39).

Use the form entitled "What Is in My Heart? Worksheet," and make a list of all the words, phrases, pictures, and emotions that come in response to your question, "Holy Spirit, what is in there?" Stay tuned to the Holy Spirit's flow, vision, and feeling as you write. Utilize the four keys to hearing God's voice as taught in Appendix A.

The Holy Spirit's flow that pours out of your heart will tend to come in categories (for example: anger, hatred, malice, and judgment may be one category; fear, doubt, and unbelief may be another category). The worksheet is designed so that you can see the groupings and so you can come back to add to them in the future if the Lord so leads.

You may return to your list on the following day or the following week, and ask the Lord if there are more issues in the same category. Since healing comes in layers, you are likely to find that more words flow out of your heart as you quiet yourself before the Lord and ask Him "What is in my heart today?" Obviously this question and this worksheet can be used whenever the desire to do so is present.

The sheet serves two primary purposes. It becomes a preliminary introductory overview of the strongholds in your life which need to be dealt with. As you add to it over the weeks and months (and after individual counseling sessions), it becomes a summary of the ground which has been covered and a pictorial overview of the healing God has accomplished in your life. Thus, it becomes a recorded testimony of God's grace toward you, and a reminder to yourself of the areas you want to steer clear of in the future.

2. Assume all seven healing approaches are needed.

When I began to seek out root, underlying causes in my own life, I would ask, "Lord, show me the root causes of this particular issue in my life." Next to each word or phrase on my list, I would put the number(s) of all appropriate root(s) that I sensed were contributing factors to this issue. I would stay tuned to the Holy Spirit's flow as I answered the questions. I found that 1, 2, 3, 4, 5, 6 and 7 all applied to essentially every heart issue on my list. I therefore suggest that you can skip the step of asking the Lord to show you the root causes of a particular issue and simply assume that all seven will apply. The worksheet discussed below assumes all seven prayers will be needed.

3. Complete a "Contributing Strands Worksheet."

By discerning specific (1) generational sins and curses, (2) ungodly soul ties, (3) underlying expectations/judgments, (4) corresponding inner vows, (5) ungodly pictures, (6) contributing demons, and (7) areas of self-effort which are contributing strands to this particular heart issue, you can effectively pray through and dismantle the sin energies, forces, and demons operating within your heart.

Discover the strands which contribute to each *major* sin/ heart issue by doing a separate "Contributing Strands Worksheet" for each major item on the "What Is in My Heart? Worksheet." Complete these "Contributing Strands Worksheets" one at a time—one worksheet for each major issue (i.e., demonic grouping). Stay tuned to the Holy Spirit's flow, pictures, and feelings as you complete the worksheet.

"Major" defined: If you have a cluster of closely associated or related words on your "What Is in My Heart? Worksheet" such as anger, hatred, malice, and judgment, you may pick the word from the list which expresses the strongest tendency in your heart and a second word which you sense is the strongest feeder to that strongest tendency in that particular cluster. Then complete one "Contributing Strands Worksheet" for those two words. You are likely to observe that this one worksheet covers the issues underlying all the related words in that cluster. In that case, you do not need to do a separate "Contributing Strands Worksheet" for each of the other related words in that cluster of heart issues.

4. Pray through the "Prayers That Heal the Heart."

When a "Contributing Strands Worksheet" is completed, pray through all issues raised on it utilizing the "Prayers That Heal the Heart Review Card."

You will record some of the things God is speaking to you on the "Contributing Strands Worksheet" mentioned above. You are encouraged to keep a **Prayers That Healed My Heart Notebook** in which you record the healing process taking place in your heart.

Make sure the prayers come from your heart and not just your head. Remember, we are seeking to heal the heart, not the head. Using vision, staying tuned to the Holy Spirit's flow and feeling (emotion) will help ensure that the prayer comes from your heart. If the word "feeling" bothers you in the previous sentence, remember we are trying to remove sin energies from the heart, not ideas from the head. Your mind probably already knows you shouldn't feel the way you do, but your mind is not able to force the feelings to change.

You may be led to repeat the prayer two or three times if you sense that your inner man needs to hear the confession of your lips more than once. Every time you speak something, you deepen it in your heart. Repetition helps drive the point home. Do not be afraid to repeat a prayer until you sense your inner being has accepted the words you are saying. We are trying to heal the heart, not just right some faulty theology in our minds.

After completing the three steps listed below (steps five through seven) for this "Contributing Strands Worksheet," go back and repeat the entire process for the next cluster on the "What Is in My Heart? Worksheet."

5. Seal the truths with a "New Truth Bible Meditation."

In the days and weeks that follow, use your devotional time to complete a "New Truth Bible Meditation" to help substantiate and deepen God's revelation of the key new truths listed on the "Contributing Strands Solutions Worksheet."

This will deepen your biblical consciousness of the new truths which are to replace the errors which you had been believing. By deepening your biblical awareness of God's truth, you lessen the possibility that Satan can get a foothold and return to your heart or your mind with his perverted half-truths and lies.

For example, you may do topics like love and forgiveness versus anger and resentment, or mercy versus judgment, or doubt versus faith.

Write at the top of a sheet of paper, "New Truth Bible Meditation Concerning _____."

Then complete the following steps.

1. It is recommended that you use a concordance and look up as many verses as possible on the topic (perhaps all verses) and take notes on what you discover, meditating upon and praying over each verse, asking God to give you a spirit of revelation (Ephesians 1:17-18) concerning each verse. Look for biblical principles and Bible stories which support the truth God wants to instill in you. As you meditate, pray continuously in your heart, "Lord, show me what I need to see in order to heal the heart issue I am struggling with."

2. Memorize verses which leap off the page, so you can easily draw them forth in time of need.

3. Pray for God to grant you experiences and insights and divinely-ordained encounters which deepen your understanding of these truths.

4. Ask your friends to contribute any principles or stories from the Bible they are aware of on this topic.

5. Perhaps you will feel led to read a book or two on the

topic. If so, ask someone whom you respect as being knowledgeable in the area to recommend a good book or two.

6. Pray over what you are learning, asking God to speak to you and to show you underlying principles which will birth within you a divinely inspired faith and a pure heart. Record the things that you are learning.

7. Record notes of what you are learning, and when done with this topic, write your personal prayerful summary of what you have learned. This summary can be your "Memorial Stone" discussed in the next session.

Examine Appendix H to discover the difference between "studying" the Bible and "meditating" upon it. Examine Appendix C and Appendix D for examples of completed "New Truth Bible Meditations."

6. Create "Memorial Stones" for remembrance and testimony.

God commanded the Israelites to establish memorials to commemorate key supernatural victories He had performed in their lives.

> *Take you up every man of you a stone upon his shoulder . . . That this may be a sign among you, that when your children ask their fathers in time to come, saying, "What mean ye by these stones?" Then ye shall answer them, "That the waters of Jordan were cut off before the ark of the covenant of the LORD; when it passed over Jordan..." and these stones shall be for a memorial unto the children of Israel forever. (Joshua 4:5-7)*

Your **Prayers That Healed My Heart Notebook** will become a travelogue and testimony of the ways God has healed your heart over the years. In this notebook you will also have completed "Memorial Stone Celebration Worksheets," which summarize the key victories over the ruling strongholds in your life. A "stronghold" is a cluster of negative energies (or demons) within one's life. Complete a "Memorial Stone Celebration Worksheet" for every stronghold God defeats in your life.

You are encouraged to create a symbolic physical memorial stone (as were the Israelites in the verses above). Symbols speak powerfully to the heart as well as to the mind. A memorial stone which is constructed as a physical symbol will be a very powerful reminder of what God has done in your life and will be a source of ongoing healing to your heart.

7. Complete the circle of life: Minister life out of death.

So then death worketh in US, but life in YOU (2 Corinthians 4:12).

How do I know when I am healed and anointed?

When I have seen the gift God produced in my life through the hurt or the pain, and I have communicated this gift to others.

If you process your healing thoroughly and completely in the ways described above, you will end up with a powerful testimony of God's healing power, which you can share in an organized and anointed way with others. As they hear your breakthrough story of how the grace and mercy of God touched your heart and transformed your life, their hearts will be quickened with faith and God's grace will come alive in them in a similar way.

Therefore, complete the work, prepare the testimony and

finalize the memorial stones, so you have a story to tell your children and others whom your life touches.

The principle of finding your life by losing your life
This principle is related to number seven above. Jesus said,

> *He that findeth his life shall lose it: and he that loseth his life for my sake shall find it. (Matthew 10:39)*

I have discovered that when I focus on myself and my needs, I am in much worse shape spiritually and emotionally than when I focus on meeting the needs of others. As I minister God's grace to another, and build that person up in the Lord, I, too, am built up in the Lord. It seems to me that as God's love and life flow through me to others, they heal me on the way through.

I feel most healed when I am ministering God's grace to others, and I feel most fractured when I focus upon myself. Somewhere in here is a principle that we must give ourselves away to others if we want to find true joy and happiness in life. So make sure you and your counselees are doing that on a regular basis, for, without giving ourselves away, it seems that healing eludes us.

Personal Application
1. Complete the worksheets following the instructions and letting the Lord show you any areas of your heart which need healing. Let Him heal them as you work through the sheets.

   Obviously, this may take you several weeks or months to complete. That is fine. Take your time and press into complete healing. You have to cover something in your daily devotions. Why not this?

Group Application

1. Have group participants share their healing experiences.

2. Answer any questions the group has about the healing process.

3. Pray as a group for a volunteer who would like healing prayer. Use the healing processes described in this chapter and the previous two chapters. Have someone take notes, completing the worksheets as the healing process unfolds. Put someone in charge of guiding the healing team and the healing process. Allow others to speak into the healing process as the Lord directs them. This approach is a standard way in which these healing prayers can be provided to those in need.

   Also, we encourage any two prayer counselors who have healed their own hearts using the healing approach provided in these last three chapters to team up and provide this healing process to those in need. In doing so, you will be a great blessing to the body of Christ. The Church needs such healing teams. Will you prayerfully consider establishing one? Generally, it is best if a more left-brain teacher/organizer team up with a more right-brain prophet/visionary (Acts 13:1). Their combined gifts flowing together are extremely effective.

4. In future weeks you may continue praying for group members using the process described in step three above. Your group may stay together for a quarter (13 weeks) or longer (perhaps 2 quarters - 26 weeks, or 3 quarters - 39 weeks) praying for one another and sharing the dreams and visions individuals receive during the week as they pray through their own issues.

Examples of worksheets follow.

Following are blank worksheets, as well as samples of completed worksheets with examples of the typical problems which people often face, and typical solutions. We trust these examples will give you a sense of how these worksheets can be used, and get you excited about completing your own worksheets on problems your heart is facing.

These worksheets work best when printed out on 8 1/2 by 11 paper. The "Contributing Strands Worksheet" is the main worksheet used in a counseling session. It works best when pages are set up double wide on 11 by 17 inch paper and then folded and stapled in the center into a little booklet. Full size copies of blank worksheets may be downloaded free of charge from http://www.cwgministries.org, or this little "Contributing Strands Booklet" may be ordered from Communion With God Ministries. See ordering information at end of this book.

What Is in My Heart? Worksheet
Name _____

Ask: "Holy Spirit, what is in my heart?" Then listen to the Holy Spirit within your heart by tuning to flow, feeling, and vision. Record below what is coming to you. Make an attempt to group related issues into the most appropriate cluster. For example, doubt, fear, and unbelief may constitute one cluster; rejection, inferiority, and abandonment may constitute another cluster. Put the word "strongest" next to what you sense is the strongest force in the cluster, and the word "feeder" next to what you sense feeds this force. As you ask, "What is in my heart?" weekly for several weeks, you will discover additional issues which become obvious and either expand a current cluster or begin a new cluster. Eventually this will serve as a review reminder and pictorial overview of the demonic strongholds and issues that have been healed in your heart.

Cluster 1 (Note the strongest & the primary feeder)

1. _____   6. _____
2. _____   7. _____
3. _____   8. _____
4. _____   9. _____
5. _____   10. _____

Cluster 2 (Note the strongest & the primary feeder)

1. _____   6. _____
2. _____   7. _____

3. _____   8. _____
4. _____   9. _____
5. _____   10. _____

Cluster 3 (Note the strongest & the primary feeder)

1. _____   6. _____
2. _____   7. _____
3. _____   8. _____
4. _____   9. _____
5. _____   10. _____

Cluster 4 (Note the strongest & the primary feeder)

1. _____   6. _____
2. _____   7. _____
3. _____   8. _____
4. _____   9. _____
5. _____   10. _____

Cluster 5 (Note the strongest & the primary feeder)

1. _____   6. _____
2. _____   7. _____
3. _____   8. _____
4. _____   9. _____
5. _____   10. _____

What Is ˙ My Heart? Worksheet
Name _____Joe ChrisTian_____

(a completed sample)

Ask: "Holy Spirit, what is in my heart?" Then listen to the Holy Spirit within your heart by tuning to flow, feeling, and vision. Record below what is coming to you. Make an attempt to group related issues into the most appropriate cluster. For example, doubt, fear, and unbelief may constitute one cluster; rejection, inferiority, and abandonment may constitute another cluster. Put the word "strongest" next to what you sense is the strongest force in the cluster, and the word "feeder" next to what you sense feeds this force. As you ask, "What is in my heart?" weekly for several weeks, you will discover additional issues which become obvious and either expand a current cluster or begin a new cluster. Eventually this will serve as a review reminder and pictorial overview of the demonic strongholds and issues that have been healed in your heart.

Cluster 1 (Note the strongest & the primary feeder)

1. anger (sTrongesT)
2. haTred
3. malice
4. judgmenT (primary feeder)
5. violence
6. murder
7. Temper
8. vengeance
9. reTaliaTion
10. unforgiveness, biTTerness

Cluster 2 (Note the strongest & the primary feeder)

1. fear (sTrongesT)
2. fear of auThoriTy
6. spiriT of rush
7. spiriT of false responsibiliTy

3. fear of men
4. doubT (primary feeder)
5. unbelief

8. dread, worry, anxieTy
9. fear of cancer
10. _____

Cluster 3 (Note the strongest & the primary feeder)

1. financial lack (sTrongesT)
2. belief in poverTy
3. robbing God by noT TiThing
4. noT believing in covenanT blessings
5. greed

6. coveTousness (feeder)
7. debT
8. dishonesTy
9. idolaTry of possessions
10. failure

Cluster 4 (Note the strongest & the primary feeder)

1. sensualiTy (sTrongesT)
2. lusT + fanTasy (feeder)
3. pornography
4. premariTal sex
5. sexual abuse

6. fornicaTion/adulTery
7. demonic sex
8. rape
9. bondage/conTrol
10. incesT

Cluster 5 (Note the strongest & the primary feeder)

1. depression (STrongesT)
2. rejecTion
3. despair
4. helplessness
5. hopelessness

6. sadness
7. self piTy (feeder)
8. withdrawal
9. suicide
10. _____

Cluster 6 (Note the strongest & the primary feeder)

1. grief (strongest)
2. despair
3. heartbreak
4. loss (feeder)
5. pain
6. sorrow
7. torment
8. weeping
9. anguish
10. agony

Cluster 7 (Note the strongest & the primary feeder)

1. shame (strongest)
2. anger
3. condemnation
4. disgrace
5. embarrassment
6. guilt (feeder)
7. hatred
8. self-hate
9. self-pity
10. inferiority

Cluster 8 (Note the strongest & the primary feeder)

1. abandonment (strongest)
2. desertion
3. divorce
4. isolation (feeder)
5. loneliness
6. neglect
7. rejection
8. self-pity
9. victimization
10. blocked intimacy

Cluster 9 (Note the strongest & the primary feeder)

1. deception (strongest)
2. cheating
6. lying
7. secretiveness

3. confusion

4. denial

5. infidelity (feeder)

8. Trickery

9. unTrusTworThiness

10. self decepTion

Cluster 10 (Note the strongest & the primary feeder)

1. menTal insTabiliTy (sTrongesT)

2. craziness

3. compulsions

4. confusion

5. hysTeria (feeder)

6. insaniTy

7. paranoia

8. schizophrenia

9.

10.

Contributing Strands Worksheet – Page 1

Restoring Faith, Hope, and Love

Prayers That Heal the Heart

1. Break generational sins and curses

2. Sever ungodly soul ties

3. Replace negative beliefs

4. Renounce inner vows

5. Receive divine visions

6. Cast out demons

7. Experience the Spirit of life in Christ Jesus

* * * *

Stay tuned to your heart - flow, vision, and feeling - as you answer the questions below.

* * * *

Dismantling Demons' Homes

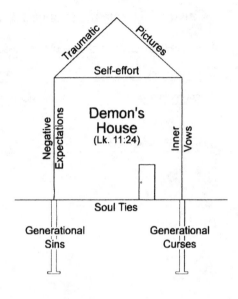

Start by welcoming the Holy Spirit's presence to guide and empower!

Name _____ Date _____

The heart issue being explored is:_____

Question: "Holy Spirit, what is in my heart?"

Step 1. Lord, what ancestors have contributed to the heart issue of _____ (heart issue listed above)? Note: We are not blaming them, just identifying entry points of negative energies.

Step 2. Lord, with whom do I have ungodly soul ties (close relationships) that are contributing to the heart issue of _____? (Examine parents, authority figures, teachers, pastors, close friends and spouse.)

Negative Expectations and
Corresponding Inner Vows - Page 2

Steps 3 & 4: Make a list of the negative beliefs which are contributing to the heart issue listed on page 1. Across from each, state the corresponding inner vow. Then go to page three and make a list of corresponding godly beliefs and Holy Spirit purposes, as the Lord reveals them to you. Finally, pray a prayer in which you repent and renounce your ungodly beliefs and vows and confess your newly established faith and purposes in the Holy Spirit. Repeat this process until all contributing negative expectations have been identified and replaced with godly beliefs.

"Lord, what negative expectations are contributing to _____?

Lord, what inner vows are contributing to _____?

I expect...

Therefore I vow to...

a. _____

a. _____

_____

_____

_____

_____

b. _____

b. _____

_____

_____

_____

_____

c. _____

c. _____

_____

_____

_____

_____

d. _____   d. _____

_____   _____

_____   _____

e. _____   e. _____

_____   _____

_____   _____

f. _____   f. _____

_____   _____

_____   _____

g. _____   g. _____

_____   _____

_____   _____

h. _____   h. _____

_____   _____

_____   _____

Contrasting Positive Beliefs and
Spirit-Empowered Purposes - Page 3

Steps 3 & 4 continued: If you become extremely disturbed when you list a particular ungodly belief, it is likely that a powerful negative picture underlies it. If this happens, deal with the picture through inner healing prayer. Record this inner healing experience on pages 4 & 5. Then, come back to this page and record godly beliefs and Holy Spirit purposes. These godly beliefs **must be deepened by the revelation of the Spirit of God.** This is facilitated by completing a "Bible Meditation Worksheet" as described on page 8.

God says...   So I purpose in the
                               Holy Spirit to...

a. _____   a. _____
   _____   _____
   _____   _____

b. _____   b. _____
   _____   _____
   _____   _____

c. _____   c. _____
   _____   _____
   _____   _____

d. _____   d. _____
   _____   _____
   _____   _____

e. _____   e. _____
_____   _____
_____   _____

f. _____   f. _____
_____   _____
_____   _____

g. _____   g. _____
_____   _____
_____   _____

h. _____   h. _____
_____   _____
_____   _____

Inner Healing through Receiving
Divine Pictures - Page 4

Step 5. "Lord, what negative pictures of people or experiences am I holding which are contributing to the heart problem of
_____?"

Healing the initial scene underlying this problem is foundational. However, if that scene is too intense to address initially, then allow the Holy Spirit to take you to other scenes and heal them first. Stay tuned to the Holy Spirit's flow. For each scene, affirm what you know to be true, "Lord, I know **You were there** in that troubling scene. Jesus, please show me where You were and what You were doing." Watch and see what Jesus does and says as He appears in the scene. Stay tuned to the Holy Spirit's flow and vision as you write. Do not manipulate the scene yourself. Follow Jesus' lead. Submit any questionable scenes you receive to the Bible and to your spiritual counselors to ensure they are from God.

Untrue and unhealed scenes	True and healed scenes
Scenes without Jesus in them	Scenes with Jesus in them

a. _____   a. _____

_____   _____

_____   _____

b. _____   b. _____

_____   _____

_____   _____

c. _____   c. _____
_____   _____
_____   _____

d. _____   d. _____
_____   _____
_____   _____

e. _____   e. _____
_____   _____
_____   _____

f. _____   f. _____
_____   _____
_____   _____

g. _____   g. _____
_____   _____
_____   _____

Casting Out Demons & Experiencing the Law of the Spirit of Life - Page 5

Step 6. "Lord, what other demons may be assisting (clustered with) the demon of _____ (i.e., heart issue from page 1) that I am struggling with?" Name the demons according to the emotion or sin they are contributing to.

To prepare for deliverance, repent of and renounce all ungodly beliefs and inner vows, and state your commitment to God's countering beliefs and the resulting new purposes you have established in the Holy Spirit, if you have not already done so. This separates you from the lies in which the demon is anchored.

If the demon still resists coming out, ask, "What is this demon attached to?" Counselee and counselor tune to flow and receive the answer from the Holy Spirit. Then, using the appropriate prayer approach, remove this demon's anchor so he will readily be cast out. Once removed, fill your heart with godly beliefs (Matthew 12:43-45).

Step 7. (To do as homework) "Lord, in what way am `I' attacking the sin of _____ in my own strength (by saying "God, help ME overcome _____"), rather than relying on the power of the Holy Spirit ("I call forth the Holy Spirit within me to overcome _____")?"

Space for Notes:

Additional therapies which are also extremely important: Excellent diet (Genesis 1:29), proper exercise, adequate rest, reduce stress (chemically, environmentally, spiritually, emotionally) and utilize natural health therapies as needed. For more information on these, read *Go Natural* and *Restoring Health Care as a Ministry* by Mark & Patti Virkler.

121

Contributing Strands Worksheet – Page 1
Restoring Faith, Hope, and Love

Prayers That Heal the Heart

1. Break generational sins and curses

2. Sever ungodly soul ties

3. Replace negative beliefs

4. Renounce inner vows

5. Receive divine visions

6. Cast out demons

7. Experience the Spirit of life in Christ Jesus

* * * *

Stay tuned to your heart - flow, vision, and feeling - as you answer the questions below.

* * * *

Dismantling Demons' Homes

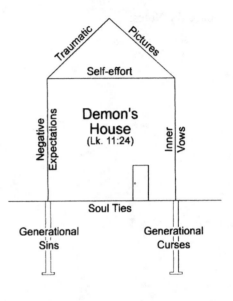

Start by welcoming the Holy Spirit's presence to guide and empower!

Name _____Joe Christian_____ Date _??/??/2000_

The heart issue being explored is:_____Anger/judgment_____

Question: "Holy Spirit, what is in my heart?"

Step 1. Lord, what ancestors have contributed to the heart issue of _Anger/judgment_ (heart issue listed above)? Note: We are not blaming them, just identifying entry points of negative energies.

Anger was present in... (list names)

Step 2. Lord, with whom do I have ungodly soul ties (close relationships) that are contributing to the heart issue of _Anger/judgment_? (Examine parents, authority figures, teachers, pastors, close friends and spouse.)

Membership in and relationships To fundamentalist churches in my youth; submission To The Teaching of fundamentalist radio Teachers when I was young; submission To The Teaching of Professor .... and NeuTheTic Counseling books.

Negative Expectations and
Corresponding Inner Vows - Page 2

Steps 3 & 4: Make a list of the negative beliefs which are contributing to the heart issue listed on page 1. Across from each, state the corresponding inner vow. Then go to page three and make a list of corresponding godly beliefs and Holy Spirit purposes, as the Lord reveals them to you. Finally, pray a prayer in which you repent and renounce your ungodly beliefs and vows and confess your newly established faith and purposes in the Holy Spirit. Repeat this process until all contributing negative expectations have been identified and replaced with godly beliefs.

"Lord, what negative expectations are contributing to ___Anger___ ?

Lord, what inner vows are contributing to ___Anger___ ?

I expect...

Therefore I vow to...

a. That life should be perfect.

a. Take control so I can make life perfect.

b. That people should not be fools.

b. educate everyone I touch.

c. That The government is immoral and out of control.

c. not trust the government.

d. ___That phariseeism is___
___contaminating the Church.___

d. ___attack phariseeism and___
___seek to destroy it.___

e. ___That evil people ought to___
___be put to death.___

e. ___wipe out evil people.___

f. ___That lack of money should___
___not hamper ministry.___

f. ___get more money for___
___the ministry.___

g. ___That life should not have___
___so many problems in it.___

g. ___doubt God if life is___
___continuously full of problems.___

h. ___That everyone should like me.___

h. ___attack those who___
___attack me.___

Contrasting Positive Beliefs and
Spirit-Empowered Purposes - Page 3

Steps 3 & 4 continued: If you become extremely disturbed when you list a particular ungodly belief, it is likely that a powerful negative picture underlies it. If this happens, deal with the picture through inner healing prayer. Record this inner healing experience on pages 4 & 5. Then, come back to this page and record godly beliefs and Holy Spirit purposes. These godly beliefs **must be deepened by the revelation of the Spirit of God.** This is facilitated by completing a "Bible Meditation Worksheet" as described on page 8.

God says...	So I purpose in the Holy Spirit to...
a. There will be Trials and Tribulations (John 16:33).	a. rejoice in The midsT of TribulaTion (Romans 5:3).
b. Some people have chosen The way of The fool.	b. noT rebuke a fool for he will haTe me (Proverbs 9:8).
c. God sTill uses immoral governmenT; discern how He wanTs me To minisTer To The needs of The governmenT.	c. minisTer unTo The fuTure governmenT by Training up SpiriT-anoinTed leaders.
d. There will always be Those who fighT againsT The SpiriT (GalaTians 4:29).	d. accepT The facT ThaT The wheaT and Tares grow TogeTher unTil The harvesT (MaTThew 13:30).

e. "Judgment is mine; I will repay," saith The Lord of Hosts (Romans 12:19).

e. leave others to God and focus on what God asks me to do (Romans 12:19).

f. If I sow seeds and have faith, God will give me a harvest (Luke 6:38).

f. will sow in faith believing (Malachi 3:10).

g. Trials and tribulations are a part of life. However, God delivers us out of them, if our faith is in Him (Psalms 34:19).

g. believe God to deliver me out of trials and tribulations (Psalms 18:2).

h. I am to rejoice when I am persecuted for righteousness' sake (Matthew 5:10-11).

h. rejoice when persecuted for righteousness' sake (Matthew 5:10-11).

Inner Healing through Receiving
Divine Pictures - Page 4

Step 5. "Lord, what negative pictures of people or experiences am I holding which are contributing to the heart problem of _____Anger/judgment_____ ?"

Healing the initial scene underlying this problem is foundational. However, if that scene is too intense to address initially, then allow the Holy Spirit to take you to other scenes and heal them first. Stay tuned to the Holy Spirit's flow. For each scene, affirm what you know to be true, "Lord, I know **You were there** in that troubling scene. Jesus, please show me where You were and what You were doing." Watch and see what Jesus does and says as He appears in the scene. Stay tuned to the Holy Spirit's flow and vision as you write. Do not manipulate the scene yourself. Follow Jesus' lead. Submit any questionable scenes you receive to the Bible and to your spiritual counselors to ensure they are from God.

Untrue and unhealed scenes Scenes without Jesus in them	True and healed scenes Scenes with Jesus in them
a. The backwardness of essentially all institutions	a. Institutions gather and preserve what has been discovered to date. Innovators challenge the institution and create the information from which new institutions are made, or by which institutions reinvent themselves.
b. The way phariseeism pulls people backward	b. Opposites show everyone's colors. People are drawn to one or to the other, and thus their true colors are shown.

c. perfecTionism of parenTs (aT least I viewed iT This way as a child)

c. I learned To be The besT I can be.

d. healing prayer ofTen seems To fail

d. I have soughT ouT The principles of healing prayer deeply.

e. being kicked ouT of The church I founded

e. I have learned noT To grasp ThaT which God has birThed Through me.

f. being kicked ouT of several pasToral roles

f. I have knowledge of many differenT church backgrounds, and now Teach and Travel widely speaking To people from many of These church backgrounds.

g. being TerminaTed unceremoniously from a church

g. I was expelled To fulfill my presenT minisTry on The road as a Teacher To The Church aT large.

Extended divine vision and revelation concerning institutionalism

My child, you see institutions as negative and bad and dead. They are not all that. Some may be partially dead, but many still have much life within them. And the finest institutions are always reinventing themselves into that which new and vital and relevant to the people whom they serve. The best churches are doing that. The best businesses are doing that, and the best governments are doing that. So do not see all institutions as being dead, for all are not.

You are to come alongside institutions and not against them. You are to offer life to them and find ways to integrate that which I have given to you to them. They are not your enemy. They are to be viewed as your friend. You are to see My hand upon them and my grace upon them. You are to see them as mine and not the enemy's. Thus you will be able to offer My life unto them.

If you close off your spirit to them, you will not be able to give My gift of life through you to them. Receive them as part of My handiwork, for all of history has been filled with institutions, and you will see in my Word that it was I who created governments and rule over them. It is I who created the Tabernacle in the wilderness with all the patterns and ceremonies that went with it. That all became an institution. A living institution. An institution created by Me and reflecting Me. That is what a true institution is to do. That which you create is to do that. That which others create is to do that.

So reject not institutions but come alongside them and see them as the work of My hand. Those that need to be reinvented into My life stream will do so or they will die. That is the pattern of the universe. That which falls out of My life stream dies. That which remains in My river bears much

130

fruit for the healing of the nations. Remain in My life stream. Do not let anger and bitterness overcome you. For thus you would fall out of My life stream.

Extended vision and revelation concerning phariseeism and the need for opposites

My child, you think phariseeism is wicked and should be destroyed. Did I destroy all Pharisees when I walked the earth? No, I think not. I let them walk and perform their deeds and I even let them do their best to destroy Me. However, what they thought would bring My destruction, My death on the Cross, actually brought forth My victory and My ministry unto all the ages.

Do you think that is any less true in your life than it was in mine? Do you think I do not work all things out for good to those whom love Me and are called according to My purpose? Of course, I do, and of course, I am in your life. If I choose to raise your ministry up higher and it is attacked by pharisees, (something you fear and which angers you) can they destroy what I have purposed to do? No, and again I say unto you, no! Not pharisees, and not Satan. They can only do that which I give them the strength and the breath to do. I am Lord of all. Satan's handiwork is only used to highlight the advance of My purposes in My universe.

Who are you to set your attention upon the wicked ones? Have I told you to do that? Have I taught you to do that? No and again I say unto you, no! I have told you to set your attention upon Me and upon My purposes in your life and in My world. So why are your eyes set upon the heathen or upon the pharisees? If I choose to use them to advance My purposes, what is that to you? You set your eyes upon your Lord and your Master, and all will go well in your life. Behold, I have spoken, and behold, it is to be done.

Casting Out Demons & Experiencing the
Law of the Spirit of Life - Page 5

Step 6. "Lord, what other demons may be assisting (clustered with) the demon of _____anger_____ (i.e., heart issue from page 1) that I am struggling with?" Name the demons according to the emotion or sin they are contributing to.

judgmenTalism, legalism, phariseeism,
narrow-mindedness, haTred

To prepare for deliverance, repent of and renounce all ungodly beliefs and inner vows, and state your commitment to God's countering beliefs and the resulting new purposes you have established in the Holy Spirit, if you have not already done so. This separates you from the lies in which the demon is anchored.

If the demon still resists coming out, ask, "What is this demon attached to?" Counselee and counselor tune to flow and receive the answer from the Holy Spirit. Then, using the appropriate prayer approach, remove this demon's anchor so he will readily be cast out. Once removed, fill your heart with godly beliefs (Matthew 12:43-45).

132

Step 7. (To do as homework) "Lord, in what way am 'I' attacking the sin of _anger/judgmenTalism_ in my own strength (by saying "God, help ME overcome _anger and judgmenTalism_"), rather than relying on the power of the Holy Spirit ("I call forth the Holy Spirit within me to overcome _anger and judgmenTalism_")?"

Space for Notes:

Journaling: You forget That you are hollow and I live in you. You forget To Turn inward To me, and ask for My Holy SpiriT To be released ouT Through you To handle The siTuaTion. InsTead you seT your will To handle iT yourself. You fighT againsT iT wiTh your sTrengTh raTher Than Turning inward and drawing upon My sTrengTh. Turn inward, for I live wiThin, and I will meeT you if you will buT call upon Me. Call upon Me and I will be your sTrengTh. Do noT walk alone. Do noT walk in your sTrengTh. Turn inward To Me, my child.

Additional therapies which are also extremely important: Excellent diet (Genesis 1:29), proper exercise, adequate rest, reduce stress (chemically, environmentally, spiritually, emotionally) and utilize natural health therapies as needed. For more information on these, read *Go Natural* and *Restoring Health Care as a Ministry* by Mark & Patti Virkler.

Models of The Seven Prayers - Page 6

(Pray all seven prayers over a life-dominating problem.)

* * * * *

To heal the heart, you must use the language of the heart, not the language of the mind! The language of the mind is analytical reason (Matthew 16:7). The language of the heart is flow (John 7:37-39), imagination (Genesis 8:21), dreams and visions (Acts 2:17), emotions (Genesis 6:6) and pondering (Matthew 5:8). **Therefore, stay tuned to flow, pictures, visions, emotions, and inner pondering as you pray.** If you neglect this, your prayers will be coming from your head and they WILL NOT HEAL YOUR HEART!

Constantly rely upon the Holy Spirit (i.e., Holy Spirit "flow") to guide you through this healing process. He can and He will respond to your faith. Pray through the issues discovered on pages 1-5 using the prayer models below.

* * * * *

If we confess our sins, he is faithful and just to forgive us our sins, and to cleanse us from all unrighteousness. (1 John 1:9)

Three steps in each prayer:
confession - forgiveness - cleansing

1. Break generational sins and curses

1. I **confess** and repent of the sin of my ancestors, my parents, and my own sin of _____, and of my anger and resentment against You, God, for allowing this to happen in my life.

2. I **forgive and release** my ancestors for passing on to me this sin and for the resulting curses of _____ (be specific). I ask You to forgive me, and I receive Your forgiveness. I forgive myself for participating in this sin.

3. I place the Cross of Christ between my ancestors and myself, as a baby in my mother's womb. I command the sin of _____ and all accompanying curses to be halted at the cross of Jesus Christ, and for freedom and release to flow down from the cross of Christ to that baby in the womb.

2. Sever ungodly soul ties

1. I **confess** and repent of my sin of an ungodly soul tie with _____, and of my anger and resentment against You, God, for allowing this to happen in my life.

2. I **forgive** _____ for their involvement in this sin. I ask You to forgive me, and I receive Your forgiveness. I forgive myself for participating in this sin.

3. Lord, sever the ungodly soul tie between me and _____ and restore the broken or torn portions of my soul. Lord, destroy anything that has come into me through this soul tie and, Lord, bring back anything godly that has been stolen from me.

3. Replace negative beliefs

1. I **confess** and repent of my sin (and if appropriate, my ancestors' sin) of believing the lie that _____ and for the ways I have judged others and/or institutions based upon this negative belief.

2. I **forgive** _____ for contributing to my forming this negative expectation/belief. I forgive myself for believing this lie.

3. I confess the countering divine truth that _____ .

4. Renounce inner vows

1. I **confess** and repent of my sin of vowing that _____ .

2. I **forgive** _____ for contributing to my forming this vow and myself for making this vow.

3. Instead, I now purpose by the power of the Holy Spirit to _____ .

5. Receive divine visions

1. I **confess** and repent of any anger and bitterness I have against You, God, for allowing this event to happen in my life. I ask You to forgive me, and I receive Your forgiveness.

2. Lord, please take me back to the appropriate memory that is underlying this issue in my heart. (See the scene. If a rape or other extremely traumatic scene, you may go back to just after it is over.)

3. Lord, show me where You were in this scene. (Look and see where Jesus is/was.) Holy Spirit, take over this scene and give me a vision, showing me what Jesus was doing. (Respond to what the Lord is showing and doing.)

6. Cast out demons

1. Make sure the demon's house is thoroughly dismantled and his anchors completely pulled up by praying through the above five prayers. If the demon does not come out, go back to the above five prayers—something has been missed. Ask God what has been missed and honor what flows back in response.

2. In the Name of the Lord Jesus Christ, I renounce and break all agreements with the demons (strongholds) of _____, _____, etc.

3. I take authority over the demons (strongholds) of _____ and I bind you and command you to leave me now in the Name of the Lord Jesus Christ.

7. Experience the Spirit of Life in Christ Jesus

1. God, the power to overcome the sin of _____ is in You, the One Who lives in me.

2. I turn away from my self-effort to overcome this sin, and embrace the power of the Holy Spirit Who flows within me.

3. Jesus, I release the flow of the power of the Holy Spirit out through me, to overcome completely the sin of _____. (May use vision, seeing this happen.)

Credits: The authors acknowledge with appreciation the contributions to these seven prayers from several ministries. Most of the ministry steps are drawn from 'Ministry Tools for Restoring the Foundations,' Proclaiming His Word, Santa Rosa Beach, FL, 1996 and 1999. All ministry steps used by permission of their authors.

Homework and additional notes

See Appendix C, "The Bible and Experience," for an example of a follow-up "New Truth Bible Meditation Worksheet" which deals with overcoming doubt, fear and unbelief. For some, these "heart issues" are a result of incomplete understanding of how the Bible and experience are to interact. Once one understands how to and how not to respond to life's experiences, they no longer have the power to produce doubt in your life.

A sample Bible meditation on "Judging" can be found in Appendix D.

All forms Copyright 1999 by Communion With God Ministries, 1431 Bullis Rd., Elma, N.Y. 14059. Phone 716-652-6990, fax 716-652-6961, e-mail: cwg@cwgministries.org. Permission given to freely reproduce and to distribute free of charge.

The previous forms have been re-typeset into an attractive, easy to use, eight page, 8½ X 11 "Contributing Strands Worksheet," which is an ideal tool for either personal use or in counseling sessions. The current price is 50 cents for this eight page worksheet. It is recommended that you order bundles of 10 for $5.00, or 50 for $25.00. This worksheet is available to order from Communion With God Ministries (contact information located in Bibliography at end of book), or can be downloaded free from the "Free Books" section of their web site.

A Memorial Stone Celebration Worksheet

* * * * *

Stay tuned to the Holy Spirit's flow,
vision and feeling as you write.

* * * * *

God has set me free from the stronghold of _____.

Foundational biblical truths which set me free:

Foundational revelation from Jesus which set me free:

The physical symbolic representation which I have created
to memorialize this healing is:

The fences which God has instructed me to build to keep
myself from temptation in this area are:

I declare I have been set completely
free from the stronghold of

_____

by my Lord and Savior Jesus Christ.

Signature_____ Date_____

A Memorial Stone Celebration Worksheet
(a completed sample)

* * * * *

Stay tuned to the Holy Spirit's flow,
vision and feeling as you write.

* * * * *

God has set me free from the stronghold of   Judging/Anger .

Foundational biblical truths which set me free:

God has severed the ungodly soul ties to my ancestors and those who formed my spirit of judgmentalism and anger in my early Christian years.

I have come to understand that God uses negative experiences in my life as His tests to see if faith is in my heart. He may allow me to come to the point of death or even to die, and at those points God wants me to express faith in Him.

When I sow righteousness, I must be patient, possibly for years, before the harvest is returned to me.

I am to minimize judging. I am only to judge as God issues forth judgment in my journal.

Foundational revelation from Jesus which set me free:

Although it is proper to allow God to establish a judgment within me, I am not to live in ongoing anger as a result of a judgment. Process all anger before going to bed. Give all anger to God daily.

It is a sin to live in the anger of a judgment against an institution.

I am to feed life into institutions rather than judge them. I am to see that they are preservers of previous revelation.

God has used the pressures in my life to mold me into the person and ministry I am and have today, so I am to celebrate and thank God for these pressures, trials and tribulations, and for the gifts God has grown in my life as a result of them. These pressures have caused me to seek out His voice, His healing, His knowledge, His health care and His financial blessing, and I am much better for them. So are those who have received my ministry in these areas.

The physical symbolic representation which I have created to memorialize this healing is:

A flowing waterfall outside my office window, demonstrating that life is a flow rather than a box with sharply defined edges. I will learn to accept and celebrate the experiences which make up the flow of life, and everything that God allows to flow into my life which creates the ultimate majesty of the sparkling river of life which I become to others.

The fences which God has instructed me to build to keep myself from temptation in this area are:

No judgments are allowed outside of my journaling times. If anger appears, go immediately to journaling about it and receive divine perspective.

I declare I have been set completely
free from the stronghold of

anger/judgmentalism

by my Lord and Savior Jesus Christ.

Signature _____Joe Christian_____ Date _November 9, 1999_

7

TIPS FOR THE PRAYER MINISTRY COUNSELOR

The Spirit of the Lord GOD is upon me; because the LORD hath anointed me to preach good tidings unto the meek; He hath sent me to bind up the brokenhearted, to proclaim liberty to the captives, and the opening of the prison to them that are bound. (Isaiah 61:1)

The prayer ministry counseling approach described in the previous chapters heals! It has healed my heart and the hearts of many for whom I have prayed. I have worked with Christian counselors in my city and seen them achieve breakthroughs with their clients in a single three-hour prayer ministry counseling session (which, of course, must be followed up with the appropriate exercises listed in the previous chapters). I have prayed for pastors and church leaders in various parts of the world and seen dramatic release through this prayer ministry counseling approach. People from all over have e-mailed me after reading the manuscript for this book, reporting that much healing has come to them over a few weeks of letting God minister to them through the use of these seven integrated prayers.

The prayer ministry approach in this book will heal your heart. You may also use it as a Christian counselor to heal the wounded hearts of those to whom you minister. Therefore, let's overview the process again so all the steps involved in utilizing this Spirit-anointed counseling approach are clear.

Three unique characteristics of the "Prayer Ministry Counseling Model"

1. It integrates many healing prayer approaches.
2. All these healing prayer approaches are used TOGETHER on a SINGLE HEART ISSUE in A SINGLE THREE-HOUR PRAYER MINISTRY COUNSELING SESSION.
3. Most of the counseling session is devoted to prayer.

1. It integrates many healing prayer approaches

Over the last thirty years, God has raised up many great men and women who have restored outstanding insights into prayer ministry counseling.

I started learning about deliverance 25 years ago from Derek Prince and Frank Hammond. Then, after a year or so, I discovered Rita Bennett and added inner healing. However, I still found counseling people so difficult and frustrating that I was glad that God called me into teaching rather than counseling. Counseling gratefully went on the back burner of my life for about twenty years. Even though I did explore John and Paula Sandford's books during these years, I never quite caught how to use the techniques easily or simply and, therefore, never used their techniques much myself, although my wife and I did go to Elijah House and receive a week of ministry from Mark Sandford. The Sandfords, of course, have contributed the understanding of bitter root judgments, inner vows, and the law of sowing and reaping.

I was pretty much unaware of the breaking off of generational sins and curses and the severing of soul ties as counseling tools until 1999.

What we have done in this book is to allow God to draw together these various streams of thought and insight, and suggested that all of these prayer ministry counseling tools be used in an integrated manner—as a single, complete, unit, rather than individual approaches.

2. All these healing prayer approaches are used TOGETHER on a SINGLE HEART ISSUE in A SINGLE THREE-HOUR PRAYER MINISTRY COUNSELING SESSION

This is at the heart of the distinctiveness of this prayer ministry counseling approach. Rather than breaking off generational sins and curses one week, and dealing with soul ties another week, and renouncing inner vows and negative expectations another week, and inner healing another week, and deliverance a final week, we integrate all these proven prayer ministry counseling tools into one three-hour counseling session.

We identify one heart issue (often stated as an emotion) which is troubling the counselee, and then we progress in an orderly way through all these six prayer approaches, AS THEY RELATE TO THE ONE TROUBLING HEART EMOTION THAT HAS BEEN RAISED BY THE COUNSELEE.

Generational sins and curses: The healing process begins where the problem probably began: that is, with generational sins and curses. If everything (blessings and curses) is passed down from four up to a thousand generations, then it is almost inevitable that the issues the counselee is struggling with have roots in previous generations, for in four generations one has 30 ancestors. In ten generations, one has 2,046. It is almost certain that what he is struggling with was in someone in the ancestral group of 30 or, in the case of sexual sin, in the ancestral group of 2,046.

Ungodly soul ties: Then we move to what is most likely the second complicating factor, which is that ungodly soul ties have been formed throughout the individual's life which have fed into this problem. These soul ties were a natural result of the generational sins and curses, for the negative spiritual energies that were being passed down through the family line are now resident within the counselee. He began sending out a message into the spirit realm as soon as he was born which was heard and responded to appropriately by other people's spirits.

For example, if a spirit of rejection was in the family line, then the child's spirit is continuously sending out a message saying, "Reject me." As a result, the soul ties created throughout the counselee's life will be with people who are designed to reject him. The counselee's friends' spirits respond readily to the message being received, and their spirits say back, "Here is a person who insists on being rejected." The laws of sowing and reaping kick in and the message "Reject me" that has been sown in the counselee's heart now reaps a harvest of rejections from many people. Obviously, since this is happening on a spirit level, and the western world is so unaware of the spirit realm, much of this is happening within the individual on an unconscious rather than conscious level.

Most likely the counselee has formed many ungodly soul ties with people who are designed to reject others.

Negative expectations and inner vows: Now the counselee's expectations of rejection are confirmed by the experiences of life, as friend after friend rejects him. As a result, the counselee commits to an ungodly belief that "People will reject me." And, of course, to defend himself from the pain of this rejection, he makes a vow: "I will maintain a distance between myself and others, and isolate myself from people."

Traumatic pictures: Of course, there are some traumatic events in his life in which people reject him big time. The memory of these scenes feeds this frenzy of passionate belief that "I will always be rejected!"

Deliverance: Now a wonderful house for a demon to live in has been built. Demons do not have bodies, so they are constantly looking for a place they can call home and they, of course, will be drawn to this individual. This house has great foundations (generational sins and curses), wonderful flooring (ungodly soul ties), excellent walls (negative expectations and inner vows), and a watertight roof (traumatic pictures which control the heart). Why wouldn't demons be more than pleased to dwell there? In they come, compounding the problem.

Will worship: And, of course, the Christian has been taught that he shouldn't feel rejection because God has loved and accepted him. So he feels guilty about feeling rejected, and sets his will to overcome this feeling of rejection. Self-will thus becomes the ceiling of the house in which the demon lives. This setting of the will doesn't work, of course, because emotions are not corrected by commands made by your will. Negative emotions are caused by sin energies which are healed by prayer.

In addition, we are not supposed to set our wills to overcome sin through our own strength or our own will-power. We are to set our wills to come to the indwelling Holy Spirit and call Him forth to do what we can't do, which is to live a victorious Christian life.[1]

Summary: So in prayer ministry counseling, we are in an orderly manner dismantling a demon's home and then casting him out, thus freeing the counselee from a lifetime of oppression by Satan (Acts 10:38). We begin by removing the strength of the foundations, then we tear up the floor boards, take down the walls, and pull off the roof. Finally, we command the demon to leave, and he must, as he no longer has a home in which to live.

I find that the seven prayers work wonderfully together in healing the strands that feed emotional and sin problems within people's lives, setting free all who are oppressed by the devil.

Dismantling Demons' Homes

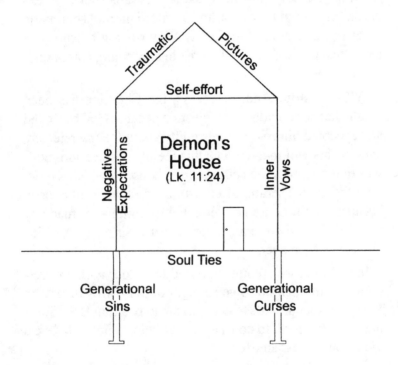

3. Most of the counseling session is devoted to prayer

This is one of the things I really love about this counseling approach. Rather than the counselee spending a great deal of time telling me about his life, we go straight into prayer ministry.

Instead of beginning the counseling session by asking him to tell me his troubles and his woes, I pray, "Holy Spirit, please reveal to us what is in the counselee's heart." Or, I may say to the counselee, "Ask the Holy Spirit, `What negative emotion is in my heart?'"

He may respond, "Anger."

I write down "anger" on the "Contributing Strands Worksheet," which is the primary worksheet used in the counseling session, and ask the second question.

Generational sins and curses: "Who in your family line exhibited anger?" He tells me, and I write the names down. Then we immediately go into prayer, placing the Cross of Christ between these individuals and the counselee (who is pictured as a baby in the womb). We are already into healing prayer within five minutes of the session beginning. While placing the Cross between him and his ancestors, I go right on into the next prayer, which is severing ungodly soul ties, because not only was sin energy coming from generational sins and curses, but it was also coming from soul ties with his parents. Therefore, asking God to sever the ungodly aspect of this soul tie with his parents is appropriate at this time.

I may follow up this prayer by laying my hand on his heart and praying for him to experience the freedom and release that Christ is offering as He halts the generational sin (and accompanying curses) of anger which are coming through the family line and cuts off the ungodly soul tie with his parents.

As a cautionary measure: When praying for a woman, I ask her to lay her hand on her own heart, and I lay my hand on her hand so no one can be offended and inappropriate touching does not take place. This is the normal procedure I am using when I say, "I lay my hand on his heart."

Why picture the Cross between the baby in the womb and his ancestors?

Of course, an adult who knows the power of the Cross of Christ could simply pray and place the Cross of Christ between him and his ancestors. However, heart-level healing occurs most completely when one goes back to the situation where the wound or hurt happened and welcomes Christ into that wound, to minister His healing from the midst of that hurtful situation. When Christ's healing and delivering power becomes present from the midst of the scene in which the hurt occurs, the healing is much more complete and powerful. And, of course, pictures are the language of the heart. So, whenever we deal with pictures we are speaking to the heart in a language to which it can readily respond.

Ungodly soul ties: I then ask, "What close relationships have you had during your life where people have demonstrated anger and fed anger to and in you? Tune to flow and pictures, and see whose names and faces come to your heart and mind."

He gives me a list of people's names which I write down, and then we pray through each one, asking God to sever the ungodly soul tie between those individuals and the counselee. I may do the praying, or I may give the worksheet to the counselee and let him pray, depending on what the Holy Spirit is saying will be most expedient. If the counselee is unsure and tentative, then I pray. If the counselee is mature and capable, then perhaps I will have him pray the prayers of severance. So again, we are in prayer. I give a copy of the "Prayers That Heal the Heart Review Card" to the counselee to aid him in his praying. I may even keep a copy of that "Review Card" on my lap to guide me in my praying, just so I don't forget any important parts of the process.

I may follow up this prayer time by laying my hand on his heart again and praying for healing and restoration of his heart.

Negative expectations and inner vows: I then ask him to tune to flow and tell me what negative expectations he has which are feeding anger in his life.

He gives me the first negative expectation which I write down. As I write, I say, "Because of this belief that _____, what promise or vow have you made to yourself?" He tells me and I write it down. As I write, I say to him, "Now tune to flow again and ask, 'God, what is Your truth which counters this negative expectation?'" He receives from his heart God's alternative positive belief, which he tells me, and I write it down. As I write, I ask, "What does God want you to purpose to do through the power of the Holy Spirit in light of this new godly belief?" He tells me and I write it down.

If he has trouble identifying what godly truth or godly purpose is to counter his ungodly beliefs and vows, I may help by offering some suggestions to him, and asking if he senses that these are correct or truthful for him and his situation. Does his spirit bear witness with my suggested answers? If he says, "Yes," then I write them down. Make sure that open, honest responses are maintained between you and the counselee, and that if he feels a need to, he can say, "No, that doesn't fit."

Now we are ready to pray again. In this prayer, the counselee repents of and renounces his negative expectation and inner vow and states his commitment to God's countering truths and Holy Spirit purposes.

Great, one ungodly belief dismantled and replaced!

Now we repeat the above process with me asking, "What other beliefs do you have in your life which are producing anger?" He gives me the next one and we repeat the exact process.

We continue this process until no more beliefs come to his mind which are producing anger in his life.

Receiving divine pictures: While going through these ungodly beliefs, you may hit some which you sense are really bedrock beliefs with traumatic pictures behind them. You will note these by the intensity in the person's voice as he states the ungodly belief. When this happens, this may be a good place to go into inner healing prayer and receive divine pictures to replace this negative picture. He is obviously looking at a very negative picture right now, which doesn't have Jesus in it.

I ask, "Is there a particular early scene in your life which connects with this belief concerning anger or with the anger you are currently feeling?" "Yes!" he will exclaim. So I suggest, "Let's go back to that scene and look around for Jesus, for He surely was there. Why don't you invite Him into that scene and see where He is and what He is doing?"

Now we are back to prayer again, and the counselee is asking, looking, listening, and sharing with me what he is seeing. I encourage him in faith to believe what he is seeing and to keep his eyes on Jesus, and to watch Him and respond to Him and to follow His lead, and to describe to me what is happening. I tell him over and over to stay tuned to the flow of the Holy Spirit, to keep his eyes on Jesus, and to respond to what He is doing. This becomes a wonderful healing time as Jesus does absolutely amazing things.

Of course, I am responsible to oversee the entire process, so if the person gets off track I am to guide him back. One counselee I was working with had grabbed Jesus' arm in the scene and was directing Him away from a dark house which Jesus wanted to enter with her. I gently said, "Let's not control Jesus. Let's follow His lead. He knows what is best. He knows how to best heal your heart. Follow Him." She did, and they entered the room. Jesus' light filled the place and He ministered to the fears she had about the room and what had happened to her there. She was healed!

Another counselee suggested that Jesus wanted to punch her abuser out. I said, "No, I don't think so. Just fix your eyes on Jesus and see what He actually is doing, not what you want Him to do."

Always remember, we are not to control or guide Jesus, or to paint scenes of our choosing. Instead, we are to fix our eyes on Jesus, and ask the Holy Spirit to grant us revelation by showing us what Jesus was doing in the situation.

If we didn't go into inner healing concerning one of the ungodly beliefs, then our next step after completing the ungodly beliefs and inner vows section will be inner healing, or the receiving of divine pictures. I will ask the counselee to go back to his early life when he had a painful memory which produced anger like he is feeling now. Back we go, and we pray an inner healing prayer as described above.

I write down the scene as he describes what Jesus is doing.

Deliverance: Now we are almost ready for deliverance. I ask him what other similar emotions come alongside anger or seem to cluster together with it or feed it. He will likely give me a list of things like hatred, wrath, envy, malice, murder, etc. I jot these down as some accompanying demons which we have probably also undermined and for which we can minister deliverance along with the demon of anger.

When casting out the demon of anger, I will be open to the flow of the Holy Spirit to give me the names of other demons in the cluster (in addition to the names the counselee has already given me). As these names come to me, I have the counselee renounce these demons also, and I cast them out.

We begin the deliverance by having the counselee repent again of the sin of anger, renounce the demon of anger, and set his will against it. The other counselor and I pray and command the demon to come out. I watch to see if I can observe a sense of release sweep over his body as we command the demon to leave. When I see this release, I ask him if he has sensed it. If so, then we pray for the Holy Spirit to come and fill this area and to take control of it. If I don't see a release after a couple of minutes of commanding the spirit to come out, I ask the counselee what he is sensing. I respond based on what he tells me. If he has felt a release, then fine, we pray for the Holy Spirit to fill the area. If he hasn't felt a release, then we ask, "What is this demon hanging on to? What is it anchored into?" The counselee and the counselors tune to Holy Spirit flow and see what ideas or pictures light upon their minds. They process appropriately whatever information they receive.

We continue deliverance prayer, dealing with each of the other demons in the cluster of anger.

Summary: That is the whole process. Plan for a three-hour counseling session to complete it. You could have the counselee read this book prior to the appointment, and come to the counseling session with a "Contributing Strands Worksheet" largely filled in. In this case, your counseling session could probably be one hour. The result should be a major breakthrough in the counselee's life.

He should go home with a copy of the completed "Contributing Strands Worksheet" for him to prayerfully review as well as some homework as suggested in Chapter Five of this book.

If he comes back for a future session, it will be to do the entire process all over again with another negative emotion which is on his heart. Or, if he needs some mopping up of remaining demons in the cluster that surround anger, then you might do some additional deliverance for things like hatred, malice, resentment, wrath, unforgiveness, murder, etc. which would all be demons which could be related in a cluster to anger. Or, you may find that not all negative beliefs were dealt with in the counseling session, and that the negative beliefs which remained became railways which the demons rode back into the person's heart. In this case, these negative beliefs will have to be dealt with and deliverance prayer prayed again.

The counselee can perhaps do this mopping up deliverance ministry on his own in his homework time, or he may need you to assist. I would not feel that I had to go through an entire "Contributing Strands Worksheet" to remove the remaining cluster demons. They probably are sufficiently undermined that they will simply come out. However, if you get stuck with one resisting exit, then you will have to discover what it is anchored to and get that anchor repented of, renounced and removed so that the demon will leave. The anchor most likely will be something which can be removed with one of the first five prayer approaches.

Dreams can assist: If you can't uncover an anchor and get a problem solved, have the counselee ask God for a dream at night which shows him what the root problem is. Have him put his journal next to his bed when he goes to sleep, and to pray as he drifts off for God to give him a dream showing him the root issue that needs to be dealt with. He can, and He will. When he awakens from a dream, he is to get up immediately and record key elements of the dream, and then tune to flow and ask God to show him the interpretation of the dream. He is to write down what comes to him and bring that into the next counseling session.

Thus we have it, prayer ministry counseling where the ministry session is focused most largely on prayer.

Prerequisites for the counselee:

1. That he has given his life to Jesus, and made Him his Lord and Savior.

2. That he be seeking to grow in the Lord, and be diligent and faithful.

3. That he know how to hear God's voice and how to see vision. "My sheep hear My voice" (John 10:27). "My words ("*rhemas*" in the Greek, meaning "spoken words") are spirit and life" (John 6:63). If one can't hear the spoken words of life from his Shepherd, Jesus, it is highly unlikely that he will be healed, because Satan surely is communicating with us on a regular basis. Therefore, if one can hear the thoughts of demons but doesn't know how to hear (or recognize) the thoughts of his Lord and Savior, he is in a mess.[2]

4. Quicker results will occur if he has read this book, for then he will understand the process and the principles and be able to work intelligently, devotionally, and wholeheartedly with them and with you, as an active participant.

5. That he know how to overcome the flesh by the power of the indwelling Holy Spirit, and not by self effort.

156

Read *Naturally Supernatural* by Mark and Patti Virkler to deepen this revelation truth.

Prerequisites for the counselor:

1. That he has given his life to Jesus, and made Him his Lord and Savior.

2. That he be seeking to grow in the Lord, and be diligent and faithful.

3. That he knows how to hear God's voice and how to see vision. (It is recommended that he has read and is practicing the principles of the book *Communion with God* by Mark and Patti Virkler.)

4. That he has the ability to interpret dreams. (The following resources are strongly recommended: *Dreams: Wisdom Within* by Herman Riffel and *Biblical Research Concerning Dreams and Visions* by Mark and Patti Virkler.)

5. That he understands how to minister out of the anointing of the Holy Spirit and has a substantial background of understanding and experience in these prayer areas. It is recommended that he read many of the books listed in the bibliography. It is also recommended that he receive some apprenticeship under people who are experienced in these ministry areas.

6. That he has processed issues in his own heart in detail, using the patterns, worksheets and procedures outlined in this book.

7. That he work in a team with one who is opposite from him in spiritual gifting. If he is more left-brain or more of a teacher, then he should team up with a person who is more right-brain or more of a prophet, and vice versa. In this way a more complete, balanced ministry is offered to the counselee.

8. **Important:** That he has revelation knowledge of the Word of God and enough Bible in him to discern the true from the false in what the counselee is bringing forth in the session. We need to frame everything in biblical truth.

9. That he knows how to guide the counselee in overcoming his flesh by the power of the indwelling Holy Spirit, and not by self effort. Read *Naturally Supernatural* by Mark and Patti Virkler to deepen this revelation truth.

An Overview of the Prayer Ministry Counseling Process:

1. **Rely upon the voice and vision of God** throughout the process. Tune to the Holy Spirit's flow and follow that flow of thoughts and pictures which alight upon you as you minister in the Holy Spirit. This flow will be instructing you how to proceed! The Holy Spirit will guide you, giving you the names of all the demons in the cluster you are evicting. If you become stuck and nothing is happening, flowing thoughts and flowing pictures from the Holy Spirit will instruct you where the blockage is and where to retrace your steps in order to get things moving again.

> *"Jesus replied, 'I assure you, the Son can do nothing of Himself. He does only what he sees the Father doing . . . I do nothing without consulting the Father. I judge as I am told. And my judgment is absolutely just, because it is according to the will of God.'"* (John 5:19, 30, NLT)

- If Jesus did not feel He could speak or minister outside of direct guidance, then surely we can't.

- The Spirit-anointed counseling model is built upon the assumptions that Jesus is alive today, speaking directly into the hearts of all believers, providing vision and healing if they will but receive and do what He says.

2. **Draw out counselee's dreams** and interpretations and work with them. The dream shows what the heart needs to deal with next. It answers the question "What is in my heart?"

   "I will bless the Lord who guides me. Even at night my heart instructs me." (Psalm 16:7, NLT)

3. **For empowered and balanced ministry, use counseling teams of two,** consisting of a right-brain prophet and a left-brain teacher (Acts 13:1). Jesus insisted that the disciples minister in teams of two (Luke 10:1). The power of the agreement of two is that anything they ask will be done for them (Matthew. 18:19). Make sure all counseling has the appearance of propriety (1 Thessalonians 5:22). Constantly guard your own heart in all counseling situations so that Satan is not given a foothold (Proverbs 4:23). If desired, a third person may be present to take notes, to be trained, and to pray quietly.

4. **Require a serious commitment by the counselee** toward healing and wholeness. This will weed out those who aren't ready yet to put forth the intensity of effort it takes to become and stay healed, and will keep the counselor from spending his valuable time on people who are not serious about being whole.

   Some people are ripe for healing; some are not. Test for ripeness. Be aware of people just wanting sympathy and looking to rehearse their pain over and over.

The counselee must complete the assigned weekly homework involving worksheets, Scripture memorization, recording his daily dialogue with God, and summaries of dreams and possible interpretations. These assignments must be completed before the next counseling session, or the session will be postponed until the homework is completed. Exercise, healthy diet, and fasting are also required as discussed below.

5. **A suggested three-month program for working with a counselee with major life-dominating problems:** We suggest six two-hour counseling sessions, every other week for six weeks, interspersed with six forty-five minute counseling sessions, every other week, for a total of twelve counseling sessions.

In the first session (which might last up to three hours), complete a "Contributing Strands Worksheet" with the client for one heart issue. Then pray through the seven prayers with him to heal that heart issue.

Assign homework for the following week, in which he completes a "New Truth Bible Meditation Worksheet" on the area(s) you have just dealt with.

The client brings this into the next week's counseling session (which is only 45 minutes long), and you review it with him, helping him see or add anything he may have missed. Then pray and discern with him what the next heart issue is that needs to be processed and send him home with a blank "Contributing Strands Worksheet" to complete. He completes this as thoroughly as he can on his own during the following week.

He brings the completed "Contributing Strands Worksheet" in to the next counseling session, which you will plan to have last about two hours. Go over it with him, deepening and expanding the answers as the Holy Spirit leads, and then praying through the seven prayers with him. He is encouraged to pray through some of the first four prayers on his own during the week as he is completing the "Contributing Strands Worksheet." In the counseling session, complete whatever prayers the counselee has not, focusing especially on the inner healing and deliverance prayers.

This whole two-week process (i.e., a two-hour session followed by a 45-minute session) is repeated six times for a total of twelve sessions over twelve weeks. By the end of this time, the counselor and counselee should expect significant, if not complete, healing.

A review of the language of the heart

1. The heart speaks in a language that is different from the mind

- The language of the mind is cognitive, analytical, rational thoughts.
- The language of the heart is spontaneous ideas, pictures emotions and pondering.
- For a detailed exploration of heart, mind, flow, and Spirit, read the books *Communion with God, Dialogue with God, The Great Mystery, Sense Your*

Spirit, and *Wading Deeper in the River of God*, by the same authors. The Holy Spirit can anoint both the mind (with anointed reason - Luke 1:1-3) and the heart (with dream, vision and prophecy - Acts 2:17).

- See also Gary Smalley's book, *The Language of Love,* in which he teaches how to touch your spouse's heart by communicating using metaphors (i.e., picture stories).

- Remember Jesus: "without a parable (i.e., picture story) He taught them not" (Matthew 13:34). Jesus, of course, ministered healing to people's hearts.

2. The heart speaks using flow

"From his innermost being shall FLOW rivers of living water, but this He spoke of the Spirit." (John 7:38-39)

- While the mind can command recall of rational thoughts, the heart responds with "flowing" ideas, pictures and emotions. Therefore, in healing the heart, we tune away from command and analytical thoughts. Instead, we still ourselves and tune to flow (Psalm 46:10, John 7:38).

- The counselor waits upon flow. The counselee waits upon flow. Flow is honored and followed. That is why we ask the question, "What is in my heart?" If we still ourselves and tune to flow, the heart will send up a response (i.e., a spontaneous thought, picture or emotion) of the issue that needs to be dealt with. Now the heart is communicating directly with us, rather than our working with and through the mind. Working with the mind does not heal the heart.

Working with the heart heals the heart. Get this, or all is lost in your attempts to heal the heart!

3. The heart speaks using emotion

- When you ask the question "What is in my heart?" the heart could answer with any emotion or character trait which it is sensing at the time. Since the heart is healed in layers, what is on the surface and needs to be healed most immediately will reveal itself and respond first. Following is a sampling of some biblically-stated emotions on the level of the spirit, any of which one could be found within an unhealed heart.

- Troubled (Genesis 41:7b-8, Dan. 2:1-3, John 13:21); anguished or oppressed (1 Samuel 1:15); angry (Ecclesiastics 10:4); discouraged (Isaiah 19:3); forsaken or grieved (Isaiah 54:6); enraged (Ezekiel 3:14); distressed (Daniel 7:15); hardened (Deuteronomy 2:30); doubting (Mark 11:23, Luke 24:25); haughty (Proverbs 16:18); defiled (2 Corinthians 7:1).

- Obviously, a healed heart is full of many positive emotions, some such as love, joy, peace are listed in Galatians 5:22.

4. The heart speaks using dream, vision and pictures.

- Dream, vision, pictures and imagination are all outworkings of the visionary capacity which the Bible says is located on the level of the heart. The heart speaks using pictures.

- Imagination is spoken of as being in the heart (1 Chronicles. 29:18; Genesis 8:21; Psalms 140:2; Proverbs 6:18; Jeremiah 7:24, 23:16). When God fills man's visual capacity, it becomes a dream or a vision (Numbers 12:6, Acts 2:17). Jesus saw vision constantly (John 5:19-20,30; 8:26, 38) and spoke continuously in a picturesque way (Matthew 13:34).

• Since the western world has focused on the mind instead of the heart, pictures, dream and vision have been lost in the shuffle.

5. What to do if the counselee cannot see vision:

• If the counselee's ability to see pictures has been stunted by western rationalism, several options are available to you: 1) you can look for vision yourself and describe what you are seeing; or 2) you can let him follow the emotion in his heart back to the initial hurt, then invite Jesus to speak into that pain, hearing His words of life; and/or 3) you can have the counselee follow the appropriate prayer approaches to heal his spiritual blindness and pray for God to heal the eyes of his heart.

• Prayer approaches for restoring vision to one who is blind might include all seven basic prayer approaches taught in this book: 1) breaking generational curses; 2) cutting off negative soul ties (from parents, pastors and teachers who do not believe in vision today); 3) replacing negative expectations ("God doesn't give vision anymore today."); 4) renouncing inner vows ("I cannot or will not see vision."); 5) healing traumatic pictures ("I never want to see again, because of the horrible flashbacks I used to have from a terrible tragedy in my life."); 6) casting out demons (e.g. spiritual blindness); and 7) experiencing the law of the Spirit of life in Christ Jesus to set you free from enslavement to sin (the sin of committing oneself to not presenting the eyes to God as a living sacrifice which is his reasonable service, thus a sin of omission [Romans 12:1, James 4:17].) Then, using vision yourself, see Jesus lay His hands on the counselee's blind eyes, and lay your own hands upon his eyes (seeing them as the hands of Christ), praying for Jesus to touch and heal his eyes. Vision should now begin to be restored to his life.[3]

If the person has dreams but cannot picture his living room couch, then he has made a vow not to see visions. When his conscious mind is in control, he doesn't see, but when he goes to sleep and his unconscious comes to the forefront, he can see. Thus, it was a "conscious" vow made at some time in his life. (However, he may not be consciously aware he made this vow until he reflects back on his life in prayer, and God shows him when he made it.) He will need to repent of the vow, and ask God to restore vision to him. Generally, when I give training seminars, two people in a hundred cannot picture their living room couch. The two basic reasons people make such vows are to either stop a replay of a traumatic scene or to overcome the sin of lust.

6. **To heal the heart we must use the language of the heart - spontaneous ideas, pictures, emotions and pondering.**

   • Emotions are by-products of pictures (and the lies that surround the picture and the demons which have taken up residence in the lies). Therefore, to heal an emotion, you must let Jesus heal the pictures by revealing to you where He was in the situation (scene) and what He was doing. The words He speaks from the midst of that scene are divine truth which replace your lies, and by His authority any resident demons are expelled. As a result, the negative emotion in the heart is healed.

- Negative emotions come from negative pictures (i.e., pictures which do not have Jesus in them).

- Positive emotions come from positive pictures (i.e., pictures which do have Jesus in them).

- Receiving divine pictures is allowing Jesus to replace pictures in your mind, removing pictures which do not have Jesus in them (which are lies) and replacing them with pictures which do have Jesus in them (which are truth). You see, *Jesus is omnipresent*. He *was* in the situation which left you with a negative picture. The reason the picture is negative is because you were not seeing truth. You did not see Jesus, Who *was* there. In healing this problem, you go back and look and see Jesus there. You see what He was doing and hear what He is saying. Now you are seeing truth and your heart is healed. Lies bring destruction; the truth brings life. "You will know the truth, and the truth will set you free."

7. Heart healing must occur on a heart level, not a mind level.

- A mentally recited biblical principle does little to heal a damaged heart.

- Jesus appearing in the negative heart picture (memory) and speaking the same truth which had been mentally recited, from the midst of the scene (through flowing thoughts coming to the counselee's mind while his eyes are fixed on Jesus), will bring total and complete healing to the damage in the heart caused by this scene!

- **Principle:** Jesus speaking from the setting of a painful memory will bring healing to that memory.

An overview of hearing from your heart through dreams

The night after I received prayer ministry in Australia, I had a dream involving a person whom I had forgotten about and with whom I had a soul tie. When I journaled about the dream upon awakening, the Lord told me that this was a key person whom I had a soul tie with, because it was the first soul tie I had established in this particular area of my life. This soul tie was a major contributor to my current problems, and needed to be severed, which I did in prayer. In the middle of the night as I journaled, I asked God to reveal any other people whom I had had soul ties with in this area and whom I had forgotten. God showed me several. I prayed for each to be severed, and that night felt an amazing release in my inner being.

Healing the **initial** event that created damage in the heart is a key to healing. Other events build upon this door-opening event. The door-opening event must be dealt with in prayer and the door closed for the healing to be thorough and complete.

Following are several principles of dream interpretation.

"I will bless the Lord who counsels me; He gives me wisdom in the night. He tells me what to do."
(Psalms 16:7, TLB)

Principles of Dream Interpretation

1. Most dreams are symbolic, so view them the same way you would view a political cartoon. Throw the switch in your brain that says, "Look at this symbolically."

2. The symbols will come out of the dreamer's life, so ask, "What does this symbol mean to me?" or, if working on another's dream, ask, "What does this symbol mean to you?"

3. The dream generally speaks of the concerns which your heart is currently facing. So ask, "What issues was I processing the day before I had the dream?"

4. The dreamer's heart will leap and "witness" and say "Aha!" when it hears the right interpretation to the dream, so never accept an interpretation that the dreamer's heart does not affirm.

5. Never make a major decision in your life based only on a dream without some additional confirmation through some of the other ways that God speaks to us and guides us.

How to recall dreams:

1. Say to yourself, "I believe dreams contain a valid message."

2. Ask God to speak to you through dreams as you fall asleep.

3. Put your journal next to your bed and immediately record your dreams upon awakening.

4. Get eight hours of sleep, as the entire last hour will be spent dreaming.

5. Awaken naturally, without the use of an alarm clock.

If you do the above five things, you will recall dreams every week.

See Appendix E for more principles on dream interpretation.

Review of the seven key prayers which heal the heart:

1. Breaking generational sins and curses
2. Severing ungodly soul ties
3. Replacing negative expectations
4. Renouncing inner vows
5. Receiving divine pictures/visions
6. Casting out demons
7. Experiencing the Spirit of life in Christ Jesus

Each of these seven prayer approaches follows naturally from one to the other in the counseling session. Each of these approaches has three parts to it (on the "Prayers That Heal the Heart Review Card"), which means you actually have twenty-one different specific prayers that can be prayed to completely heal a negative power within a person's heart.

Do you need to pray all twenty-one? Is that too many? Does this become too legalistic? Well, a few thoughts. No, I don't think you need to pray all of them. God can heal in less than twenty steps. I generally do not go through all of the prayers when I am working in a counseling session. However, if I get stuck and a demon is hanging on and not coming out, then I review these steps to see which ones I forgot, as they may be allowing a foothold to which the demon is anchoring itself.

Is twenty-one too many? I doubt it. If a person has been struggling for many years with a life-dominating problem and in a few hours you can take him through twenty or so prayers to ensure that the problem and all its roots have been fully dealt with, and the life-dominating problem vanishes, will the counselee be glad you have taken him through the twenty prayers? I certainly assume so, for I am sure if he is a Christian he has prayed many more than twenty ineffective prayers about this problem. To pray twenty-one effective prayers which actually healed it at its core would be astounding.

Why twenty-one specific prayers? They ensure that you get all the roots and angles to the problem dealt with so the healing is 100% complete.

Is it legalistic? I think so.

Do I believe in legalism? Yes, under a certain, specific circumstance.

What circumstance? When I am learning a new skill, I put myself under law in order to master it. After I have mastered the new skill, I then revert to grace and simply ask the Holy Spirit to guide me. It is easier for Him to guide me when I have His Word, His principles and His ways hidden in my heart. Then He actually has something He can draw upon when His Spirit wants to bring specific truths back out of my heart which apply to the specific situation I am facing.

So, my suggestion is, why not pray all these prayers ten or twenty times, until you are comfortable with them and their flow and the structure they have and the reasons they are there in the first place? Once you have internalized this, then go back to simply asking the Holy Spirit to guide you (i.e., "flow") as you pray for yourself and for others.

Would I ever simply pray deliverance prayer in a situation? Perhaps. Has it worked? Yes. However, now when it doesn't, I know what to do. I go back and start with prayer one and work through the series of prayers, dismantling the demon's home so that he will surely have to come out.

When only ONE prayer was needed to cast out a demon

I was on the phone recently with a student of mine taking a course from Christian Leadership University. She shared that she was having a great struggle with anger. I suggested it may be a demon and if she wanted I would pray and cast it out of her. She was a bit shocked, but she agreed to have me pray. So, with a simple prayer of deliverance and in less than two minutes, she was freed of a demon of anger. She felt it trembling in her stomach as I prayed and then felt it leave through her breath. She was astounded. I was thrilled.

A couple of weeks later I received her completed course work, and along with it came a note which she (Connie Zachrich) has allowed me to share with you. In part it said:

> I want to thank you for praying for me over the phone. I am so very thankful and so relieved to be free of that ugly spirit of anger. I have been carrying that with me for at least three years. At first I just thought it was mood swings . . . I felt so defeated as a Christian. . . . When I got hold of a teaching on "Forgiveness Therapy" and the book, *Making Love Last a Lifetime,* God began showing me how angry and bitter I had become. I did not like what I saw. I finally had come to the point of godly sorrow and repentance, but still couldn't disconnect the emotion of anger every time I had a memory of some of the things perpetrated against me. I walked around in pain every moment of every day. I cried a lot and was depressed to the point of wanting to die so all the pain would end. Then God led me to you with His perfect timing that I never take for granted. I see now how He was gently leading me to the point in time where you could be used by Him to do that which He has been wanting to do for me for such a long time. . . . Now I am interested in learning about deliverance, so I can be used by God in order that those I know and love who find themselves in need of deliverance, can be set free. The Scripture, "Those who God sets free **are free indeed!**" is so alive in me now!

Thank you for your sensitivity to my circumstances and for walking in obedience by faith. I can't thank you enough. I have that peace that passes all understanding, and joy has returned to my camp!

What a wonderful letter to receive! Can you see why only a simple deliverance prayer was necessary to set her free— why we didn't need to go through the other prayers to dismantle the demon's home? She had taken the time to prepare her heart for deliverance. She hated the sin of anger. She had repented of it. She wanted it gone. She was standing against it. The stage was set. All we needed now was a simple deliverance prayer. So, yes, a person can be set free in less than twenty or even seven prayers. It can be done with a simple command, *when the heart is ready.* I am sure that is exactly what the situation was with the crowds which followed Jesus and sought His hand of deliverance. They had prepared themselves, and the deliverance came readily, especially when Jesus prefaced His healing and deliverance ministry with an anointed time of teaching.

The seven key prayers I want to memorize

In my heart, I think of it this way: There are seven key prayers I want to pray. They are:

1. Lord, I place the Cross of Jesus between me and my ancestors. I command the sin and curses of _____ to be halted at the Cross and I pray for freedom and release to flow down from the Cross upon that baby in the womb.

2. Lord, sever that ungodly soul tie between me and _____ and release me from the ungodly flow of _____ from him to me. Restore back to me any parts which have been taken, and send back any parts of others which have been received.

3. I confess and repent of my negative belief and expectation that _____ and replace it with your godly belief that _____ .

4. I confess and repent of the vow I have made that _____ and replace it with Your godly, Spirit-anointed purpose to _____ .

5. Lord, please show up in the midst of this troubling scene and speak to me, and show me what You are doing.

6. In the Name of Jesus Christ, I cast out the demon of _____ .

7. Homework: Thank You, Holy Spirit, that You live within me. I release the Holy Spirit's power to overcome _____ .

If there are any key things I want to memorize so I can walk through them forward and backward and even upside down, it is these seven prayers. Internalize them so you can quickly process what is in one's heart, whether it is your heart or someone else's.

In addition, I would suggest you memorize the following lists so that they can flow out of you effortlessly when ministering either to yourself or to others.

The three sub-parts to each prayer

Rather than memorize the individual sub-parts of the seven prayer approaches, they are essentially as follows:

Confession, Forgiveness, Cleansing - 1 John 1:9

Memorize the seven initial clues which indicate prayer ministry is needed

1. Pressures within you that are being held at abeyance, and are not truly gone.

2. Issues which come back continuously.

3. Any habitual or stubborn sin pattern.

4. Habitual weaknesses - mental, emotional, spiritual, physical.

5. Anything within that is contrary to peace, hope and love.

6. Anything within that lines up with any activity of Satan.

7. Addictions or out-of-control areas.

Memorize the seven steps to discovering and healing a hurt in your heart

1. Ask the right question ("What Is in My Heart? Worksheet").

2. Assume all seven healing prayer approaches apply.

3. Ask more specific questions to reveal contributing strands to any heart issue ("Contributing Strands Worksheet").

4. Pray through the seven healing prayers.

5. Seal it with a "New Truth Bible Meditation Worksheet."

6. Create "Memorial Stones" declaring God's supernatural deliverance.

7. Complete the circle of life; Minister life out of death.

Memorize the following overview of the language of the heart

1. The heart speaks in a language that is different from the mind. The language of the mind is logical ideas. The language of the heart is emotion, flow and pictures.

2. Heart healing must occur on the level of the heart, not merely in the mind. To heal the heart we must use the language of the heart.

The heart is healed in layers, so give time to complete the healing!

Jesus spent forty days alone in prayer and fasting in the wilderness, processing temptations which Satan threw at him (Luke 4:1-14).

Would it be reasonable to expect that it might take an equal amount of time for me to process the attacks of Satan within my own heart? I think so.

And if I didn't want to take forty days alone fasting, but instead decided to spread the healing out over time, could I anticipate it taking a year of my devotional and Bible meditation time to process and heal my heart? I think so.

I challenge you to take a year (if necessary) to process your heart in-depth, using the healing prayer approaches taught in this book. You can pray over and over the initial prayer, "What is in my heart?" and then process the issues that come forth.

Healing will occur in layers. You get one layer off and a few days or a week or two later another layer surfaces. What surfaces may be similar to or different from what you already prayed for. If it is different, then you are off to removing the next cluster of demons.

If it is similar, it probably means you did not get the whole cluster out (i.e., some in a particular cluster were left in). In this case, you will need to go back and get the rest. For example, you may have cast out lust and lust of the eyes, but missed pornography, fornication, adultery, perversion, fantasy, homosexuality, lesbianism, rape, bondage, etc. Review cluster groupings in the book *Pigs in the Parlor*, and ask the Holy Spirit, "What else do I have within me in this or a related category?" Tune to flow. Receive God's answer as spontaneous thoughts which light upon your mind. Then pray through the additional issues God has brought to your attention.

If similar urges return after a few weeks, you might need to go back and extend the prayers you have already prayed. For example, ask God to remind you of any additional soul ties which you forgot to break in the earlier session. Then ask God to sever them. You may also ask, "God, are there additional negative expectations or vows which I need to repent of in this area to more fully clean this area out? God, are there additional pictures which You need to walk into? Are there additional demons connected to this area from which I need to be delivered?"

If the pressure in an area is partially released but not fully gone (or comes back) that means you have dealt with the issues partially but not fully. Keep going back through these prayers in the above manner until there is a peace in the area and a release from all pressure. Do not accept partial healing. Keep going back and asking God to show you additional things you need to pray through until your healing is full and complete. Do not settle for simply "feeling better." Do not quit until your heart abounds in faith, hope and love.

Remember the heart is healed in layers! And also remember that as we confess our sins to one another and pray for one another, we are healed (James 5:16). Do not shy away from confessing your sins to a prayer partner and being set free from them as he agrees with you in prayer for demonic strongholds to be uprooted and cast out of you.

Eventually, what will come forth when you ask the question, "What is in my heart?" will not be negative spirit emotions, but positive spirit emotions of love, peace, joy, faith, hope and power. This will be the evidence that you are healed and have been empowered within by the penetration of the Holy Spirit through the areas of your heart and soul. We will examine this in more detail in the next chapter.

Jesuit priests do a nine-day retreat every January to examine their lives. That may be a good idea for us, also. Once we are healed and restored, wouldn't it be wise to take a few days every January again to ask the question "What is in my heart?" and keep asking it until it is pure? I think so.

Counsel for the counseling session

1. Honor the flow of the Holy Spirit: The counselor is to be constantly open and seeking flowing thoughts and visions from God's Holy Spirit within him. He must remain open to flow throughout all the prayers and the entire process. This keeps the prayers from becoming mechanical formulas which rule out the presence and power of the Holy Spirit. Also, the Holy Spirit will bring things to mind which have been forgotten or never known by the counselee. Honor "flow" in the counseling session!

Flow may guide you to change the order of the prayers. For instance, I sometimes find I go from 1) generational sins to 2) soul ties to 5) inner healing to 6) deliverance. Then the counselee's homework is to pray prayers 3) renouncing negative expectations, 4) inner vows and 7) appropriating the Spirit's power to overcome the sin.

However, sometimes the demon is so entrenched in the negative expectations and inner vows that the counselee must identify, renounce, and separate himself from these things before the demon is ready to come out. Be aware of this possibility if you are attempting deliverance and the demon is not coming out.

2. Touching and praying for the heart: I often lay my hand on the person's heart and speak directly to it while freeing it from generational curses and sins and soul ties. (Men, be careful about laying your hand on a woman's heart - avoid touching her inappropriately. Also, realize that often sexual abuse victims don't want to be touched at all, so, men, especially, be sure to ask if it is all right to touch a female counselee before you touch her. Or, another possibility is for the counselee to put her own hand on her heart and for the counselor to put his hand upon the counselee's hand. This is especially wise if the counselor is a male and the counselee is a female.) Address the heart directly. Speak freedom and release and healing to it. It can hear and will respond to your direct words.

3. Expecting and discovering demonic clusters: Recognize that demons are in clusters. They like clusters of at least three because of the truth of Ecclesiastes 4:12. The person's heart can tell you what is in the cluster. Also, it may be helpful for you to be aware of likely clusters, such as those listed in the book, *Pigs in the Parlor*. As you become more experienced and as you stay tuned to the flow of the Holy Spirit, words will just pop into your head of additional demons in a cluster which the counselee should rebuke and which you should cast out. Maintaining a running, constantly-updated "What Is in My Heart? Worksheet" will help you discover clusters. If you have prayed for anger and seen partial release but not total freedom from anger, then ask the Lord, "What other demons are in this cluster with anger?" Tune to the Holy Spirit's flow and into your mind may pop words like hatred, malice, resentment, unforgiveness. These then are parts of the cluster which must be removed in future prayer sessions.

4. Tips on the deliverance prayer: Address the demon several times, commanding it to leave. Generally, there will be evidence of its leaving in (a) heavy breathing or coughing by the counselee (so keep your eyes open and be observant) and/or (b) the counselee feeling a sense of release. You can ask the counselee if he senses it is gone. The word for "spirit" and "breath" is the same in the Greek, so often when spirits leave, they leave through the breath. I feel that if the prayers have been effective then the counselee should, at a minimum, be feeling a sense of inner release.

Other demonic manifestations **during** the deliverance session may include trembling, shaking, lumps in the throat, pain in the stomach or chest or shoulders, bands around the head, etc.

If the demon is manifesting an inner tension in the counselee but not coming out, ask God what area in the earlier five prayers needs to be revisited so the demon's home can be more completely dismantled and the demon's anchors fully dislodged. Bind demons and command them to separate.

Also, if a demon is hanging on and not coming out, ask, "What is this demon anchored to?" Both the counselor and the counselee should then tune to flow and a response should be forthcoming. You can then pray through the issue indicated as the anchor. One deliverance was blocked by the fact that the counselee had, in his younger days, made a pact with the devil while listening to Satanic secular music. This pact, of course, needed to be renounced in prayer and the effects of this vow in his life cut off in the name of the Lord Jesus Christ.

5. Tips on receiving divine pictures: If you have returned to the first traumatic scene that gave birth to the emotional problems the counselee is facing, and the counselee is so emotionally distressed that he cannot see Jesus in that scene, ask him to look for a later occasion in his life where he felt this similar emotion. Invite Christ into that scene. Once healing of this less traumatic incident is complete, repeat the process with another future event. Then you should be able to return to the initial scene and bring Christ into it also, after some of the fear has been dealt with.

If the counselee has disconnected or dissociated himself from his childhood and is therefore unable to go back and picture it (probably because it was so painful), ask Jesus to meet him as an adult, take his hand, lead him back to a childhood scene, and show him the scenes necessary to heal the particular heart emotion being dealt with. We have seen that the Lord does honor that prayer and the counselee sees a vision of himself either as an adult together with Jesus watching a movie of a scene in which Jesus is ministering to the child in a troubling situation, or he may go back and actually be in the scene. We have seen both happen with good results. Often scenes appear which the counselee has forgotten or pushed from his mind.

6. Working backwards from a sickness: Often sicknesses and infirmities have contributing strands coming from our souls and spirits. 3 John 2 offers a prayer that we would prosper and be in good health just as our souls prosper, indicating a link between our souls' health and our bodies' health. Jesus healed "all who were oppressed by the devil," indicating that many sicknesses have a spiritual and/or demonic root (Acts 10:38). James 5:14-16 says we should confess our sins so we can be healed, also indicating that outer infirmity is a result of inner infirmity.

Therefore we need to learn to look at a sickness or infirmity as an outgrowth of a disturbance in our souls and our spirits. To heal the infirmity, we would heal the underlying disturbance on the level of the soul/spirit.

Think of it this way. An injury to your skeleton, muscles or ligaments will heal faster if the organ underlying that area is strong and healthy. Likewise, your organs will heal faster if the spiritual and soulish counterparts underlying that organ are healthy.

Or, we could say it another way. Imbalances in our spiritual or soul area (demons or soul ties) cause reactions which must be stored some place in the body. Various parts of the body store various illnesses (i.e., spiritually-caused illnesses).

It is like a family of maggots. Will they live in a new, clean trash can, or do they thrive in the areas of filth and impurity? The same principles apply in the spiritual realm. If our bodies are whole and clean, we will not only prevent evil and germs from entering and taking root in us, but by cleaning the soul and the spirit, demons or other uncleanness no longer find it a nice habitation and are much more willing to flee the area.

You may therefore start with a sickness and work backwards, asking the heart, "What is causing this sickness?" The heart knows, and, if one tunes to flow, his heart (and the Holy Spirit within his heart) will tell him. Then you can process the issue revealed, using the seven prayers.

Some specific questions you could ask about a sickness in order to discover contributing strands

- What bodily organ is affected or underlies the area of my body which is sick or infirm? If you need to, get your encyclopedia out and look at some pictures of the human body and refresh your memory as to what organs underlie various body parts.

- What does the Bible say about the relationship between this part of the body and an emotion or attitude? For example, a stiff neck is related to rebellion (Deuteronomy 31:27); gall is identified with bitterness (Acts 8:23); bones may be dried up because of a loss of hope (Ezekiel 37:11);

181

shoulders may represent government or authority (Isaiah 9:6); feet are associated with peace, loins with truth, heart/ lungs with righteousness (Ephesians 6:14-15) and the mind with hope (1 Thessalonians 5:8). Clues of underlying spiritual factors may be discovered by asking, "What spiritual or emotional condition could be contributing to this bodily weakness?"

- Natural health practitioners recognize other relationships between the body and character, emotion, and attitude which could be explored. These include:

> pineal gland - intuitive
> pituitary gland - analytical
> thyroid gland - self-pity
> heart - joy
> lungs - grief
> thymus - self-esteem
> liver - anger
> gallbladder - bitterness
> bladder - irritation
> spleen - jealousy
> colon - holding it in
> lymph - reliving it
> small intestine - gullible
> kidneys - fear
> pancreas - joy

- Ask, "What is happening to this part of the body - infection, injury, itching, pain, weakness, paralysis? In what way am I experiencing a counterpart to this physical experience in my heart, spirit or soul?"

- Consider the timing - "What happened in my life at the same time this infirmity began?" There could easily be a connection.

- Find additional clues for what is causing this infirmity by completing a "Contributing Strands Worksheet" and then receiving healing by praying through the seven prayers.

For example, I suddenly found myself extremely short of breath when I exercised. I asked Reuben DeHaan (my mentor in the area of health) what he suggested. He recommended an herbal combination called HIGS II. I discovered through muscle testing that I had an infection in my lung and verified that HIGS II would provide my body what it needed to restore the lung.

That night, I asked the Lord to show me any infection in my heart or spirit. (Lungs relate directly to breath, and breath and spirit are the same word in the Greek and in the Hebrew). I had a dream which, when God showed me the interpretation, indicated that the infection in my spirit arose from a sin of which I needed to repent. My journaling concerning the dream confirmed and enlarged my understanding of my sin and my need for repentance. I repented, and then prayed in faith for God to heal the infection in my spirit and my lung. I also began taking the herbal combination HIGS II. Within a couple of weeks, the infection was gone.

The restoration process above involved: 1) counsel from my mentor in the area of health; 2) confirmation through Muscle Response Testing; 3) confirmation and deeper understanding through a dream, its interpretation, and journaling; 4) repentance; 5) the prayer of faith for healing; and 6) taking an appropriate herb. I encourage you to use all these avenues when you need to restore health.

The end result of using these prayers (whether starting from a sickness and working backward, or starting with an emotional disturbance in one's heart) will often be freedom and release from physical sickness. Most sicknesses are caused indirectly by inner emotional and spiritual disturbances. As these disturbances are healed, the body, too, will be healed within a short time. Also, according to Jesus' ministry in the Gospels, some physical infirmities are caused by demons. So the casting out of demons which are directly causing certain infirmities can and will bring immediate healing.

7. Occult backgrounds: If the counselee has an occult background, he should not try self-deliverance. It is best for a mature, experienced counselor to assist.

8. Striving! Striving occurs when the counselor or counselee dismisses Jesus from the process and does it on his own. Do not let this happen. If it does, repent and turn your eyes and your heart away from self and back to Christ. Then pick up the activity again from a posture of Christ-consciousness (Galatians 2:20). This principle is taught in our book, *Naturally Supernatural*. We encourage all counselors and counselees to read this book and internalize this truth because it makes all the difference.

People can begin striving in the following ways: fighting with negative demonic thoughts themselves, rather than binding and casting out demons in the Name of Jesus; expressing their pain and sorrow, and not seeing Jesus there removing it by touching and healing it; thinking THEY have to come up with all the soul ties and the negative expectations and inner vows they have made, rather than relaxing and tuning to Holy Spirit flow and asking Him to show them each of these; thinking that they are the center of anything or any part of the process, rather than realizing that the Holy Spirit and the Lord Jesus Christ are the center of each part of

184

this healing process. If you are still living self conscious rather than Christ conscious, then you need a deeper revelation of Galatians 2:20.

9. How much time should be given to letting the counselee tell his story? (answer from Kay Cox)

In regard to the counseling sessions, Mark, I tend to take things as they fall. Yes, in my normal counseling sessions (which last for two hours), I would listen to the counselee telling his/her story with as little interruption as possible. I would work through the prayers regarding generational sins and breaking soul ties. Then I would isolate a particular issue, discuss this and then pray into that area, forgiveness and repentance being the major focus. I would concentrate on inner healing prayers after that, then go on to the next issue, discuss, forgive, etc., with prayers for that, and so on.

If I only had two-and-a-half hours with someone, and that was all I was likely to get, I would approach it as I did with you: listen, discuss, break soul ties, repent, forgive, pray, as we went along. A sort of short version, so to speak.

Many a time, when we are in the middle of a dinner party with our friends, someone will say something, recognize there was an issue in what he had said, repent, forgive and ask for prayer right at the table. It all depends where I am, who I am with, what the time limit is, how eager the person is, what is happening, what degree of confidence they need. At church, people approach me and want prayer right at the front step. When a soul is hurting and wants to repent of some particular sin, I just do what is necessary at the time. The inner healing first usually allows the demonic to come away very gently without much fuss and bother. Most of the deliverance sessions are very quiet.

10. Does prayer ministry work with drugged clients?

The following answer was provided by Mike Chaille from Ellel in Canada.

I don't know if you are familiar with the ministry of Jackie Pullinger in Hong Kong with drug addicts, but she has people praying in tongues for the addicts in their presence around the clock for one week. She has remarkable success because the prayer in the Spirit is going up to God, but also into their human spirits and building their spirits up to stand against the addiction.

One thing we are always careful about is to make sure we don't pray for anyone who doesn't understand what we are praying for. We never pray for anyone against their will. I guess my question would be, "Is the client aware of what you are praying and does she choose to be free?" The addicts in Hong Kong have chosen to leave their addictions and Jackie is praying for them to build up their spirits so they will have the strength to fight in their spirits against the desire of their soul to remain addicted. It is the battle of Romans 7 in which the spirit is strengthened to rule over the desires of the flesh.

We deal all the time with persons on anti-depressants. The anti-depressants affect body and soul, not spirits. We always pray the Lord causes the drugs to work to His advantage and they serve the proper purpose. We deal with any spirits of addiction attached to the drugs as well.

The main thing in all cases of depression is to get to the roots. It is usually rejection, self-rejection, or fear of rejection. Also, they usually have damaged or sick spirits from deep rejection or abuse. That is why we pray into their spirits a lot of Holy Spirit life. It would be helpful for you to read the book, *Healing the Human Spirit* by Ruth Hawkey. We carry it.

Freed parents praying for their children

If parents have received deliverance and broken off generational sins, they will now need to see that their children are ministered to, also. They should construct a list of the generational sins which are in their two family lines using the "What Is in My Ancestors?" and "What Is in My Children? Worksheets." While doing this, they can examine their children's lives for evidences of things which have been passed on.

They should then meet with their children and as a family go through the prayers for healing. Perhaps the father can speak the prayers and the wife and children can repeat them after him, encouraging all to speak them from their heart.

Parents can pray for (or be prayed for) in proxy for their young children's deliverance and freedom (Mark 7:24-30).

Praying over homes and businesses

Similar prayers should be prayed over homes, ground and businesses which one may purchase. Pray specifically for generational sins and curses to be broken, soul ties to be cut, the offense of sin committed to be repented of, cleansed and forgiven, and for the Holy Spirit to anoint the land, home or business. Perhaps anoint the building or business with consecrated oil.

The concept of land becoming cursed

Cursed is the ground for thy sake; in sorrow shalt thou eat of it all the days of thy life. (Genesis 3:17)

The curse upon the land reinforced through sin

And he said, What hast thou done? the voice of thy brother's blood crieth unto me from the ground. And now art thou cursed from the earth, which hath opened her mouth to receive thy brother's blood from thy hand; When thou tillest the ground, it shall not henceforth yield unto thee her strength; a fugitive and a vagabond shalt thou be in the earth. (Genesis 4:10-12)

Because of the evil of your doings, and because of the abominations which ye have committed; therefore is your land a desolation, and an astonishment, and a curse, without an inhabitant, as at this day. (Jeremiah 44:19-23)

Therefore the wild beasts of the desert with the wild beasts of the islands shall dwell there, and the owls shall dwell therein: and it shall be no more inhabited for ever; neither shall it be dwelt in from generation to generation. (Jeremiah 50:39)

Note also the curses of Deuteronomy 28 and Leviticus 26. Notice the process used to cleanse an unholy building (2 Chronicles 29:3-19).

Summary: Objects, land and buildings can be cursed and become demonized through sin.

The concept of land being holy

And the angel of the LORD appeared unto him in a flame of fire out of the midst of a bush: and he looked, and, behold, the bush burned with fire, and the bush was not consumed . . . . And he said,

Draw not nigh hither: put off thy shoes from off thy feet, for the place whereon thou standest is holy ground. (Ezekiel 3:2, 5)

The concept of a holy building

And thou shalt take the anointing oil, and anoint the tabernacle, and all that is therein, and shalt hallow it, and all the vessels thereof: and it shall be holy. And thou shalt anoint the altar of the burnt offering, and all his vessels, and sanctify the altar: and it shall be an altar most holy. And thou shalt anoint the laver and his foot, and sanctify it. (Exodus 40:9-11)

So that the priests could not stand to minister by reason of the cloud: for the glory of the LORD had filled the house of God. (2 Chronicles 5:14 - read chapters 5-7)

Summary: Receiving God's anointing comes as a result of dedication, consecration, and obedience.

Some incidentals that can only help!

Since our body, soul and spirit are so closely linked, taking good care of your body can only assist the healing and growth of your heart and soul.

Provide your body with a healthy diet (Daniel 1:12), plenty of water, exercise, proper rest and regular fasting (Isaiah 58:6,8). Test for chemical imbalances underlying emotional imbalances. Use herbs (Psalms 104:14) and other natural biblical remedies as necessary.

Utilize accountability relationships to make sure you are doing what you are responsible to do.

Personal Application

1. Memorize the lists above as recommended.

2. Continue processing your own heart using the seven prayer approaches.

3. Have you used the language of the heart to heal the heart, or have you used the language of the mind in trying to heal the heart? Record a journal entry concerning what the Lord speaks to you concerning this issue.

4. Come to your group meeting prepared to share, to minister and to receive ministry.

Group Application

1. Share the lists you have memorized with one another in the group.

2. Have students share their journaled responses to question three of the Personal Application above.

3. Let group participants share their ongoing healing experiences with one another.

4. Pray for a volunteer in the group, using the seven healing prayer approaches.

What Is in My Ancestors? Worksheet

Ask: "What is in my ancestors?" Then picture each of your ancestors on both sides of the marriage. Listen to your heart by tuning to the Holy Spirit's flow, feeling and vision. Record below what comes to you.

Husband's side:

• Dad _____

_____

_____

• Mom _____

_____

_____

Grandfather on Dad's side _____

_____

Grandmother on Dad's side _____

_____

Grandfather on Mom's side _____

_____

Grandmother on Mom's side _____

_____

(continued next page)

Wife's side:

• Dad _____

_____

_____

• Mom _____

_____

_____

Grandfather on Dad's side _____

_____

Grandmother on Dad's side _____

_____

Grandfather on Mom's side _____

_____

Grandmother on Mom's side _____

_____

Other Ancestors to 4th generation _____

_____

_____

What Is in My Children? Worksheet

Ask: "What is in my children?" Then picture each of your children. Listen to your heart by tuning to the Holy Spirit's flow, feeling and vision. Record below what comes to you.

First born_____

_____

_____

_____

Second born_____

_____

_____

_____

Third born_____

_____

_____

_____

Fourth born_____

_____

_____

_____

Fifth born_____

_____

_____

_____

Compare the above with the answers you have written on the "What Is in My Ancestors? Worksheet." Gather your children and pray with them, leading them in the prayers.

If there was a miscarriage or abortion, before which child did it occur? List children's names on following line.

Demons can easily be connected with an aborted or miscarried child. These will often hang around and attach themselves to the next-born child causing him difficulties. They should be renounced, cut off and cast out of the next born.

If you had a child which you didn't want or s/he was not the sex you were hoping for, check for spirits of rejection.

What Is in My Land, City, Nation, Home, Business, Congregation, Ministry? Worksheet

Ask: "What is in my land, city, nation, home, business, congregation, ministry?" Then picture the item you are praying about and listen to your heart by tuning to the Holy Spirit's flow, feeling and vision. Record below what comes to you.

_____

_____

_____

_____

_____

_____

_____

_____

_____

_____

_____

_____

_____

_____

_____

_____

_____

_____

_____

_____

_____

_____

Pray the seven prayers for these things to be cleansed and broken. You will want to identify with the sins of the people/ institutions involved (Daniel 9:1-22) and repent of them.

Pulling down Principalities

Cities get as demonized as people. If you are praying for your city, one way of determining the principalities that need to be cast down is for you to observe the ongoing needs and sins of your city. This can be done by reading the newspaper and listening to the news. As you do so, listen to the Holy Spirit (i.e., tune to flow, emotions and pictures) to give you the names of the principalities which rule over your city or region.

You may need to do some historical research to fully know how to pray effectively through the seven prayers for your city or region. In your research, you want to discover what the generational sins and curses are, what the soul ties are, what the ungodly beliefs and inner vows of the city fathers were, and what traumatic scenes of the city's history need healing prayer. Once you have discovered and prayed through these issues, you should have undermined the ruling principalities over the area and you should be ready to cast them down. It would be best for leading pastors and intercessors in the city to agree in prayer and to, as a group, pray through these seven prayers to set their city free.

[1] See our book *Naturally Supernatural* for an expansion of this idea.

[2] The books *Dialogue with God* and *Communion with God* by Mark and Patti Virkler provide training in how to do these two things. Understanding and practicing the principles taught in these books gives a foundation for the deeper healing of the heart which is to come.

You can offer the course Communion with God in your church or community as a 12-week course. Student texts, a teacher's guide, videos and audio cassettes are available. Students will journal and use vision during about 10 weeks of this course. Hearing God's voice and seeing God's vision are foundational to the healing of one's heart.

[3] The course Communion with God, and the book *Dialogue with God* will help introduce people to the use of vision.

8

A HEALED, ANOINTED, AND EMPOWERED HEART

From pain to power

A false assumption you might have is that once one's heart is healed and restored by the power of Almighty God, it will now be neutral, no longer being pulled down by negative sin energies from the spirit world.

Well, you are in for a big surprise, because you go right beyond neutral to a positive, divine anointing which enables you to live in God's faith, hope, love, peace, power and joy!

You see, there really aren't any neutral areas in the spiritual world. What is not filled with God is quickly filled with Satan. As one's heart is healed through the power of God, the Holy Spirit of God who resides deep within provides an anointing and a divine charge to all one thinks, does, believes, and experiences.

You go soaring right past neutral to being filled with the anointing of God! Or, at least you should do that. If you don't, and you stay neutral, you will quickly find yourself falling back into the depths of despair from which God pulled you initially.

Jesus taught that once your being has been swept clean of demonic forces, you need to fill yourself with the Holy Spirit or the demons will come back and bring seven even worse demons with them (Matthew 12:44-45). Indeed, we want to fill our hearts with the voice and vision of Almighty God (Acts 2:17).

How does one charge himself up with the power of Almighty God? We have written about this in-depth in our books, *Developing Heart Faith* and *Spirit Born Creativity*, but below is a summary of the way it is done.

Five heart senses God wants to fill

God has created man with five senses in his heart that God wants to fill. These senses are:

Conception

1. Ears in our hearts which can hear God's voice (John 5:30)
2. Eyes in our hearts which can see God's vision (Revelation 4:1)

Incubation

3. Minds in our hearts which can ponder God's thoughts (Luke 2:19)
4. Wills in our hearts which can guide our speech (Acts 19:21)
5. Emotions in our hearts which can move us to action (Genesis 17:23)

Birth

When these five senses of our hearts are filled thoroughly with God, we find His miraculous power beginning to flow out through our lives, creating the visible from the invisible (Galatians 4:4a).

The process

Hearing God always. Instead of hearing the lies of the enemy Satan, I now make sure to only allow in my heart the truths which God has given to me from His Word and by His Spirit.

Seeing God always. Next, I make sure that any ungodly pictures in my heart or mind have been replaced with divine pictures which demonstrate God's love and faithfulness to me in the midst of all of life's adversities and trials.

Pondering God always. Then I am careful to ponder only the truths and divine pictures which God has placed in my heart. I am careful to ensure that all negative expectations and inner vows have been pulled out and replaced with godly expectations and godly purposes in my heart and mind. I make sure that any picture I hold within is a picture which has Jesus in it, for I am without hope when I am without Christ (Ephesians 2:12). Therefore, every picture I hold within must have Christ in it so it builds faith, hope and love. Any picture that does not have Christ in it, I renounce as being untrue (as it is), and I invite Jesus to walk into the picture and show me what He indeed was doing.

Speaking the purposes of God always. I purpose in my spirit to follow the revelation of God within me. I speak out of this purpose and the godly dreams and visions which fill my heart. I speak godly beliefs. My speech is constantly positive, spiritual and anointed, never negative or demonic.

Obeying God always. My heart is moved by the pictures it holds within it. These godly pictures produce godly emotions. These godly emotions move me to act in faith and power and with conviction.

I wait in faith for God to fulfill what He has spoken and what He has shown. I do not rely on the strength of my flesh to accomplish the divine purposes of God, but I believe that God can do what no man can do (Galatians 3:3). I believe that God can do through me what He has said He will do through me.

Demonstrated in Abraham, the Father of Faith

God filled all five senses of Abraham's heart with Himself, and as a result, Abraham became the father of faith and an example of how God births a supernatural lifestyle out through us (Romans 4).

Abraham Hears God's Promise. In Genesis 12:1-3, God speaks to Abraham.

> *Now the LORD had said unto Abram, Get thee out of thy country, and from thy kindred, and from thy father's house, unto a land that I will show thee: And I will make of thee a great nation, and I will bless thee, and make thy name great; and thou shalt be a blessing: And I will bless them that bless thee, and curse him that curseth thee: and in thee shall all families of the earth be blessed. (Genesis 12:1-3)*

Abraham Sees God's Promise. In Genesis 15:5-6, God adds a vision to the earlier, spoken promise. This vision deepens Abraham's faith.

> *And He (God) brought him (Abram) forth abroad,*
> *and said, Look now toward heaven, and tell the*
> *stars, if thou be able to number them: and He said*
> *unto him, So shall thy seed be. And he believed in*
> *the LORD; and He counted it to him for righteous-*
> *ness. (Genesis 15:5-6)*

Abraham Ponders God's Promise. Even though Abraham and his wife are old, and, in the natural, the fulfillment of the promise appears impossible, Abraham chooses to believe.

> *He (Abram) staggered not at the promise of God*
> *through unbelief; but was strong in faith, giving*
> *glory to God; And being fully persuaded that, what*
> *he had promised, he was able also to perform.*
> *(Romans 4:20-21)*

Abraham Speaks God's Promise. God finally asks Abraham to begin confessing that he is the father of a multitude of nations (i.e., the literal meaning of the name "Abraham"). This confession is requested even before his wife Sarah has become pregnant.

> *Neither shall thy name any more be called Abram,*
> *but thy name shall be Abraham; for a father of*
> *many nations have I made thee. (Genesis 17:5)*

Abraham Acts on God's Promise. Abraham has come to a point where he is instantly obedient to the ongoing instructions of Almighty God. When God asks him to circumcise his family, note how quickly he obeys.

> *And Abraham took Ishmael his son, and all that*
> *were born in his house, and all that were bought*
> *with his money, every male among the men of*

*Abraham's house; and circumcised the flesh of
their foreskin in the selfsame day, as God had said
unto him. (Genesis 17:23)*

**Abraham Waits in Faith for God to Fulfill What He
Has Spoken and What He Has Shown.** Abraham first falls
into self-effort as he tries to bring forth the nations through
his wife's maidservant, a plan which is not divinely ordained
and is rejected by God (Genesis 16:2; 17:18-19). Then Abraham waits upon God to perform the miracle through his wife
Sarah.

*And the LORD visited Sarah as he had said, and
the LORD did unto Sarah as he had spoken. For
Sarah conceived, and bare Abraham a son in his
old age, at the set time of which God had spoken
to him. (Genesis 21:1-2)*

*But when the fulness of the time was come, God...
(Galatians 4:4)*

A healed heart and a Spirit-anointed lifestyle

This is the divine pattern for a healed and Spirit-anointed
heart and lifestyle. If one keeps asking the question, "What
is in my heart today?" the answer he will begin receiving
will be words like, "Faith, hope, trust, power, anointing,
peace, love, joy."

When your heart begins responding to your question with
words like this, then you know that your heart is healed.
Even more than that, then you know that your heart is empowered with the strength and anointing of Almighty God.
Then you know that you are ready to be used by God to
change the world in which you live, to bring life out of death,
to bring hope out of sorrow, to bring peace out of anger, to
bring the kingdom of God out of the ravages of Satan

(1 Timothy 1:12). Then your heart is whole!

May you be a Spirit-anointed world-changer!

Specific ways to ensure complete healing

No one should be satisfied with partial healing. Each of us should seek full and complete healing in every area of our lives. Life is just a lot more fun if we can walk through it healed. Following are ways to accomplish this healing.

Invite your friends to help you see your blind spots. Have a few close spiritual friends who are willing to take on the responsibility of sharing with you anytime they sense something within you that is not fully healed. They may sense this by the words you are speaking or your attitudes or actions. Ask them to inform you anytime they see anything that doesn't look fully healed. Then take what they offer you to prayer. Work through a "Contributing Strands Worksheet" and see what God shows you.

Ask God detailed questions in your morning devotional and journaling time. God answers in light of what we ask (James 4:2b; Matthew 7:7-8). So the better questions we ask God, the better answers we receive. Following are some detailed questions you could ask God to help you discover ungodly beliefs or inner vows. Make them part of your devotional time for awhile.

Lord, what negative beliefs/expectations or inner vows do I have concerning life in general, my present life, my younger years, my older years, my spouse, my children, my parents, my friends, my pastor, my church, the Church in general, previous churches I have attended, my current health, my future health, my work, my finances, my play time, my sexuality, my spouse's sexuality, my past education, my present education, my future education, my house, my time, my responsibilities, my death, the anointing of God upon my life, my capacity to minister as Jesus did, my country, my city, my denomination, other denominations, renewal groups, conservative groups, liberal groups, New Agers, other religions? Let God weed out negative beliefs and expectations.

Joyful, free, light, energetic. These words describe the spirit of many young children. We only lose these cherished characteristics as we take on additional responsibilities (which we should be leaving with God) and judgments and reproaches (which we should be asking God to heal). So ask God the above questions in your journaling time and let Him heal you from the inside out, so you can become a child again (Matthew 18:3-4)!

Personal Application

1. Continue asking the question "Holy Spirit, what is in my heart?" until your heart responds with divine positives, not demonic negatives.

2. Continue journaling and applying the prayers and exercises of Chapter Five until your heart is completely healed.

3. Begin living in God's supernatural faith, hope and love, being a conduit through whom God releases miracles into His world.

Group Application

1. Let group members share their answers from the Personal Application activities above.

2. Pray for a volunteer, using the approaches in Chapter Five.

3. Continue week by week with activities 1 and 2 until all are healed and filled with the power and vision and faith of Almighty God.

9

TESTIMONIES OF HEALING
FROM KAY COX

Mark's introduction to this chapter

One of the things I realize is that in real life, the Lord heals differently every time. That is why, even though we have taught a process of healing in this book, we have encouraged you over and over to stay tuned to the Holy Spirit's flow and let God guide you as He desires through the healing process. This cannot be overemphasized.

Therefore, I asked Kay to write a chapter demonstrating through example the principle that we must always stay tuned to flow, and not just mechanically go through the seven prayers in an exact order. It is not the ritual that heals, it is the power of the Holy Spirit.

Every healer must be led by the anointing of the Holy Spirit as he releases the power of God through the avenues of faith, hope and love (i.e., the realities which abide - 1 Corinthians 13:13). Ministering faith, hope and love while staying tuned to flow is, in my estimation, the path which releases the anointing. May each of us walk this path.

Kay's testimonies

Mark has asked me to recall some of the experiences I have had in counseling to demonstrate the validity of the principles he has laid out in this book. Every case and person is unique, so it is very important to follow the direction of the Holy Spirit as you ask questions about their life and minister to their needs. In most cases I will cut generational soul ties, but do not always use all the prayers listed by Mark as a routine. They all have a place in specific cases at different times and represent a good basis from which to work.

I did not want to be a counselor. When my last child Michael went to school four years ago, I stood in the kitchen and said to the Lord, "Here I am, Lord, do with me what You will." One week later, I was working with Pastor Darryl Goodsell, who had spent 23 years counseling according to biblical principles and trusting in God for all his material needs. He is a godly and gentle man who shared his understanding and revelation and experience with me and others unselfishly. Darryl was my mentor for 18 months, until the Lord told us both separately it was time for me to work on my own.

I did not know where the Lord was taking me. While sitting in on sessions with Darryl, I would be given a word of knowledge from the Lord like "jealousy" or "adultery" which was relevant to the person receiving counseling. I began to trust that the Lord wanted these issues dealt with and found that when prayer and submission were applied, great changes began to occur. The Lord led me then to Peter Horrobin's seminar on healing through deliverance and Ellel Ministry, which reinforced and built upon what I had learned with Darryl. I do not see visions as I counsel, but often find it useful to have someone minister with me who does. It frequently helps us focus our prayer on specific areas.

I am a housewife and mother of three doing what the Lord asks. Nothing more. These are some of the ways I have seen the Lord express His power in my life.

* * * * *

One afternoon in May 1998, a 37-year-old lady came to see me complaining of nagging abdominal pain. She had seen several doctors who had done various tests, performed certain procedures and carried out three operations on her, but they had not really come to any conclusion as to why the pain was still there. She had approached yet another surgeon and another operation was looming in the near future. Someone had suggested that she come and see me before going in for the surgery again.

After taking quite a detailed history of her family illnesses, etc., I asked if she could tell me when she had first noticed the pain. She could give me the exact month, and when I asked her what she had done that was different to her usual behavior, she said the only thing that she did was to have her Tarot cards read. I asked her if she could forgive the lady who had done the reading, repent of looking to the other side for answers regarding her life, and renounce any future participation in the occult. We then cut any ungodly soul ties to the medium. As I prayed and bound the spirit of witchcraft, she said the pain seemed to rise up in her abdomen in a dragging motion, and then she felt something break and the pain was gone. I asked the Holy Spirit to restore any damage that had been done to her internal organs.

On her return visit to the doctor, she told him that the pain had gone following prayer and that the Lord had healed her. She said he just smiled, and told her to make another appointment when the pain returned. Praise the Lord, that was nearly twenty months ago and there is still no sign of the pain. She came to know Jesus for the first time that day. She received a healing and was baptized in the Spirit and is still following the Lord today.

* * * * *

One night in February 1999, we were working with a group of Christian folk, breaking judgments and inner vows that we had made as children, especially judgments on our parents, teachers, friends, enemies, and anyone else that the Holy Spirit showed us. After we had repented of these judgments and vows and cut any ungodly soul ties to these people, we were praying and forgiving those who had hurt or wounded us in any way. One man came out of the group and told me that, as he was forgiving his mother-in-law, the pain in his knees became almost unbearable and then it was like something popped, and the pain left. He had been in severe knee pain for years and didn't realize that the bitterness and unforgiveness that he had held towards his mother-in-law was manifesting in his bones. How many of us find it difficult to forgive our brothers and sisters, or difficult to not hold grudges? "A merry heart doeth good like a medicine, but a broken spirit drieth the bones" (Proverbs 17:22).

* * * * *

One Sunday morning just before church, a woman approached me and asked if she could have some prayer before the service started. She had been experiencing pain in her right forearm for quite some time and it was really beginning to annoy her. We prayed quietly for a few minutes and asked the Holy Spirit to show us what the root cause of the pain was. After a few moments she opened her eyes and said that the Holy Spirit had shown her that she had been involved in a séance as a child. She repented of this, asked the Lord to forgive her and renounced any further involvement in witchcraft. As I bound the spirit of necromancy, the pain moved up her forearm and came out through her fingers. She was thrilled that once again the Lord had answered her prayers and that she had been healed.

* * * * *

One Saturday afternoon about eighteen months ago, there was a knock on my door and standing in the doorway was a 34-year-old woman named Tracey. Tracey lived a couple of blocks from our house and had known my husband when they attended the same church. I invited her in for a cup of tea, and as she made her way slowly down our long hallway, with the aid of a walking stick, I noticed she grimaced in pain with every step that she took. She told me that in 1996 she had fallen at the local hospital and injured herself, and that she was still experiencing pain in her knee. Then, six months later, she had been involved in a bus accident in which, as she was making her way to the back of the bus, the driver had put his foot on the brake to prevent an accident, sending her flying through the air. She ended up at the front of the bus, down in the stairwell. Her body had not recovered from either of the accidents and she now felt that she needed the walking stick to assist her, making walking a little less painful.

A few months before Tracey arrived on the scene, I had attended one of Peter Horrobin's Ellel conferences where we were taught about the effects of shock and trauma. Peter demonstrated very clearly how, when we are involved in accidents, our physical bodies are attended to, but our souls and our spirits are sadly neglected. As Tracey chose to forgive the people responsible for her accidents and repented of any bitterness and resentment that she felt toward any of them, I prayed and the Holy Spirit ministered to her. She testifies that a warm feeling came over her and she began to feel her body being healed. Her excitement was infectious as she ran out of the room to tell our children of her healing. An hour later my husband arrived home from work and she raced down the hallway to greet him with a big hug and to share her wonderful news. Tracey no longer needed her stick as the pain was totally gone. Jesus had healed her broken body.

* * * * *

Just recently, another person to whom I have been ministering rang to say, "Thank you." She was supposed to have an operation, but since having two sessions breaking soul ties, judgments and inner vows, and experiencing the inner healing that went with it, she no longer needs the operation, and the doctor has given her the all clear. Praise the Lord!

* * * * *

A young girl rang from a coastal town asking if she could come and see me as she had been bleeding for years and, at only 19 years of age, was going to have a hysterectomy. She was having the operation on Friday, so I managed to change some of my booked clients and spent the day counseling her. We dealt with some pretty tragic issues and the Holy Spirit led us to pray about some specific hurts. By the end of the afternoon, as she made her way to the hospital for her anesthetic check, she seemed happy and relieved. The next day, when her gynecologist examined her, she told him that the bleeding had stopped. The operation was canceled at the last minute and she went back to her family. She rang me a few months later to tell me that she was still fine and the bleeding had not returned. It was like a last-minute rescue, and the Lord had answered her prayers.

* * * * *

A 28-year-old woman from Macksville was visiting with her sister, and made an appointment while she was down here. She had difficulty trying to forgive her Dad for abandoning her when she was a baby. As a result, she had not spoken to him for 13 years. As we went through breaking generational soul ties and repenting of bad attitudes and judgments, she felt a huge burden lift from her as she asked the Holy Spirit to help her come to a place where she could forgive him for not being there for her. She cried a lot of tears, and eventually she was able to forgive him. She rang him when she got home and told him that she forgave him and that she loved him very much. A new relationship commenced on that day and she found it much easier to "honor her father" as the Lord would have us all do. Jesus can fill up any hole we have; we just have to ask.

* * * * *

This last healing occurred just a few months ago and the lady, Helen Henderson, has very graciously agreed to share her testimony with you. I thank Helen for her honesty and openness. She has given much of her time and energy to share her testimony with many of the churches and schools in the Newcastle area, and she goes on giving praise and glory to our Almighty God for her wonderful healing. Such faith I have never seen before! Here is Helen's own story.

The story begins 6:00 A.M. September 9, 1999. Told my husband John that I felt unwell - dizzy. 8.00 A.M. - school (I am a schoolteacher) - told a friend that if I didn't feel better soon I was going home, then proceeded to collapse onto the cold floor.

I woke very confused and with left-side weakness. I was taken to the hospital where I was diagnosed as having had a stroke (Cerebro vascular accident, in medical terminology). Transferred to Warners Bay Private Hospital under a medical specialist. I was completely paralyzed on my left side and had difficulty recognizing friends and acquaintances.

Final Diagnosis - My brain had just shut down and was not functioning right. Why? The doctor could not tell me.

The weeks that followed my admission to hospital were the darkest of my life. People would come to visit me and comment on how calm and serene I appeared to be. In truth, I spent most of my waking hours focusing on my sin. Satan had a field day convincing me that I was not worthy of God's love. I had no ability to see the possibility of my ever being restored to physical or, for that matter, spiritual health. I regularly cried myself to sleep and had horrific nightmares when I did sleep. Physically, I was making small steps. I began to sit out of bed for small periods of time that were gradually increased. I had daily physiotherapy and began to use my arm to do small tasks, but I was still unable to use my leg. My foot was floppy and I had to wear a foot-drop splint to hold my foot in place.

The real story, however, begins several months earlier. My dear father died on the 10th of June, 1999. His death caused me to go into deep sorrow bordering on despair. I could not come to grips with the loss of my dad. To top it off, I had an operation one week after Dad's funeral. On my follow-up visit, my surgeon, who is a Christian, said I was physically fine. Then he asked how I really was. I explained that I felt I was in real trouble, because a padded room and a bed looked good to me. He asked what I wanted to do. "See your wife Kay," I replied.

It was a struggle all day, but I finally rang her and arranged a visit, not really knowing what to expect but open to what God was going to do in my life. God in his graciousness blessed me that day. The burdens of a lifetime were lifted from me. I was completely exhausted but elated at what God had done for me. I suppose I expected life to get easier. It didn't!! But I was more able to cope with the things that came to me. I believe that I was attacked in not just the physical realm but in the spiritual realm, also. Satan was having a field day with me. I think on the twentieth of September he thought he had won, but God had other plans.

During my time in hospital, friends came to see me - so much love, so much kindness. Total strangers sent me flowers and inquired as to my well-being, but this had no real effect on me. I became darker and darker. I have a very close friend, Margaret. We have been friends for the whole of our lives. She recognized and knew what I was experiencing because her husband Neil had been through a similar experience. She was the only person that I allowed to see what was really happening to me. I vented my frustration, anger and resentment on her and she just sat and let me do it and in great love ministered to me of God's love. It was not that I did not appreciate the love and concern shown to me. I just could not allow others to see my real feelings . . . FEAR and complete unworthiness of God's love. At this point I had been hospitalized for over nine weeks and things were not looking too good for me.

My medical specialist is a very clever man and very astute. He is not a Christian, but God was not limited by this. He asked my surgeon to arrange for his wife Kay to come and see me, as I was not getting much better. Why hadn't I done this? It goes back to how I felt about myself at the time.

When Kay rang me to arrange an appointment, I knew that God was in control of the situation. I knew and believed God would heal me. Not just the physical healing I obviously needed, but also more importantly the mental, emotional and spiritual problems that had beset me. Believing that I would be healed, I began to tell everyone I came in contact with: nurses, doctors, friends and family, in fact just about everyone, with varying degrees of belief expressed by all. I asked my family to pray and also my KYB group.

Kay arrived on time with Jenny Parkinson, her intercessor, and we seemed to get down to business almost immediately. There were various issues that had to be addressed regarding sin in my life and sin of past generations of my family. The prayer I was asked to pray was very difficult as I had to say aloud those things that I did not really want others to know about. Fortunately, the Lord enabled me to do it.

When Kay began to pray for my physical healing, she did not pray generally, but very specifically, for each part of my body that needed to be healed. She began by praying for my brain - every individual part: the neurons, the blood vessels, the nerves, the gray matter, the white matter, etc. This process was followed for my limbs. When Kay had finished praying for my arm, she told me to raise it up - and I did, right above my head! Previously I could only raise it with great concentration and not above my head. Kay continued down my body, finally praying for my leg and foot. She took the splint off my leg and told me to lift my leg onto her knee. I did this automatically! I was completely amazed! I could not do that before, and yet now I could. Then she told me to walk around my room. I did that, too! Then she flung the door open and I ran down the the hallway full pelt. I was overwhelmed with happiness and thanksgiving to God for doing this for me.

News soon spread in the hospital and nursing staff were coming from everywhere to witness the "unbelievable," in human terms. One nurse was so confused by what she saw, she took my arm and carefully walked me back to my room. I rang my husband to tell him what had happened and he thought I'd gone completely demented. He could not comprehend what I was telling him. Finally Kay got on the phone with him to convince him that I was telling the truth. He arrived at the hospital in record time. The joy on his face when he saw me is something that I will never forget.

Most reactions to my healing were positive, except for one nurse. She was very negative and hostile. This reaction had an interesting effect on me. It made me very fearful, so much so that I did not want to leave my room. I rang my friend Margaret, who recognized what was happening. Satan was trying to rob me of the victory and the blessing that the Lord had given me. When I prayed, the problem was gone. When I came out of my room, that particular nurse had just left the nurses' station.

I had to wait twenty-four hours to see my doctor and to be discharged. When he spoke with me, he said that I was one of three miraculous healings he had seen in his time as a doctor and he could not explain any of them. He also did not want to see me for any follow-up - I was cured.

On Tuesday, the 16th of November, God healed me. The most important thing for me in all of this is that I recognized that nothing I did or could do was going to change my situation. In His graciousness, God made me whole. He gave me back my life. I do not know why He chose to do this for me. I definitely do not deserve it. All I know is that the glory belongs to the Lord. Only He is worthy of our praise, and I want to tell others of His greatness and love.

* * * * * * * * * * * * * *

In his subsequent letter to the other doctors involved in Helen's care, her medical specialist described her recovery as . . . faith healing. Helen had faith and was willing to be healed. The Lord was glorified and many saw His power that night and received the good news of Jesus as Jenny and I were able to talk to patients and staff who filled the corridors after the commotion.

Throughout my meager three-and-a-half years of doing the Lord's work, I have had the privilege of seeing many wonderful healings - physical healings, emotional healings and spiritual healings - and I never get tired of seeing the amazing power of the Holy Spirit at work. Never get tired of seeing the faces radiating as the Holy Spirit turns God's precious people's mourning into dancing. Some mornings I'll still be awake at 4:00 A.M. wondering, "Did that really happen?" and saying, "Thank you, Jesus, that through the shedding of Your precious blood we are set free. We do have resurrection life! You are real! We do have authority on this earth when we allow You to use us."

APPENDIX A

FOUR KEYS TO HEARING GOD'S VOICE

The age in which we live is so married to rationalism and cognitive, analytical thought that we almost mock when we hear of one actually claiming to be able to hear the voice of God. However, we do not scoff, for several reasons. First, men and women throughout the Bible heard God's voice. Also, there are some highly effective and reputable men and women of God alive today who demonstrate that they hear God's voice. Finally, there is a deep hunger within us all to commune with God, and hear Him speak within our hearts.

As a born-again, Bible-believing Christian, I struggled unsuccessfully for years to hear God's voice. I prayed, fasted, studied my Bible and listened for a voice within, all to no avail. **There was no inner voice that I could hear!** Then God set me aside for a year to study, read, and experiment in the area of learning to hear God's voice. During that time, God taught me **four keys that opened the door to two-way prayer.** I have discovered that not only do they work for me, but they have worked for many thousands of believers who have been taught to use them, bringing tremendous intimacy to their Christian experience and transforming their very way of living. This will happen to you also as you seek God, utilizing the following four keys. They are all found in Habakkuk 2:1-2. I encourage you to read this passage before going on.

Key #1 - God's voice in our hearts sounds like a flow of spontaneous thoughts. Therefore, when I tune to God, I tune to spontaneity.

The Bible says "the LORD answered me, and said, . . ." (Habakkuk. 2:2). Habakkuk knew the sound of God's voice. Elijah described it as a still, small voice. I had always listened for an inner **audible** voice, and surely God can and does speak that way at times. However, I have found that for most of us, most of the time, God's inner voice comes to us as **spontaneous thoughts, visions, feelings, or impressions**. For example, haven't each of us had the experience of driving down the road and having **a thought come to us** to pray for a certain person? We generally acknowledge this to be the voice of God calling us to pray for that individual. My question to you is, "What did God's voice sound like as you drove in your car? Was it an inner, audible voice, or was it a spontaneous thought that lit upon your mind?" Most of you would say that God's voice came to you as a spontaneous thought.

So I thought to myself, "Maybe when I listen for God's voice, I should be listening for a flow of spontaneous thoughts. Maybe spirit-level communication is received as spontaneous thoughts, impressions, feelings, and visions." Through experimentation and feedback from thousands of others, I am now convinced that this is so.

The Bible confirms this in many ways. The definition of *paga*, the Hebrew word for intercession, is "a chance encounter or an accidental intersecting." When God lays people on our hearts for intercession, He does it through *paga*, a chance encounter thought, accidentally intersecting our thought processes. Therefore, when I tune to God, I tune to chance encounter thoughts or spontaneous thoughts. When I am poised quietly before God in prayer, I have found that the flow of spontaneous thoughts that comes is quite definitely from God.

Key # 2 - I must learn to still my own thoughts and emotions, so that I can sense God's flow of thoughts and emotions within me. Habakkuk said, "I will stand on my guard post and station myself on the rampart." (Habakkuk 2:1). Habakkuk knew that in order to hear God's quiet, inner, spontaneous thoughts, he had to first go to a quiet place and still his own thoughts and emotions. Psalm 46:10 encourages us to be still, and know that He is God. There is a deep inner knowing (spontaneous flow) in our spirit that each of us can experience when we quiet our flesh and our minds.

I have found several simple ways to quiet myself so that I can more readily pick up God's spontaneous flow. Loving God through a quiet worship song is a most effective means for me (note 2 Kings 3:15). It is as I become still (thoughts, will, and emotions) and am poised before God that the divine flow is realized. Therefore, after I worship quietly and then become still, I open myself for that spontaneous flow. If thoughts come to me of things I have forgotten to do, I write them down and then dismiss them. If thoughts of guilt or unworthiness come to my mind, I repent thoroughly, receive the washing of the blood of the Lamb, and put on His robe of righteousness, seeing myself spotless before the presence of God.

As I fix my gaze upon Jesus (Hebrews 12:2), becoming quiet in His presence, and sharing with Him what is on my heart, I find that two-way dialogue begins to flow. Spontaneous thoughts flow from the throne of God to me, and I find that I am actually conversing with the King of kings.

It is very important that you become still and properly focused if you are going to receive the pure word of God. If you are not still, you will simply be receiving your own thoughts. If you are not properly focused on Jesus, you will receive an impure flow, because the intuitive flow comes out of that upon which you have fixed your eyes. Therefore, if you fix your eyes upon Jesus, the intuitive flow comes from Jesus. If you fix your gaze upon some desire of your heart, the intuitive flow comes out of that desire of your heart. To have a pure flow you must first of all become still, and secondly, you must carefully fix your eyes upon Jesus. Again I will say, this is quite easily accomplished by quietly worshiping the King, and then receiving out of the stillness that follows.

Key #3 - As I pray, I fix the eyes of my heart upon Jesus, seeing in the spirit the dreams and visions of Almighty God.

We have already alluded to this principle in the previous paragraphs; however, we need to develop it a bit further. Habakkuk said, "I will keep watch to see," and God said, "Record the vision" (Habakkuk 2:1-2). It is very interesting that Habakkuk was going to actually start looking for vision as he prayed. He was going to open the eyes of his heart, and look into the spirit world to see what God wanted to show him. This is an intriguing idea.

I had never thought of opening the eyes of my heart and looking for vision. However, the more I thought of it, the more I realized this was exactly what God intends me to do. He gave me eyes in my heart. They are to be used to see in the spirit world the vision and movement of Almighty God. I believe there is an active spirit world functioning all around me. This world is full of angels, demons, the Holy Spirit, the omnipresent God, and His omnipresent Son, Jesus. There is no reason for me not to see it, other than my rational culture, which tells me not to believe it is even there and provides no instructions on how to become open to seeing this spirit world.

The most obvious prerequisite to seeing is that we need to look. Daniel was seeing a vision in his mind and he said, "I was looking . . . I kept looking . . . I kept looking" (Daniel 7:1, 9, 13). Now as I pray, I look for Jesus present with me, and I watch Him as He speaks to me, doing and saying the things that are on His heart. Many Christians will find that if they will only look, they will see. Jesus is Emmanuel, God with us. It is as simple as that. You will see a spontaneous inner vision in a manner similar to receiving spontaneous inner thoughts. You can see Christ present with you in a comfortable setting, because Christ is present with you in a comfortable setting. Actually, you will probably discover that inner vision comes so easily you will have a tendency to reject it, thinking that it is just you. (Doubt is Satan's most effective weapon against the Church.) However, if you will persist in recording these visions, your doubt will soon be overcome by faith as you recognize that the content of them could only be birthed in Almighty God.

God continually revealed Himself to His covenant people using dream and vision. He did so from Genesis to Revelation and said that, since the Holy Spirit was poured out in Acts 2, we should expect to receive a continuing flow of dreams and visions (Acts 2:1-4). Jesus, our perfect example, demonstrated this ability of living out of ongoing contact with Almighty God. He said that He did nothing on His own initiative, but only that which he **saw the Father doing, and heard the Father saying** (John 5:19-20, 30). What an incredible way to live!

Is it actually possible for us to live out of the divine initiative as Jesus did? A major purpose of Jesus' death and resurrection was that the veil be torn from top to bottom, giving us access into the immediate presence of God, and we are commanded to draw near (Hebrews 10:19-22). Therefore, even though what I am describing seems a bit unusual to a rational twentieth century culture, it is demonstrated and described as being a central biblical teaching and experience. It is time to restore to the Church all that belongs to the Church.

Because of their intensely rational nature and existence in an overly rational culture, some will need more assistance and understanding of these truths before they can move into them. They will find this help in the book *Communion With God* by the same author.

Key #4 - Journaling, the writing out of our prayers and God's answers, provides a great new freedom in hearing God's voice.

God told Habakkuk to record the vision and inscribe it on tablets (Habakkuk 2:2). It had never crossed my mind to write out my prayers and God's answers as Habakkuk did at God's command. If you begin to search Scripture for this idea, you will find hundreds of chapters demonstrating it (Psalms, many of the prophets, Revelation). Why then hadn't I ever thought of it?

I called the process "journaling," and I began experimenting with it. I discovered it to be a fabulous facilitator to clearly discerning God's inner, spontaneous flow, because as I journaled I was able **to write in faith for long periods of time**, simply believing it was God. I did not have to test it as I was receiving it, (which jams one's receiver), because I knew that when the flow was over I could go back and test and examine it carefully, making sure that it lined up with Scripture.

You will be amazed when you attempt journaling. Doubt may hinder you at first, but throw it off, reminding yourself that it is a biblical concept, and that God is present, speaking to His children. Don't take yourself too seriously. When you do, you become tense and get in the way of the Holy Spirit's movement. It is when we cease **our labors** and enter His rest that God is free to flow (Hebrews 4:10). Therefore, put a smile on your face, sit back comfortably, get out your pen and paper, and turn your attention toward God in praise and worship, seeking His face. As you write out your question to God and become still, fixing your gaze on Jesus, who is present with you, you will suddenly have a very good thought in response to your question. Don't doubt it, simply write it down. Later, as you read your journaling, you, too, will be amazed to discover that you are indeed dialoguing with God.

Some final notes. No one should attempt this without having first read through at least the New Testament (preferably, the entire Bible), nor should one attempt this unless he is submitted to solid, spiritual leadership. All major directional moves that come through journaling should be submitted before being acted upon.

Appendix B

Confession, Repentance, Forgiveness, Cleansing

Summary - We are to:

- Confess our sins (acknowledge our specific sins to God);
- Repent (turn away from our sin);
- Forgive (others, ourselves, and 'God');
- Be forgiven (receive God's forgiveness and healing);
- Celebrate (thank God for His cleansing and healing).

Repentance and forgiveness are at the heart of one's healing. The word "repent" in its various forms is found 112 times in the Bible, so it is important to understand this word. In the New Testament, there are two basic words translated repent: *metamelomai* and *metanoes*. Their combined meanings give us the following definition of repentance:

> Repentance is the informing and changing of the mind; the stirring and directing of the emotions to urge the required change; and the action of the

yielded will in turning the whole man away from one thing and to something else.

Repentance is one of the foundational doctrines (Hebrews 6:1-2).

From that time Jesus began to preach, and to say, Repent: for the kingdom of heaven is at hand. (Matthew 4:17)

And the times of this ignorance God winked at; but now commandeth all men everywhere to repent. (Acts 17:30)

When we repent and return to God, it brings great joy in the heavens. (Luke 15:1-10)

Likewise, I say unto you, there is joy in the presence of the angels of God over one sinner that repenteth. (Luke 15:10)

Sin provides demonic footholds

Repentance ushers healing into our lives by removing any foothold or opportunity or right that Satan or a demon may have in our lives. Ephesians 4:27 tells us not to give the devil a place or an opportunity or a foothold by sinning. The verses which surround this command list the kinds of sins which can give Satan a foothold (i.e., falsehood, anger, stealing, speaking unwholesome words, having bitterness, wrath, clamor, slander, malice). See also 2 Corinthians 2:10-11.

Repentance removes demonic footholds, by disarming demons

Colossians 2:13-15 describes the disarming of rulers and authorities (i.e., demonic forces) through Christ's death and shed blood at the Cross. We receive the effects of Christ's death on the Cross in our own lives by personally repenting of our sins and being cleansed by the application of Christ's blood.

> *When He had disarmed the ruler and authorities, He made a public display of them, having triumphed over them through Him. (Colossians 2:15, NASB)*

Functioning in our role as "royal priests"

The role of the priest is to confess the sins of the people before God. God has made us "royal priests" (1 Peter 2:9), and as priests we can and we ought to confess the sins of others before God so that judgment may be stayed upon the people (Leviticus 16:21).

Moses and Daniel identified with and confessed the sins of others

> *And Moses made haste, and bowed his head toward the earth, and worshipped. And he said, If now I have found grace in thy sight, O Lord, let my Lord, I pray thee, go among us; for it is a stiffnecked people; and pardon our iniquity and our sin, and take us for thine inheritance. (Exodus 34:8-9)*

> *And whiles I was speaking, and praying, and confessing my sin and the sin of my people Israel, and presenting my supplication before the LORD my God for the holy mountain of my God; Yea, whiles I was speaking in prayer, even the man Gabriel, whom I had seen in the vision at the be-*

*ginning, being caused to fly swiftly, touched me
about the time of the evening oblation. And he
informed me, and talked with me, and said, O
Daniel, I am now come forth to give thee skill and
understanding. (Daniel 9:20-22)*

See also: Ezra 9:5-15; Nehemiah 1:6, 9:1-2; Psalm 106:6;
Jeremiah 3:25, 14:7, 20; Daniel 9:1-23; 10:2-3, 12-13. Note
plural Greek pronouns in 1 John 1:9 and James 5:16.

Meditation on "confess" (found 28 times in the KJV Bible)

One is to confess the ways he has sinned

*And it shall be, when he shall be guilty in one of
these things, that he shall confess that he hath
sinned in that thing. (Leviticus 5:5)*

Priests can serve as intermediaries and confess the sins of others

*And Aaron shall lay both his hands upon the head
of the live goat, and confess over him all the iniquities of the children of Israel, and all their transgressions in all their sins, putting them upon the
head of the goat, and shall send him away by the
hand of a fit man into the wilderness. (Leviticus
16:21)*

It is proper to confess the sins of your fathers

*If they shall confess their iniquity, and the iniq-
uity of their fathers, with their trespass which they
trespassed against me, and that also they have
walked contrary unto me. (Leviticus 26:40)*

Confession is to bring about restitution

Then they shall confess their sin which they have done: and he shall recompense his trespass with the principal thereof, and add unto it the fifth part thereof, and give it unto him against whom he hath trespassed. (Numbers 5:7)

Unconfessed sin brings defeat in one's life

When thy people Israel be smitten down before the enemy, because they have sinned against thee, and shall turn again to thee, and confess thy name, and pray, and make supplication unto thee in this house . . ." (1 Kings 8:33; see also 2 Chronicles 6:24-25)

Unconfessed sin can bring drought in one's life

When heaven is shut up, and there is no rain, because they have sinned against thee; if they pray toward this place, and confess thy name, and turn from their sin, when thou afflictest them . . ." (1 Kings 8:35; see also 2 Chronicles 6:26-31)

Confession unto the Lord brings forgiveness from God

I acknowledged my sin unto thee, and mine iniquity have I not hid. I said, I will confess my transgressions unto the LORD; and thou forgavest the iniquity of my sin. Selah. (Psalms 32:5)

Confess your faults one to another, and pray one for another, that ye may be healed. The effectual fervent prayer of a righteous man availeth much. (James 5:16)

If we confess our sins, he is faithful and just to forgive us our sins, and to cleanse us from all unrighteousness. (1 John 1:9)

Meditation on "repent" and its various forms (found 112 times in the KJV Bible)

God repents

If that nation, against whom I have pronounced, turn from their evil, I will repent of the evil that I thought to do unto them. (Jeremiah 18:8)

If it do evil in my sight, that it obey not my voice, then I will repent of the good, wherewith I said I would benefit them. (Jeremiah 18:10)

And the LORD repented of the evil which he thought to do unto His people. (Exodus 32:14)

And Samuel came no more to see Saul until the day of his death: nevertheless Samuel mourned for Saul: and the LORD repented that he had made Saul king over Israel" (1 Samuel 15:35)

And he remembered for them his covenant, and repented according to the multitude of his mercies. (Psalms 106:45)

Man commanded to repent so he can be saved:

Therefore I will judge you, O house of Israel, every one according to his ways, saith the Lord GOD. Repent, and turn yourselves from all your transgressions; so iniquity shall not be your ruin. (Ezekiel 18:30)

And saying, Repent ye: for the kingdom of heaven is at hand. (Matthew 3:2)

When Jesus heard it, he saith unto them, They that are whole have no need of the physician, but they

232

that are sick: I came not to call the righteous, but sinners to repentance. (Mark 2:17)

And they went out, and preached that men should repent. (Mark 6:12)

I tell you, Nay: but, except ye repent, ye shall all likewise perish. (Luke 13:3)

Then Peter said unto them, Repent, and be baptized every one of you in the name of Jesus Christ for the remission of sins, and ye shall receive the gift of the Holy Ghost. (Acts 2:38)

Repent ye therefore, and be converted, that your sins may be blotted out, when the times of refreshing shall come from the presence of the Lord. (Acts 3:19)

And the times of this ignorance God winked at; but now commandeth all men every where to repent. (Acts 17:30)

For godly sorrow worketh repentance to salvation not to be repented of: but the sorrow of the world worketh death. (2 Corinthians 7:10)

Man is to bring forth fruits in keeping with his repentance

Bring forth therefore fruits meet for repentance (Matthew 3:8)

Repentance of a sinner brings great joy in heaven

Likewise, I say unto you, there is joy in the presence of the angels of God over one sinner that repenteth." (Luke 15:10)

Repentance must be continuous

And if he trespass against thee seven times in a day, and seven times in a day turn again to thee, saying, I repent; thou shalt forgive him. (Luke 17:4)

God chastens us so that we will repent

As many as I love, I rebuke and chasten: be zealous therefore, and repent. (Revelation 3:19)

Meditation on "forgive" (found 56 times in the KJV Bible)

Pray for God to forgive our sin

Then hear thou in heaven, and forgive the sin of thy servants, and of thy people Israel, that thou teach them the good way wherein they should walk, and give rain upon thy land, which thou hast given to thy people for an inheritance. (1 Kings 8:36)

Every man receives from God according to the ways of his heart

Then hear thou in heaven thy dwelling place, and forgive, and do, and give to every man according to his ways, whose heart thou knowest; for thou, even thou only, knowest the hearts of all the children of men. (1 Kings 8:39)

Then hear thou from heaven thy dwelling place, and forgive, and render unto every man according unto all his ways, whose heart thou knowest; for thou only knowest the hearts of the children of men. (2 Chronicles 6:30)

God will forgive and heal us if we confess our sins and repent

If my people, which are called by my name, shall humble themselves, and pray, and seek my face, and turn from their wicked ways; then will I hear from heaven, and will forgive their sin, and will heal their land. (2 Chronicles 7:14)

For thou, Lord, art good, and ready to forgive; and plenteous in mercy unto all them that call upon thee. (Psalms 86:5)

If we confess our sins, he is faithful and just to forgive us our sins, and to cleanse us from all unrighteousness. (1 John 1:9)

Forgiveness must be continuous

Then came Peter to him, and said, Lord, how oft shall my brother sin against me, and I forgive him? till seven times?' Jesus saith unto him, 'I say not unto thee, Until seven times: but, Until seventy times seven. (Matthew 18:21-22)

God forgives us as we forgive others

And forgive us our debts, as we forgive our debtors. (Matthew 6:12)

For if ye forgive men their trespasses, your heavenly Father will also forgive you. (Matthew 6:14)

And his lord was wroth, and delivered him to the tormentors, till he should pay all that was due unto him. So likewise shall my heavenly Father do also unto you, if ye from your hearts forgive not every one his brother their trespasses. (Matthew 18:34-35)

And when ye stand praying, forgive, if ye have ought against any: that your Father also which is in heaven may forgive you your trespasses. (Mark 11:25)

But if ye do not forgive, neither will your Father which is in heaven forgive your trespasses. (Mark 11:26)

Judge not, and ye shall not be judged: condemn not, and ye shall not be condemned: forgive, and ye shall be forgiven. (Luke6:37)

And forgive us our sins; for we also forgive every one that is indebted to us. And lead us not into temptation; but deliver us from evil. (Luke 11:4)

When we are wounded by man's inhumanity, we are to forgive

Then said Jesus, Father, forgive them; for they know not what they do. And they parted his raiment, and cast lots. (Luke 23:34)

APPENDIX C

THE BIBLE AND EXPERIENCE

*In everything (i.e., all experiences) give thanks
(1 Thessalonians 5:18).*

*For everything (i.e., all experiences) give thanks
(Ephesians 5:20).*

Should experiences be put in opposition to the Bible?

Experiences are probably set in opposition to the Bible because one observes from time to time that an experience does not line up with his understanding of a Bible promise. Then one may question, "Is the Bible wrong, since my experience contradicts it?" This produces doubt and undermines his walk with God, and thus becomes extremely destructive.

Therefore, some people suggest as a solution: "Do not seek, expect, look at, or trust in experiences, but rather study the Bible and trust the Bible. Experiences lie, but the Bible is true.

The unfortunate consequence

Renouncing experiences removes several wonderful ways which God has chosen to reveal Himself to us.

This results in cutting off several of the ways God would use to reveal truth to His children. God can reveal truth through experiences, dreams and visions, and revelation in one's heart. Even negative experiences can be the stimulus to searching out a deeper truth than one initially perceived (i.e., Habakkuk 1-3).

The wise men found Jesus because of the experience of following a star. The shepherds found Jesus because they followed the leading of an experience they had involving a vision of angels. King Ahasuerus's negative experience of not being able to sleep was the stimulus which brought Israel's deliverance (Esther 6).

The scribes and Pharisees all missed Jesus, because their current interpretation of the Bible left no place for the Messiah to be born in a manger. They were not open to, not looking for, and not listening to the voice of the Spirit or to God speaking to them through experience.

Since the Pharisees interpretation of the Bible led them to reject Jesus, they ignored all experiences with Jesus as inaccurate deceptions which did not line up with the Scriptures. When Jesus raised Lazarus from the dead, the Pharisees were even willing to put Lazarus to death again just so they could remove any experiential evidence which was contrary to their understanding and interpretation of the Word.

Seven improper ways of relating to experiences

1. One can camp out at the experience and let this experience be the end of his spiritual pilgrimage. (The Mount of Transfiguration - Luke 9:29-33.)

2. One can worship the experience. (The pole with a serpent on it in the wilderness was continually worshiped - Numbers 21:6-9; 2 Kings 18:4.)

3. One can let a negative personal experience cause him to doubt the truth of the Bible (such as God's love and protection - Romans 8:28, 38-39).

4. One can not believe in some aspect of God, just because he has not yet experienced that aspect. (Thomas would not believe what he had not personally experienced - John 20:29.)

5. One can seek experiences (which is acceptable according to 1 Corinthians 14:1 and John 5:39-40) without also seeking a biblical understanding and framework for the experience (which is not acceptable). After one has an experience in God, he should go back to Scripture and seek to ground the experience within its pages (1 Thessalonians 5:21). The Bible should either teach about the experience specifically, or allow for the experience through the application of biblical principles.

6. One can observe another Christian's life and his negative experiences, and create a bitter root judgment about God's unfaithfulness toward His children (Hebrews 12:15). This is improper because he has no idea what is going on in that person's life - what spiritual forces are surrounding him and working within him, or if God is testing him. Thus he does not have enough knowledge to make a judgment (Romans 14:4).

7. One can measure his spiritual experiences against another's and decide he is not as spiritual. For example, "I didn't get a vision of an angel, I didn't fall down or tremble or shake when I was prayed for, therefore I am not as spiritual as those who do." All such comparisons are foolish according to 2 Corinthians 10:12. The experience we are all to seek is exemplified in John 5:19-20, 30.

Seven proper ways of relating to experiences:

1. One can understand that life *is* an experience, and that life with God is to be an experience of enjoying an intimate love relationship with God as Adam and Eve did in the Garden of Eden (Genesis 1-2). For the Christian, this includes dreams, visions, God's voice, and the experience of His heart of compassion toward him and through him to others (Acts 2:17; I John 2:5).

2. One can let an experience lead him to search Scripture for new insights. For example, Paul's visionary experience on the Damascus Road (Acts 9:1-19) was followed by three years in the Arabian desert (Galatians 1:15-18), where he adjusted his theology based on the new insights he had received from his Damascus Road experience.

3. One can let an experience lead him to seek God in repentance and deeper obedience. For example, since we know that healing is a conditional covenant (Exodus 15:26), if one found himself sick, he would be wise to seek the Lord concerning any statutes he is not obeying that are bringing this sickness upon him. As God reveals to him the statute or commandment, he can repent and be healed (James 5:14-16). Actually, every promise God has given us is conditional upon our responses to it (Ezekiel 33:13-16; Jeremiah 18:7-10).

4. God uses experiences to test our hearts to see if there is faith there. Abraham was asked to put his son on an altar and raise a knife to kill him in obedience to God (Genesis 22:1-19). God tested the Israelites ten times in the wilderness, and they failed each test by not believing God in the midst of the adversity. Therefore God said they would receive the destruction they ex-

pected (Numbers 14:22-23, 27-28; 1 Corinthians 10:1-11). Some of these tests brought the Israelites to the point of perishing (i.e., three days with no water - Exodus 15:22).

5. One must apply a proper understanding of the principle of sowing and reaping (Galatians 6:7) which is that, after you sow biblical truth and practices in your life, you will need to wait awhile for a harvest of biblical blessings. The experience of the harvest will not be immediate. There is a growing period between sowing and reaping which may take many years, even generations (e.g., the sin of 490 years of not letting the land lie fallow every seventh year was finally reaped in Habakkuk's lifetime when the Israelites were taken into Babylonian captivity for 70 years).

6. If the experiences of life require us to die in faith, we are to do so, still believing in God! That is what the heroes of faith in Hebrews chapter eleven did.

7. An experience can build one's faith. For example, on the Emmaus Road in Luke 24, the disciples experienced a conversation with Jesus (perhaps in a vision - since He instantly disappeared at the close of His discourse). Jesus re-interpreted Scripture by illuminating various Old Testament passages to them. This caused the disciples' hearts to burn within them (an experience) and the result of this experience was that their faith grew (verse 34). They began sharing their experiences with the other disciples, most likely causing the faith of the other disciples to rise, as well.

Summary: Properly understanding how to relate to experiences can provide many precious biblically-stated and illustrated ways in which God can guide and lead and interact with His children. An improper understanding of how to relate to experiences can cause much anguish in one's Christian life. Cutting all experiences off is not proper. Seeing God at work in and through experience is the proper goal.

APPENDIX D

MEDITATION ON JUDGING

Upon discovering that my tendency to judge was contributing to my increasing anger, I asked the Lord,

"What do You want to show me about judging?"

He replied,

"My child, your anger was not a matter of judging. It was a matter of not forgiving once the judgment was made. A godly judgment is fine. However, to hold a resulting anger in your heart because of a judgment you have made is where you fell into trouble. You may judge with righteous judgment, determine a godly verdict and then commit the matter into My hands after you have done that which I have told you to do. So it is a matter of committing the judgment to Me after your work is done. That is where you have failed, My son. That is where the sin was."

Following is my Scripture meditation on "judging."

Verses on judging organized into categories

God is the Judge over nations and people

And also that nation, whom they shall serve, will I judge: and afterward shall they come out with great substance. (Genesis 15:14)

That be far from thee to do after this manner, to slay the righteous with the wicked: and that the righteous should be as the wicked, that be far from thee: Shall not the [Judge] of all the earth do right? (Genesis 18:25)

The adversaries of the LORD shall be broken to pieces; out of heaven shall he thunder upon them: the LORD shall [judge] the ends of the earth; and he shall give strength unto his king, and exalt the horn of his anointed. (1 Samuel 2:10)

The LORD shall judge the people: judge me, O LORD, according to my righteousness, and according to mine integrity that is in me. (Psalms 7:8)

God judgeth the righteous, and God is angry with the wicked every day. (Psalms 7:11)

And he shall judge the world in righteousness, he shall minister judgment to the people in uprightness. (Psalms 9:8)

Arise, O LORD; let not man prevail: let the heathen be judged in thy sight. (Psalms 9:19)

Judge me, O LORD my God, according to thy righteousness; and let them not rejoice over me. (Psalms 35:24)

Judge me, O God, and plead my cause against an ungodly nation: O deliver me from the deceitful and unjust man. (Psalms 43:1)

And the heavens shall declare his righteousness: for God is judge himself. Selah. (Psalms 50:6)

O let the nations be glad and sing for joy: for thou shalt judge the people righteously, and govern the nations upon earth. Selah. (Psalms 67:4)

A father of the fatherless, and a judge of the widows, is God in his holy habitation. (Psalms 68:5)

He shall judge thy people with righteousness, and thy poor with judgment. (Psalms 72:2)

He shall judge the poor of the people, he shall save the children of the needy, and shall break in pieces the oppressor. (Psalms 72:4)

But God is the judge: he putteth down one, and setteth up another. (Psalms 75:7).

A Psalm of Asaph. God standeth in the congregation of the mighty; he judgeth among the gods. (Psalms 82:1)

How long will ye judge unjustly, and accept the persons of the wicked? Selah. (Psalms 82:2)

Arise, O God, judge the earth: for thou shalt inherit all nations. (Psalms 82:8)

Lift up thyself, thou judge of the earth: render a reward to the proud. (Psalms 94:2)

Say among the heathen that the LORD reigneth: the world also shall be established that it shall not be moved: he shall judge the people righteously. (Psalms 96:10)

For the LORD is our judge, the LORD is our lawgiver, the LORD is our king; he will save us (Isaiah 33:22)

Henceforth there is laid up for me a crown of righteousness, which the Lord, the righteous judge, shall give me at that day: and not to me only, but unto all them also that love his appearing. (2 Timothy 4:8)

For we know him that hath said, Vengeance belongeth unto me, I will recompense, saith the Lord. And again, The Lord shall judge his people. (Hebrews 10:30)

And the nations were angry, and thy wrath is come, and the time of the dead, that they should be judged, and that thou shouldest give reward unto thy servants the prophets, and to the saints, and them that fear thy name, small and great; and shouldest destroy them which destroy the earth. (Revelation 11:18)

And I saw heaven opened, and behold a white horse; and he that sat upon him was called Faithful and True, and in righteousness he doth judge and make war. (Revelation 19:11)

And I saw the dead, small and great, stand before God; and the books were opened: and another book was opened, which is the book of life: and the dead were judged out of those things which were written in the books, according to their works. (Revelation 20:12)

And the sea gave up the dead which were in it; and death and hell delivered up the dead which were in them: and they were judged every man according to their works. (Revelation 20:13)

God delegates judging to spiritual leaders to perform

And it came to pass on the morrow, that Moses sat to judge the people: and the people stood by Moses from the morning unto the evening. (Exodus 18:13)

When they have a matter, they come unto me; and I judge between one and another, and I do make them know the statutes of God, and his laws. (Exodus 18:16)

And let them judge the people at all seasons: and it shall be, that every great matter they shall bring unto thee, but every small matter they shall judge: so shall it be easier for thyself, and they shall bear the burden with thee. (Exodus 18:22)

And they judged the people at all seasons: the hard causes they brought unto Moses, but every small matter they judged themselves. (Exodus 18:26)

And thou shalt come unto the priests the Levites, and unto the judge that shall be in those days, and inquire; and they shall show thee the sentence of judgment. (Deuteronomy 17:9)

And the man that will do presumptuously, and will not hearken unto the priest that standeth to minister there before the LORD thy God, or unto the judge, even that man shall die: and thou shalt put away the evil from Israel. (Deuteronomy 17:12)

If there be a controversy between men, and they come unto judgment, that the judges may judge them; then they shall justify the righteous, and condemn the wicked. (Deuteronomy 25:1)

And it shall be, if the wicked man be worthy to be beaten, that the judge shall cause him to lie down, and to be beaten before his face, according to his fault, by a certain number. (Deuteronomy 25:2)

And Deborah, a prophetess, the wife of Lapidoth, she judged Israel at that time. (Judges 4:4)

And he judged Israel twenty and three years, and died, and was buried in Shamir. (Judges 10:2)

And after him arose Jair, a Gileadite, and judged Israel twenty and two years. (Judges 10:3)

And Samuel judged Israel all the days of his life. (1 Samuel 7:15)

For I verily, as absent in body, but present in spirit, have judged already, as though I were present, concerning him that hath so done this deed. (1 Corinthians 5:3)

Guidelines concerning how we are to judge

Ye shall do no unrighteousness in judgment: thou shalt not respect the person of the poor, nor honour the person of the mighty: but in righteousness shalt thou judge thy neighbour. (Leviticus 19:15)

Judges and officers shalt thou make thee in all thy gates, which the LORD thy God giveth thee, throughout thy tribes: and they shall judge the people with just judgment. (Deuteronomy 16:18)

And the judges shall make diligent inquisition: and, behold, if the witness be a false witness, and hath testified falsely against his brother. (Deuteronomy 19:18)

Give me now wisdom and knowledge, that I may go out and come in before this people: for who can judge this thy people, that is so great? (2 Chronicles 1:10)

And all Israel heard of the judgment which the king had judged; and they feared the king: for they saw that the wisdom of God was in him, to do judgment. (I Kings 3:28)

Judge not according to the appearance, but judge righteous judgment. (John 7:24)

For what have I to do to judge them also that are without? do not ye judge them that are within? But them that are without God judgeth. Therefore put away from among yourselves that wicked person. (1 Corinthians 5:12,13)

Do ye not know that the saints shall judge the world? and if the world shall be judged by you, are ye unworthy to judge the smallest matters? (1 Corinthians 6:2)

Know ye not that we shall judge angels? how much more things that pertain to this life? (1 Corinthians 6:3)

I speak to your shame. Is it so, that there is not a wise man among you? no, not one that shall be able to judge between his brethren. (1 Corinthians 6:5)

Let no man therefore judge you in meat, or in drink, or in respect of an holyday, or of the new moon, or of the sabbath days. (Colossians 2:16)

The way Jesus judged

And shall make him of quick understanding in the fear of the LORD: and he shall not judge after the sight of his eyes, neither reprove after the hearing of his ears: But with righteousness shall he judge the poor, and reprove with equity for the meek of the earth: and he shall smite the earth with the rod of his mouth, and with the breath of his lips shall he slay the wicked. (Isaiah 11:3-4)

I can of mine own self do nothing: as I hear, I judge: and my judgment is just; because I seek not mine own will, but the will of the Father which hath sent me. (John 5:30)

Ye judge after the flesh; I judge no man. And yet if I judge, my judgment is true: for I am not alone, but I and the Father that sent me. (John 8:15-16)

And if any man hear my words, and believe not, I judge him not: for I came not to judge the world, but to save the world. (John 12:47)

He that rejecteth me, and receiveth not my words, hath one that judgeth him: the word that I have spoken, the same shall judge him in the last day. (John 12:48)

Guidelines to avoid undue judgment

Agree with thine adversary quickly, whiles thou art in the way with him; lest at any time the ad-

versary deliver thee to the judge, and the judge deliver thee to the officer, and thou be cast into prison. (Matthew 5:25)

Judge not, that ye be not judged. (Matthew 7:1)

For with what judgment ye judge, ye shall be judged: and with what measure ye mete, it shall be measured to you again. (Matthew 7:2)

Judge not, and ye shall not be judged: condemn not, and ye shall not be condemned: forgive, and ye shall be forgiven. (Luke 6:37)

Therefore thou art inexcusable, O man, whosoever thou art that judgest: for wherein thou judgest another, thou condemnest thyself; for thou that judgest doest the same things. (Romans 2:1)

And thinkest thou this, O man, that judgest them which do such things, and doest the same, that thou shalt escape the judgment of God. (Romans 2:3)

Let not him that eateth despise him that eateth not; and let not him which eateth not judge him that eateth: for God hath received him. (Romans 14:3)

Therefore judge nothing before the time, until the Lord come, who both will bring to light the hidden things of darkness, and will make manifest the counsels of the hearts: and then shall every man have praise of God. (1 Corinthians 4:5)

For if we would judge ourselves, we should not be judged. But when we are judged, we are chastened of the Lord, that we should not be condemned with the world. (1 Corinthians 11:31-32)

Speak not evil one of another, brethren. He that speaketh evil of his brother, and judgeth his brother, speaketh evil of the law, and judgeth the law: but if thou judge the law, thou art not a doer of the law, but a judge. There is one lawgiver, who is able to save and to destroy: who art thou that judgest another? (James 4:11-12)

God's delegation of judgment to Jesus

For the Father judgeth no man, but hath committed all judgment unto the Son. (John 5:22)

The principles underlying judgment

For as many as have sinned without law shall also perish without law: and as many as have sinned in the law shall be judged by the law. (Romans 2:12)

Who art thou that judgest another man's servant? to his own master he standeth or falleth. Yea, he shall be holden up: for God is able to make him stand. (Romans 14:4)

But why dost thou judge thy brother? or why dost thou set at nought thy brother? for we shall all stand before the judgment seat of Christ. (Romans 14:10)

Let us not therefore judge one another any more: but judge this rather, that no man put a stumblingblock or an occasion to fall in his brother's way. (Romans 14:13)

But he that is spiritual judgeth all things, yet he himself is judged of no man. (1 Corinthians 2:15)

252

*Let the prophets speak two or three, and let the
other judge. (1 Corinthians 14:29)*

A summary on judging: God is the Ruler and ultimate
Judge over the world (Revelation 19:11, 20:12-13; Hebrews
10:30; Isaiah 33:22). God has delegated judgment to Jesus
(John 5:22) and to spiritual leaders (Exodus 18:13, 16, 22,
26; Deuteronomy 17:9; 25:1-2; 1 Corinthians 5:3).

God gives us numerous guidelines for how we are to judge.
They include: not giving special respect to the rich or to the
poor (Leviticus 19:15; James 2:2-4); judging justly
(Deuteronomy 16:18); making diligent inquisition
(Deuteronomy 19:18); praying for divine wisdom (2
Chronicles 1:10); not judging according to appearance but
with righteous judgment (John 7:24); judging those within
the church, not without (1 Corinthians 5:12); and not judging concerning meat or drink or in respect to a holiday, a
new moon or the sabbath (Colossians 2:16).

Jesus judged not by sight, but with righteous judgment
(Isaiah 11:3-4). He only judged according to what the Father was showing Him (John 5:30). The words of Jesus will
be used to judge people at the last day (John 12:48).

It is best to minimize judgment. Ways of minimizing judgment include: not judging unless absolutely necessary (Matthew 7:1); agreeing with thine adversary quickly so you are
not taken before a judge (Matthew 5:25); knowing that you
will be judged with the same harshness that you judge others (Matthew 7:2); not judging others for the same things
that you yourself are doing (Romans 2:1); not judging others
for what they eat (Romans 14:3); waiting and letting God
judge the hearts of man at the final judgment (1 Corinthians
4:5); judging ourselves so God doesn't have to judge us (1
Corinthians 11:31-32); and not speaking evil of our brother
(James 4:11-12).

Principles which underlie judgment include: determining whether a person had access to the law or not (Romans 2:12); letting God judge His servants (Romans 14:4); and not judging our brothers (Romans 14:10, 13). Prophets are to be judged (1 Corinthians 14:29). The spiritual judge the carnal; the carnal cannot judge the spiritual (1 Corinthians 2:15)

My personal summary concerning judging: It is wisest to minimize judging in my life as excessive judgment can easily lead to sin, which brings with it much negative repercussion in one's life.

Any judgments I make must flow out of my journaling time with the Lord. If God issues a judgment I am to perform what He tells me to do and then set aside any and all personal anger concerning the judgment before the sun goes down, or else the judgment has moved into sin on my part. "Let not the sun go down on your wrath" (Ephesians 4:26).

This is an important distinction I had not made in the past. I would carry the anger of the judgment for days, weeks, months and years. I also felt that living in judgment and anger against an institution was acceptable. These are the places where I have sinned. These are the reasons why judgment within me was feeding a spirit of anger. Thank You, Lord, for showing me this.

APPENDIX E

MORE TEACHING ON DREAM INTERPRETATION

Concerning dreams

1. Do not pose as an expert on interpreting others' dreams until you have been interpreting your own dreams for at least five years.

2. If you get stuck, ask your spiritual counselor for help in interpreting your dreams.

3. Read some good books on Christian dream interpretation. *Dreams: Wisdom Within* by Herman Riffel and *Biblical Research Concerning Dreams and Visions* by Mark and Patti Virkler are recommended.

4. Realize that dreams are not to be viewed with a fatalistic attitude; when they are **acted** upon, the anticipated results may change.

5. Act on your dreams.

Training in symbolism

One of the best ways to get the feel for how to work constructively with symbols is to purchase and play the game Bible Pictionary. Just as you draw pictures to get people to guess the word you are working on, so your heart draws pictures to get your mind to understand a message it is seeking to communicate to your conscious self.

Discerning objective and subjective dreams

Subjective dreams

Most dreams (perhaps 95%) are subjective, meaning that they are talking about *you*. The people in these dreams are, in this case, *parts of yourself*. You can determine what part of yourself they are representing by simply asking, "What is the dominant personality characteristic of this person, as I know him?" The answer to that question tells you what part of yourself you are dreaming about.

Animals in subjective dreams are often your emotions. Ask, "What emotion might this animal be symbolizing?" (For example: an *angry* bull, a *curious* cat, a *sly* fox, a *contented* cow!)

The best way to interpret a dream is to start with the first symbol, try to interpret it, and then go on to the next symbol, etc. Ask the question, "In what way am I experiencing this symbol in my life at this time?" For example, if the symbol is that your car is going backward, ask, "In what way do I feel that I am going backward?" If your mom or dad is driving your car in the dream, ask, "In what way is someone in authority driving my life at this time (i.e., my reactions, attitudes, behaviors)?"

Objective dreams

Perhaps only 5% of our dreams are objective. An objective dream is not talking about parts of yourself, but about outer realities. For example, I have found three different women who have all scored 7.7 on the left/right brain hemisphere test found in the *Communion with God* book (i.e., the highest score I have seen). All these women have vivid dreams at night where they see the murders, rapes, and thefts which are taking place in their communities that night. Obviously, not all objective dreams need to be showing these fearsome of pictures. These are just given as examples.

Objective dreams are shared publicly much more often than subjective dreams. That is why the vast majority of the dreams in the Bible fall into the category of objective dreams.

Three clues which can indicate to you that your dream may be objective and not subjective

1. The dream just does not fit subjectively. The first question you should always ask God is, "Lord, show me any way the events in this dream are revealing struggles my heart is currently facing." If you cannot see that the dream is talking about a struggle you are facing, and your spiritual counselor cannot help you see how this may be something your heart is currently processing, then you can assume that the dream is not subjective - it does not fit subjectively.

2. The events happen in the dream exactly as they could in real life (i.e., no flying houses, etc.).

3. You are intensely, emotionally related in real life to the person who shows up in the dream (i.e., you are processing some intense emotions with the person in real life, and then you dream about that same person).

An example of dream interpretation

I had the honor of teaching a Communion with God seminar last week at the Toronto Airport Christian Center to about 35 pastors who had come for a week of school. Toward the end of the week, one of them named Rev. Mike Bastien had voiced some concerns that he was not getting all the information I was cramming down their throats at breakneck speed. I assured him he probably wasn't, but that that was all right because he could take the *Communion with God* book, cassettes, and videos home with him and review them at his leisure. However, this advice was not heard by all parts within Mike, as he e-mailed me a day or two later with a troubling dream he had had. Following are the e-mails which went back and forth between us over the next few days. Mike has given me permission to share these e-mails and his dream.

The dream as Mike sent it to me

Here it goes: The school bus was coming to my home when I was in high school. I was running late and saw the bus coming and was running towards it and I saw my father-in-law (Fred) get on the bus and before I could get on. Just before I reached it, it left. I was a bit upset that he didn't wait for me. I tried to look to see if it was George driving the bus and thought it was. (George and I talked once in awhile, and he was the actual bus driver when I was in high school.)

But soon after I saw another school bus coming and knew it was going to the public school in the same town and asked the lady if I could take it and she said yes. So I got on. Don't remember any of the ride. Next I remember talking to my father-in-law and asking him why George left me and didn't wait. He gave me a mumbled answer which didn't make sense and which I can't remember at all now.

And that was the dream. One thing that really concerns me is that my father-in-law died this past December of cancer at the age of 61.

My first response

I'll be glad to offer a few questions and suggestions for you to consider.

The symbols in the dream include:

- school = place where we get educated and learn
- bus = transportation to the place of learning
- getting left behind = fear of being left behind

So the question you would ask yourself is, "In what sense am I being educated at this time in my life, and am I afraid I am going to be left behind?"

I suspect the answer is that you are being educated in the area of Communion with God, and that there is a part of you that is afraid that you are being left behind (i.e., not going to get it all). You actually expressed exactly that fear in class. I assume it is that fear in your heart which was expressed in your dream.

However, God showed you in the dream that there was hope. Another bus came along and took you to school. So you do not need to fear missing some parts of the teaching the first time around. There is another way to get it. For example, reading the whole *Communion with God* book; taking the three-month Communion with God course with Christian Leadership University and having me as a mentor; purchasing the videos which were made; purchasing the cassettes of me teaching the entire course; purchasing the CWG Teacher's Guide; getting a couple of spiritual counselors in your church or area who are right-brain and sharing your journaling with them and having them cover it, etc.

Don't be concerned that the person in your dream had died a year ago. People in our dreams most often are parts of ourselves. The way we discover what part is to ask, "What is the dominant characteristic of the person?" Then, it is usually that part of ourselves we are dreaming about. The dream is not about you dying.

Mike's second letter

Thank you, Mark, for responding. To be honest it was not what I expected. It sounds good but I have this big question... why was my father-in-law in this dream and why was it so evident that he was in it? He must have something to do with the dream?

My second response

When you think of your father-in-law, Fred, what is the most dominant characteristic of him? That is your key. Once you identify that characteristic, you are then talking about that part of yourself. Your heart is drawing pictures (like Bible Pictionary - if you have ever played it), to communicate a message to you.

Whatever part of you Fred is representing, that part of you is comfortable with the message of CWG and is getting along with it and on time (as evidenced by the fact that he got on the bus all right). Some other part of you is struggling with the message of CWG, being afraid you are not getting it all.

Any chance that Fred is a "heart" kind of a guy, as opposed to a "head" kind of a guy?

My guess is that your heart is fine with the CWG message but your left-hemisphere is afraid that it hasn't got all the pieces yet (which is true - it hasn't). However, as I mentioned earlier, your head doesn't need to get all the pieces in my four mornings of teaching you, because I have provided books and cassettes and videos which you can take home and study in detail.

My guess is that your left-hemisphere (your analytical, reasoning brain) is uptight, but that your heart (as perhaps represented by an "easy-going Fred") is fine with the message of Communion with God.

What do you think?

Mike's final response

Mark. Wow. That's exactly how he was. Easy going. Laid back.

Blessings

Mike

APPENDIX F

BUT WASN'T IT ALL COMPLETED AT CALVARY?

The Question

There are so many verses which say that Jesus accomplished my complete salvation at Calvary. Why would I want to believe there are issues from my pre-Christian days which are still affecting me, if all has become new? Why ask Jesus to walk with me through traumatic pictures in my pre-Christian days? We are new creatures in Christ, old things have passed away and behold, all things are new. Why dig around in the past if all things are new?

The Answer

For starters, we don't dig around. If there is any digging around to do, we allow the Holy Spirit to do it by asking our hearts and the Holy Spirit in our hearts, "What is in my heart?" Thus, if the Holy Spirit brings something forth, it wasn't me digging around, it was the Holy Spirit revealing things. That, of course, is fully acceptable. The Holy Spirit may reveal what He wants when He wants.

And yes, it was all done at Calvary. However, I now need to apply what was done at Calvary to my own life. And I do that a step at a time. I appropriate salvation through confessing my sin, repenting, and making Jesus Christ my Lord and Savior. I appropriate healing by believing in faith that by His stripes I am healed.

I appropriate deliverance by using the authoritative name of Jesus Christ who has dismantled all rulers by His death at Calvary, and I cast out demons which are intruders into my life.

It is as I appropriate what was done at Calvary into area after area in my own life that the fullness of the effects of Calvary become real in me.

I am to work out my soul's salvation with fear and trembling, for it is Christ Who is at work in me both to will and to do of His good pleasure (Philippians 2:12-13). At salvation, I receive the indwelling Holy Spirit. As I grow in the Lord, I allow the indwelling Holy Spirit to rule and control more and more areas of my soul and body. This is exactly where the seven prayers that heal the heart come in - in assisting in this outworking.

The children's teeth are no longer set on edge

What about the prophecies of Ezekiel and Jeremiah? Do their prophecies not imply that the children cannot be harmed as a result of the sins of the fathers, by saying that the children's teeth will not be set on edge (Jeremiah 31:29; Ezekiel 18:1-4)?

No, they don't. These passages are referring to **guilt** for the sins of the fathers - not the **damage** done as a result of the sin. The child will not be guilty before God for his father's sin, but he may be damaged by his father's sin and have additional issues which he will have to work through in his own life because of the sins of his ancestors.

Notice how it is **guiltiness** being discussed, not effects.

> ***But every one shall die for his own iniquity:*** *every man that eateth the sour grape, his teeth shall be set on edge. (Jeremiah. 31:30)*

> *Behold, all souls are mine; as the soul of the father, so also the soul of the son is mine:* ***the soul that sinneth, it shall die.*** *(Ezekiel 18:4)*

APPENDIX G

THE MIND AND THE HEART

The western culture, including myself, has worshipped at the throne of rationalism. Rationalism is "reliance upon reason to establish religious truth" (Webster). This, of course, is nowhere taught in Scripture, and is directly against Scripture. For the Bible says, "Trust in the LORD with all thine heart; and lean not unto thine own understanding" (Proverbs 3:5).

When I rely on my mind, rather than relying on the revelation of God, I have put trust in my mind rather than in my God. My mind has become an idol. In understanding this truth, some Christians have chosen instead to reject the mind entirely and go with the Spirit. So they have become anti-mind. I don't think either of these extremes is where I want to stand.

The rest of this appendix is quoted from the book *Wading Deeper Into the River of God* by Mark and Patti Virkler. Read that entire book for a deeper understanding of the roles of the mind and the heart. For an exhaustive understanding of these truths, read *How Do You Know?* by Mark and Patti Virkler.

There are four examples of reason in the Gospels

In all four occurrences of the word "reason" in the Gospels, Jesus rebuked the individuals for faulty reasoning because they were not incorporating faith, divine revelation, or the power of God into their reasoning processes.

1. Matthew 16:5-12. The disciples are rebuked by Jesus for reasoning **without faith** or revelatory understanding of what He was saying.

2. Mark 2:5-12. Jesus rebuked the Pharisees for reasoning **without revelation** knowledge of who He was.

3. Mark 8:15-18. The disciples are rebuked by Jesus for reasoning **without perception** (i.e., a spirit phenomenon), without understanding, with a hardened heart, and eyes that see yet can't see, and ears that hear yet don't hear.

4. Luke 5:21-22. Jesus rebuked the scribes and Pharisees for reasoning against Him, because they did so **without revelation** of who He was.

Summary of the examples of faulty reasoning

This is quite astounding. It is clear that faulty reasoning occurs when we reason without incorporating faith, divine revelation, and God's ability to do the miraculous into our reasoning process.

Get this, because if you don't, you will find Jesus rebuking you for your faulty reasoning process.

I personally believe that all reasoning processes I was taught in school and college were faulty in light of the biblical examples, and must be replaced by an understanding of what the Bible exemplifies as anointed reasoning.

Spirit-anointed reasoning defined

The Holy Spirit granting divine perspective and understanding by guiding the analytical and visionary processes through Holy Spirit flow, while infusing the heart with faith.

A biblical example of anointed reasoning

The phrase "anointed reasoning" is not found in Scripture, but I believe the experience of it is found in the passage below.

> *Inasmuch as many have undertaken to compile an account of the things accomplished among us, just as those who from the beginning were eyewitnesses and servants of the word have handed them down to us, it seemed fitting for me as well, **having investigated everything carefully** from the beginning, to write it out for you in consecutive order, most excellent Theophilus; so that you might know the exact truth about the things you have been taught. (Luke 1:1-4, NASB)*

Careful investigation is involved in anointed reasoning

Luke investigated everything carefully, which sounds to me like some left-brain processes at work because, as you will recall, examination and analysis are left-brain functions.

If flow guides the reasoning process, you can have anointed reasoning

If reason itself could allow us to do research and come up with illumined, prophetic, revelatory truth, then all of us could easily be writing out prophecies by just investigating things carefully and writing about them. However, I think we would all agree that more than careful investigation was at work when Luke wrote his gospel. The Holy Spirit was inspiring him. "All Scripture is given by inspiration of God" (2 Timothy 3:16). So inspiration or flow from the river within was guiding his reasoning process as he investigated. This is what I believe we are to do. We are to come to God in faith as we begin the reasoning process, and invite the river of God within us to guide our reasoning through flow. Then we stay tuned to flow as we reason, and find that flow causes our thoughts to follow certain tracks and avoid others. The Holy Spirit's flow puts things together with great insight, which reason might never relate to each other, because flow gives us God's perspective, where reason alone (i.e., without flow) only gives us man's perspective.

> **Note:** Are we adding more Scripture to the Bible? I have no plans to add the anointed reasoning which I write down to the Bible. I am satisfied that it is complete and that it is wiser to submit my anointed reasoning to the Scriptures, rather than add it to the Scriptures. This has been the consensus of Christendom for nearly 2000 years.

This reminds me of a quotation from Albert Einstein: "I want to know God's thoughts . . . the rest are details." Of course, Einstein's theory of relativity and his work in the area of quantum physics radically altered the sciences and the Newtonian premises which had been science's foundation for hundreds of years.

Einstein tells how he "developed" his theories: "The ideas danced in my mind." This sounds like spirit flow to me. He also tells of lying on his back on a grassy slope, looking into the sky through half-closed eyelids and wondering what it would be like to ride on a ray of sunlight. Then the theory of relativity struck him. This is whole-brain thinking, which involves left-brain questions, right-brain pictures, and third-brain illumination. This is an example of the proper functioning of the brain, using it as God intended.

The third brain is the cerebellum, which is under the cerebrum. This is thought by scientists to be the place where we receive transcendent (i.e., spiritual) experiences. However, science is not sure, as they have only mapped about half the brain so far. So whether spiritual experiences come from the heart or the third brain, as the most cutting-edge scientific experiments might be indicating, is not a critical matter to me. I am glad to call it the heart even if it is registered in the third brain. I suppose it is possible that the Bible might have been speaking symbolically when it referred to the heart. Or perhaps it wasn't. I don't think I know enough to know for sure. I don't think it matters to me. The important thing is that one have spiritual experiences, not whether these experiences come through the heart or through the third brain. The point is, HAVE THEM!

APPENDIX H

BIBLICAL MEDITATION

Biblical meditation results in illumination, revelation knowledge, and anointed reasoning.

Do Not Do This: LEFT-BRAIN STUDY/RATIONAL HUMANISM	But Do This: WHOLE-BRAIN/HEART MEDITATION/DIVINE REVELATION
1. Have unconfessed sin	1. Be washed by Jesus' blood
2. Have a pre-conceived attitude	2. Have a teachable attitude
3. Be independent: "I can..."	3. Pray: "Lord, show me"
4. Read quickly	4. Slow down, ponder, muse
5. Rely on reason & analysis only	5. Combine anointed reason, flowing pictures, music & speech
6. Read without specific purpose	6. Read with focused purpose
7. Take credit for insights	7. Glorify God for insights

The Seven Steps of Biblical Meditation Explained

1. **Lord, cleanse me by Your blood.** Since receiving divine revelation is at the heart of biblical meditation, you must prepare yourself to receive from the Holy Spirit by repenting and being cleansed by the blood of the Lamb. You must be obedient to previous revelations from God (Matthew 7:6), and confess any sin in your life, so you are not cut off from ongoing revelation (Isaiah 59:1-2, 1 John 1:9).

2. **Lord, grant me a teachable attitude.** Revelation is given to those who maintain an attitude of humility, and it is withheld from the proud and the arrogant. So keep an open, humble attitude before God, allowing Him the freedom to shed greater light on any ideas you currently hold and to alter them as He sees fit (James 4:6, 2 Peter 1:19).

3. **Lord, I will not use my faculties myself.** You can do nothing of your own initiative but only what you hear and see by the Spirit (John 5:19-20, 30). You do not have a mind to use, but a mind to present to God so He can use it and fill it with anointed reason and divine vision (Proverbs 3:5-7, Romans 12:1-2). If you use your mind yourself, it is a dead work (Hebrews 6:1-2).

4. **Lord, I pray that the eyes of my heart might be enlightened.** Slow down as you read, mulling the text over and over in your heart and mind, praying constantly for God to give you a spirit of wisdom and revelation in the knowledge of Him (Ephesians 1:17-18, Psalms 119:18).

5. **Lord, I present the abilities to reason and to imagine to You to fill and flow through by Your Spirit.** Meditation involves presenting your faculties to God

for Him to fill and use. These include your left-brain reasoning capacities as well as your right-brain visual capacities. Look for the river of God (i.e., "Spirit flow") to guide and fill both hemispheres, granting you anointed reasoning and dream and vision. Music can assist you, as can muttering, speaking, and writing as you go through the discovery process (John 7:37-39).

6. **Lord, show me the solution to the problem I am facing.** Focused attention brings additional energies of concentration of heart and mind, which help release revelation. For example, note the difference between a ray of sunlight hitting a piece of paper, and sunlight going through a magnifying glass to hit a piece of paper. The focused energy creates a ray so concentrated that the paper bursts into flames. When you have a hunger to master a new understanding and discipline, that hungry and searching heart will cause you to see things you would not normally see (Matthew 5:6).

7. **Thank You, Lord, for what You have shown me.** Realizing that the revelation came from the indwelling Holy Spirit, give all the glory to God for what has been revealed (Ephesians 3:21).

The Hebrew and Greek Definitions of "Meditation"

According to *Strong's Exhaustive Concordance*, there are several Hebrew and Greek words which underlie the words "meditate" and "meditation" in the Old and New Testaments. The Strong's numbers for these words in the Old Testament are: 1897, 1900, 1901, 1902, 7878, 7879, 7881. The New Testament numbers are 3191 and 4304.

The literal meanings of "meditate" and "meditation" as listed by _Strong's Exhaustive Concordance_

To murmur; to converse with oneself, and hence aloud; speak; talk; babbling; communication; mutter; roar; mourn; a murmuring sound; a musical notation; to study; to ponder; revolve in the mind; imagine; pray; prayer; reflection; devotion.

Left-hemisphere functions listed above include: study, revolve in the mind, murmur, mutter, converse, speak, talk, communication (Note: Reason and speech are left-brain.)

Right-hemisphere functions listed above include: imagine, a musical notation, mourn, babbling (Note: Tongue speaking has been registered in experiments at Fuller Theological Seminary as taking place in the right hemisphere. Pictures, music and emotion are also right-brain.)

Heart (or third-brain) functions listed above include: pray, prayer, devotion, reflection, ponder (i.e., enlightened reasoning by adding Spirit-flow to the reasoning process - Ephesians 1:17-18)

Meditation results in illumined verses every time you read the Bible and every time you meditate on any subject. Illumination is experienced as insights jumping off the page and hitting you between the eyes.

Meditation is a whole-brain and heart process, and study is often left-hemisphere only

I asked a pastor who scored as extremely left-brain (2.4) on the Brain Preference Indicator Test how he studied the Bible. Did he use pictures a fair amount? He replied, "Never." Then I asked a right-brain pastor (6.7) how he studied the Bible. Did he use pictures much? He said, "Always." He had a constant stream of flowing pictures when he studied. (Note: 5.0 is perfectly balanced.)

Do you see that a left-brain person will tend to study the Bible differently than a right-brain person? We tend to miss this, because we assume that everyone else studies the way we do. This could not be further from the truth. Left-brain people study using primarily logic, reason, and analysis. Right-brain people study (or could we say, meditate) using primarily pictures and flow combined with reason, analysis, speech, and song.

Repenting for studying

So, in meditation, the whole brain is being controlled and guided by the indwelling Holy Spirit, whereas in study, primarily the left brain is being used, and it is under the control of self.

Wow! What a startling insight, especially when we realize that the Bible (NASB) **never** encourages study, but twenty times does encourage meditation! Look up the Greek in the three instances that the King James Version uses "study," and you will see that they are all inaccurate translations. So I, a left-brain individual, repented for studying, and purposed in my heart to only meditate from now on when I come to the Word of God or to any topic that God sets before me to explore.

Another great aid to "seeing" - writing out Scripture

When you write or type out a verse, you discover words which you otherwise might have missed.

The following is the law which God gave for new kings who had just been crowned and were coming to sit upon their throne for the first time.

Now it shall come about when he sits on the throne of his kingdom, he shall write for himself a copy of this law on a scroll in the presence of the Levitical priests. (Deuteronomy 17:18)

Since we are kings and priests (1 Peter 2:9), are we to do any less? Let us make the writing out of Scriptures an important part of our lives.

APPENDIX I

HOW OFTEN DID JESUS MINISTER DELIVERANCE?

The following table lists forty-one different times when it is recorded in the Gospels that Jesus prayed for people to be healed. Of these forty-one, twelve incorporated prayers for deliverance. That means that in one-fourth to one-third of Jesus' prayers for healing, the Gospel writers specifically mention the fact that they involved the casting out of demons. Obviously, additional healing prayers of Jesus may have involved deliverance which was just not specifically mentioned, so the proportion could actually be higher.

Therefore, if I am praying for people to be healed, I would assume that between one-fourth and one-third of my prayers would involve deliverance. After all, if I am not going to pattern my healing prayer ministry after Jesus, who am I going to pattern it after? Jesus is the greatest healer the world has ever known.

Evaluate your own prayer ministry approach to see if you are minimizing or over-doing deliverance prayer.

The Healing Ministry of Jesus

(D) means **D**eliverance was mentioned

(NDM) means **N**o **D**eliverance Mentioned

Description, Reference, and Parallel passages

1. Man with unclean spirit. Mark 1:23-25 **(D)**, Luke 4:33-35 **(D)**

2. Peter's mother-in-law. Matthew 8:14-15 (NDM), Mark 1:30-31 (NDM), Luke 4:38-39 (NDM)

3. Multitudes. Matthew 8:16-17 **(D)**, Mark 1:32-34 **(D)**, Luke 4:40-41 **(D)**

4. Many demons. Mark 1:39 **(D)**

5. Leper. Matthew 8:2-4 (NDM), Mark 1:40-42 (NDM), Luke 5:12-13 (NDM)

6. Paralytic. Matthew 9:2-7 (NDM), Mark 2:3-13 (NDM), Luke 5:17-25 (NDM)

7. Man with withered hand. Matthew 12:9-13 (NDM), Mark 3:1-5 (NDM), Luke 6:6-10 (NDM)

8. Multitudes. Matthew 12:15-16 (NDM), Mark 3:10-11 (NDM)

9. Gadarene demoniac. Matthew 8:28-32 **(D)**, Mark 5:1-13 **(D)**, Luke 8:26-33 **(D)**

10. Jairus' daughter. Matthew 9:23-25 (NDM), Mark 5:35-43 (NDM), Luke 8:49-56 (NDM)

11. Woman with issue of blood. Matthew 9:20-22 (NDM), Mark 5:25-34 (NDM), Luke 8:43-48 (NDM)

12. A few sick people. Matthew 13:58 (NDM), Mark 6:5-6 (NDM)

13. Multitudes. Matthew 14:34-36 (NDM), Mark 6:55-56 (NDM)

14. Syro-phoenician's daughter. Matthew 15:22-28 **(D)**, Mark 7:24-30 **(D)**

15. Deaf and mute man. Mark 7:32-35 (NDM)

16. Blind man. Mark 8:22-26 (NDM)

17. Child with evil spirit. Matthew 17:14-18 **(D)**, Mark 9:14-27 **(D)**, Luke 9:38-43 **(D)**

18. Blind Bartimaeus. Matthew 20:30-34 (NDM), Mark 10:46-52 (NDM), Luke 18:35-43 (NDM)

19. Centurion's servant Matthew. 8:5-13 (NDM), Luke 7:2-10 (NDM)

20. Two blind men. Matthew 9:27-30 (NDM)

21. Mute demoniac. Matthew 9:32-33 **(D)**

22. Blind and mute demoniac. Matthew 12:22 **(D)**, Luke 11:14 **(D)**

23. Multitudes. Matthew 4:23 **(D)**, Luke 6:17-19 **(D)**

24. Multitudes. Matthew 9:35 (NDM)

25. Multitudes. Luke 7:21 **(D)**

26. Multitudes. Matthew 14:14 (NDM), Luke 9:11 (NDM), John 6:2 (NDM)

27. Great multitudes. Matthew 15:30 (NDM)

28. Great multitudes. Matthew 19:2 (NDM)

29. Blind and lame in temple. Matthew 21:14 (NDM)

30. Widow's son. Luke 7:11-15 (NDM)

31. Mary Magdalene and others. Luke 8:2 **(D)**

32. Crippled woman. Luke 13:10-13 **(D)**

33. Man with dropsy. Luke 14:1-4 (NDM)

34. Ten lepers. Luke 17:11-19 (NDM)

35. Servant's ear. Luke 22:49-51 (NDM)

36. Multitudes. Luke 5:15 (NDM)

37. Various persons. Luke 13:32 **(D)**
38. Nobleman's son. John 4:46-53 (NDM)
39. Invalid. John 5:2-9 (NDM)
40. Man born blind. John 9:1-7 (NDM)
41. Lazarus. John 11:1-44 (NDM)

Special Note: The following occurrence is worthy of special mention for it specifically mentions that this woman's infirmity was caused by a spirit.

> *And He was teaching in one of the synagogues on the Sabbath. And behold, there was a woman who for eighteen years had a sickness caused by a spirit; and she was bent double, and could not straighten up at all. And when Jesus saw her, He called her over and said to her, "Woman, you are freed from your sickness." And He laid His hands upon her; and immediately she was made erect again, and began glorifying God. (Luke 13:10-13, NASB)*

The Healing Ministry of the Disciples

The following references will assist those who want to explore the ongoing healing ministry of the disciples.

1. Jesus' ministry described. Matthew 11:2-6, Luke 7:18-23
2. The twelve sent. Matthew 10:1-11:1, Mark 3:13-19, Luke 9:1-11
3. The seventy-two sent. Luke 10:1-24
4. Disciples attempt to cast out demons. Matthew 17:14-21, Mark 9:14-29, Luke 9:37-45

5. Power to bind and loose. Matthew 16:13-20
6. Great Commission. Matthew 28:16-20, Mark 16:14-20, Luke 24:44-53, Acts 1:1-11
7. Signs and wonders at Apostles' hands. Acts 2:22, 42-47
8. Healing of lame beggar. Acts 3:1-4
9. Prayer for confidence and healing signs. Acts 4:23-31
10. Signs and wonders at Apostles' hands. Acts 5:12-16
11. Ministry of Stephen. Acts 6:8-15
12. Ministry of Philip. Acts 8:4-13
13. Ananias and Saul. Acts 9:10-19
14. Peter heals Aeneas (Lydda). Acts 9:32-35
15. Peter heals Dorcas (Joppa). Acts 9:36-43
16. The ministry of Jesus. Acts 10:34-41
17. Magician struck blind by Paul. Acts 13:4-12
18. Paul and Barnabas in Iconium. Acts 14:1-7
19. Lame man at Lystra. Acts 14:8-18
20. Paul raised at Lystra. Acts 14:19-20
21. Slave girl at Philippi. Acts 16:16-40
22. Paul at Ephesus. Acts 19:8-20
23. Eutychus raised from the dead. Acts 20:7-12
24. Paul recalls Ananias. Acts 22:12-21
25. Paul on Malta. Acts 28:1-10
26. Galatians 3:5
27. Hebrews 2:4

APPENDIX J

IMPASSIONED REPENTANCE WORKSHEET ON LUST

Lust is an issue that nearly all men encounter and probably 95% of women. Following is a completed sample of an "Impassioned Repentance Worksheet" on the topic of lust, pornography, and adultery/fornication. Obviously, greater detail can be added in answering each of the questions below.

A detailed picture of the devastation and destruction of the sin of lust, pornography, and adultery/fornication

"Lord, show me the destruction it will bring into my life if I continue in the sin of lust/pornography." Tune to Holy Spirit flow and pictures as you write.

A detailed picture of the sin and the way it grows in one's life

Lust is an appetite of the flesh which has become perverted and grown quickly out of control. It is the twisting of love, which focuses on giving to others, into lust, which focuses on demanding from others. It believes that greater satisfaction is achieved by grasping from others to meet one's needs rather than experiencing the joy of giving to others. This is a lie.

As with all appetites of the flesh (eating, sleeping, sex), when indulged, it continues to grow until it is out of balance and disruptive to one's life. It believes that if it can just have more, it will be satisfied. This is a lie. It will never be satisfied by more. Its appetite will just continue to grow, becoming larger and larger with its passions becoming more and more perverted and demonic as it goes along, incorporating many unspeakable images and acts.

It provides pleasure for the moment, but leaves destruction in its wake. It leads from lust to pornography to sexual immorality and adultery/fornication. Pornography is a lie. It does not depict life as it really is.

Every sexual union causes you to join your life force with the prostitute you are with and with the other hundreds or thousands with whom that prostitute has joined herself. Your life force becomes scattered, and you pick up the life force of many others, many of which are demonic and destructive and negatively impact your life.

Biblical (and other) principles which relate to this sin

- Whatever I fix my eyes upon, grows within me. If I fix them on lust and perversion, then lust and perversion grow within me. If I fix my eyes upon God and a wholesome love toward my spouse, then that grows within me. Watch over your eyes with all diligence.

- Sexuality is a constant inner God-given drive. However, this appetite can get out of control and become one's master.

- Pornography involves lust, which is forbidden in Scriptures.

- At times, the "call for sexuality" should be transformed into other creative energy releases. The river of the life force within a person can be expressed through many channels, including sex, companionship, creative expression, expressing one's heart motivation, etc. The urge toward sexuality may actually be an inner call for intimacy, physical sensation, or sex. The call for intimacy can also be met by an intimate conservation and/or companionship (either in person, or by phone or letter, or by journaling with the Lord). The call for physical sensation and release can be met through exercise.

- Meditate upon Proverbs chapter five, "the pitfalls of immorality," and chapter seven, "the wiles of the harlot." Perhaps memorize these chapters. At a minimum, make a list of the important truths God gives you from these chapters.

A detailed picture of what it will do to my physical health

Assuming that lust eventually leads to sexual immorality, my body will be consumed with various sexual diseases such as venereal disease and AIDS. This leads to a pain-ridden life and a painful death, as well as public humiliation.

A detailed picture of what it will do to my soul's health

My soul will become twisted as it views people of the opposite sex as sex objects rather than people. I will not see straight. I will not enjoy the pleasures of life. I will see only one thing, perverted sex, everywhere I look.

A detailed picture of what it will do to my spiritual health

I will experience guilt and sinfulness, and be cut off from spiritual growth and development. A person's morality determines his theology. Since I will feel separated from God, I will lose my spiritual passion. I will become lukewarm and spiritually rebellious. I will be hardened inside, rather than tender.

A detailed picture of what it will do to my relationship with God

My guilt over my sexual sin will cause me to hide from God, to fear God, to be angry at God. I will seek to steer clear of spiritual things, or I will turn into a hypocrite. I will no longer be honest within. I will be dishonest, evil and vile. I will likely become a mocker of religious things.

A detailed picture of what it will do to my acquaintances

All people of the opposite sex will become objects rather than friends. People will not trust me, for if I break my marriage vows, I will break any and every vow I ever make. Wholesome people will shy away from me. Perverts will be drawn to me.

A detailed picture of what it will do to my spouse

My marriage will lose its passion as I find sexual satisfaction elsewhere. I will begin to disdain my spouse and my marriage. Adultery will probably cause the break-up of my marriage. I will lose my spouse, my happiness, and my joy of being married. I will be left alone in life. I will come home to an empty house, day after day. If I didn't maintain my vow to my spouse, I probably will not maintain any vow to anyone. I will drift from relationship to relationship, eventually being left alone.

A detailed picture of what it will do to my children

I will probably lose my children's love, honor and respect. They will have anger at me for violating my marriage vow, and for harming and humiliating their father/mother and themselves. They will be damaged as they grow up in a single-parent household, and will have a distorted view of God, life and family. They will be unhappy and tend to pass my sins on to their families and children. I will probably lose a close relationship with my grandchildren. My chance to pass on a godly heritage will be gone.

A detailed picture of what it will do to my ministry

I will likely lose my ministry position. I will cut off my service to God and to the building of the kingdom of God. Many people will judge me, will not trust me, and will reject me. Any joy I have found in ministering to others will be a thing of the past.

A detailed picture of what it will do to my job/finances

If I am employed in the ministry, I will likely lose my employment. I will have two homes to support rather than one, so I will be reduced financially. Paying prostitutes for sex will cause a great financial drain on my life. The curse of God will be upon my finances. Proverbs says I will be reduced to a loaf of bread.

A detailed picture of what it will do to my eternal life

Because of the hardening of my heart toward the things of God, I am likely to not repent, but to begin a life of ongoing rebellion toward God. Thus I would fall from God's grace through Christ and spend eternity in torment in hell (Galatians 5:4; Hebrews 6:4-6; Matthew 7:21-23; Colossians 2:189).

As a result of this meditation, here is my confession as to what I will do (speak this aloud several times, and whenever tempted)

I will establish the following fences in my life: I will cut off all potential sources of pornography. I will not shop in stores which sell it. I will only use internet web services which screen out all pornography. I will not maintain any pornography in my possession. I will not go near any location where I could be tempted.

When tempted to lust, I will picture Jesus instead. I will commune with Him and worship before His throne. I will also exercise, and have honest conversations with friends and family so that the desire for intimacy can be met through this means. When tired or discouraged, and thus more susceptible to temptation, I will be extra careful. Sleep will be the best remedy.

When I feel attraction toward a person of the opposite sex, I will put in place the extra safeguard of never being alone with him/her. I will seek to avoid a relationship with him/her to protect both him/her and me.

I will meditate upon Proverbs 5 and 7, and record what God shows me.

If I am still unable to overcome this temptation, I will seek counseling and/or establish an accountability relationship in this area. Lust should respond well to the seven prayers in this book. I will pray through these prayers as they relate to the problem of lust.

A picture of the blessing of the righteous act of pure sexual love

"Lord, show me the blessing it will bring into my life if I continue in the righteousness of pure sexual love." Tune to Holy Spirit flow and pictures as you write.

A detailed picture of this act of righteousness and the way it grows in one's life

Since pure sexual love is an activity between a husband and a wife, both the husband and the wife should explore this topic of the deepening of pure marital sexual love. It will take two to make this happen. So agree to both work through the following process.

Pure sexual love which is expressed within marriage is intended to produce an ongoing bond and union between the marriage partners, bringing joy and passion throughout the entire marriage. The physical union of the two marriage partners makes them one, and this joining causes a sharing of the gifts and life flow of one to the other. Eventually, they will begin to look alike, think alike, and respond alike.

Studies show that married people have sex more often than non-married people, therefore you will have greater sexual fulfillment than the immoral unmarried person.

A married couple is to grow together sexually throughout their marriage, as well as in every other way.

Biblical (and other) principles which relate to this act

- But if they do not have self-control, let them marry; for it is better to marry than to burn with passion (1 Corinthians 7:9, NASB).

- Being together with your spouse provides sexual safety. This should be sought. Traveling alone should be avoided.

- Having a warm, loving relationship with your spouse enhances sexuality. This should be sought. Pursuing deeper intimacy and companionship with your marriage partner is one of the best things you can do to enhance one's sexuality.

- Give and it will be given back to you. Give love in the way which represents love to your partner. Women want companionship, love and relationship. Men tend to want more the act of sex.

- Read a good book on sexuality in marriage. Read Song of Solomon to gain an understanding of sexual fulfillment in marriage. Make a list of key things God shows you from the Song of Solomon.

- Sexuality is richest when it is an expression of love.

- God recognizes our weaknesses and the mistakes we make in life, and meets the repentant sinner with His mercy and grace. The blood of Jesus washes away all sexual sin. Seek God's perfect will in sex, rather than His permissive will.

- Flee youthful lusts or you will be ensnared. Put up fences which protect yourself from sexual temptation. No pornography, no sexual movies, television, or books. No going to places where sexual temptation abounds. No doing any activity which leads you to sexual temptation.

- If necessary, get capable, spiritual counseling to overcome sexual problems. Inner healing and deliverance can help deal with sexual problems.

- No demanding of sexual exploits from one's marriage partner which violates his/her heart, soul or mind.

- One is drawn to that on which he fixes his eyes. Fix your eyes upon a strong, healthy, passionate, fulfilling marriage, and that is what you will get. Receive pleasure and fulfillment from this vision.

A detailed picture of what it will do to my physical health

Sex within marriage will be a blessing to my physical health. It will produce love, joy, and peace, which all produce positive health responses because of psychosomatic effects. The receiving of my partner's life force through this sexual union will complete and deepen and enlarge me.

A detailed picture of what it will do to my soul's health

It will produce love, joy, and peace, which will heal and restore my soul. I will feel satisfied and fulfilled and enlarged and blessed to be given such a gift from my Maker and from my spouse.

A detailed picture of what it will do to my spiritual health

The growth in all levels of intimacy with my spouse will encourage a continuing growth of intimacy with the Lord. My marriage will be a picture of the spiritual intimacy the Lord and I are to have, and thus a constant encouragement toward that intimacy. I will continue to seek the Lord.

A detailed picture of what it will do to my relationship with God

I will be at peace with God, and thankful for the love He has given me through my spouse. I will have a clear conscience, and thus be able to maintain a passionate desire to grow and to go on with God. My zeal will increase. God's revelation will increase within me. My knowledge and wisdom will increase.

A detailed picture of what it will do to my acquaintances

I will maintain the trust and companionship of my friends, as they will sense that I am a moral and trustworthy person. My number of acquaintances shall continue to grow, and they will be moral and trustworthy people.

A detailed picture of what it will do to my spouse

My spouse will continue to grow and to bloom, because he/she will know that he/she is loved, honored, and respected. Our marriage will continue to grow in love and intimacy and closeness. It will remain warm throughout our marriage, as we each seek to express love to the other in ways that are meaningful to them.

A detailed picture of what it will do to my children

My children will continue to grow in their respect, love, and honor of me. We will maintain a close relationship throughout our lives. I will enjoy the friendship of my grand-children, and I will pass on a godly anointing through several generations.

A detailed picture of what it will do to my ministry

It will enhance my ministry. People will be able to look upon me with trust and respect. God's grace, knowledge, wisdom, and anointing will be able to flow unrestricted through me. I will be able to help others in the areas of sexual purity because I have discovered God's grace in this area myself. My ministry will continue to grow and enlarge.

A detailed picture of what it will do to my job/finances

God's blessing will continue to flow upon my job and my finances. He will bless everything I put my hand to. My barns will overflow. God's blessing and prosperity will be drawn to me.

A detailed picture of what it will do to my eternal life

My heart will remain strong, pure, and fervent. I will go on to heaven, and spend eternity in the presence of my Father. I will enjoy an eternity of joy, blessing, and rest.

As a result of this meditation, here is my confession as to what I will do (speak this aloud several times, and whenever you need to reinforce these truths in your life)

I will build intimacy and friendship with my spouse by loving him/her in the ways that are most meaningful to him/her.

(For the man.) This will include taking her out on dates, eating meals out, purchasing flowers, writing love notes, holding hands, touching in non-sexual ways, caring, and daily expressing love, appreciation, and approval verbally. I will also avoid criticizing my wife or trying to remake her into my image or the image of what I think she should be. I will accept her for who God has made her to be. I will not seek to dominate, manipulate, or pressure her. I will respect her.

(For the woman.) This can include making his favorite meal, honoring and respecting him, letting him see and enjoy me naked, dressing in enticing lingerie, letting him regularly enjoy a sexual love feast with me, including much touch and caressing and intercourse and sexual variations.

(For both.) I will not close off my spirit from my spouse. I will remain open and loving and kind and compassionate. I will repent of any negative judgments, bitter root expectations, and inner vows I have toward them. I will believe the best—that they do love and cherish me and that they want to satisfy me sexually and can and will and do satisfy me sexually, and that I can satisfy them sexually. I renounce any belief or inner vows to the contrary—that they don't love me, don't want to satisfy me sexually, or that they can't and don't satisfy me sexually, or that I will never be able to satisfy them sexually. These are lies from the pit of hell. I reject them as feeders to demonic activity within me. I will only feed on the truth of the Holy Spirit, not the lies of the enemy.

I also renounce any inner vows I have made that I will not or cannot give myself wholeheartedly sexually to my spouse. I purpose through the Holy Spirit to give myself wholeheartedly sexually to my spouse.

I will meditate upon Song of Solomon and record what God shows me.

If I am still unable to overcome this temptation, I will seek counseling and/or establish an accountability relationship in this area. Most sexual problems should respond well to the seven prayers in this book. I will pray through these prayers as they relate to my sexual problem.

Concluding instructions

Meditate upon this completed "Impassioned Repentance Worksheet" daily in your devotional time for the next two weeks, asking God to deepen, expand, and internalize the truths given above. Read it aloud, for speaking is part of meditating and speaking it aloud deepens the truths within you. Whenever tempted, come back and read this meditation aloud.

APPENDIX K

PROVERBS AND THE SONG OF SOLOMON ON THE TOPIC OF SEX

Insights from Proverbs 5 and 7 and the Song of Solomon on healing lust and growing into pure, vibrant marital love. Read this appendix aloud to yourself whenever you are tempted.

- Keep this teaching as the apple of your eye (look at it)
- Bind it on your fingers (let it guide your actions)
- Write it on your heart (memorize it)
- Make it your intimate friend (keep it close to you)
    So you may be kept from an adulteress

(Proverbs 7:2-5)

Proverbs Chapter Five (NASB) - The Pitfalls of Immorality

The adulteress:

- Her lips are smooth, enticing and drip honey.
- She does not ponder the path of life.

- Her ways are unstable and she does not know it.
- The end of an encounter with an adulteress is bitter as wormwood.
- She cuts sharp as a two-edged sword.
- Her path leads to death.
- She goes to Sheol.

Avoiding relationships with an adulteress:
- I keep far away from her.
- I do not go near the door of her house.

What an encounter with an adulteress will do to me:
- I give my vigor to her.
- I give over years of my life to a cruel taskmaster.
- She is filled with my strength.
- My hard-earned goods go to her house.
- I will groan in the latter end when my flesh is consumed.

Enjoying your wife's love instead of an adulteress:
- Drink from her love.
- Don't let her love go to another; let it be yours alone.
- Be blessed with her love.
- Rejoice in her.
- Let her breasts satisfy you at all times.
- Be exhilarated always with her love.

God is watching my actions:
- God sees all my paths.
- My iniquities will capture me.
- I will be held with the cords of my sin.
- I will die for not listening to instruction.

Proverbs Chapter Seven (NASB) - The Wiles of the Harlot

How to get led astray by an adulteress:

- Be simple and lack sense.
- Go near her place.
- Have darkness cover your dark actions.
- See the seductive way she dresses.
- You are an ox being led to the slaughter.
- You are in bondage to a fool.
- Your liver is pierced.
- This will cost you your life.

How an adulteress leads you astray:

- She is cunning as she reels you in.
- She is boisterous and rebellious and brazen.
- She goes out to meet her prey.
- She initiates physical contact.
- She claims to be good and godly.
- She flatters you.
- She offers you a full night of lovemaking.
- She continues until you are seduced and follow.

LISTEN:

- Do not let your heart turn aside to her ways.
- Do not stray into her paths.
- She has many she has killed.
- She will take you to Sheol and to death.

——————— Transitional Thoughts ———————

*But if they do not have self-control, let them marry;
for it is better to marry than to burn with passion.
(1 Corinthians 7:9, NASB).*

- If you are not married and are having trouble handling your sexual desires, then seek God to lead you to a marriage partner as you also seek Him for grace to handle your sexuality while waiting for marriage to occur.

- While seeking God in faith for a marriage partner, follow His Spirit's leading. You may be led to go to a certain place and/or to look for a certain sign to find your marriage partner, as Isaac's servant was (Genesis 24:1-14). Or you may be led to simply continue in your everyday work, and your marriage partner will come to you, as Rebekah did (Genesis 24:15-67). Follow the Lord's leading as you pray for God to bring you and your partner together.

- A spouse should be someone who will assist in fulfilling God's destiny for your life.

- While deepening a relationship with a potential spouse, stay in public places, and use discretion in your actions (especially as they relate to touching) so as to not fall into fornication.

- In marriage, one's physical needs can be met, however one still must watch over his/her mind and not allow lust to reign.

- The safeguard of not going near a harlot's house, and thus being enticed by her and having your liver pierced through, should be obeyed whether married or single (Proverbs 7:8-23). In today's world, that would mean creating fences such as the following:

1. Do not go into adult sections of video rental stores.
2. Do not go in a store which sells adult magazines.
3. Do not go to "R" or "X" rated movies.
4. Do not have cable or satellite television, or, if you do, purchase a television with a chip that blocks out "R" and "X" rated movies.
5. If you are on the internet, obtain a service that blocks out all sexually-oriented materials.
6. Do not go near sections of town which have adult services.
7. Do not go near a person's home to whom you are drawn sexually, or, if you must, never go alone.

Song of Solomon (NASB) - The Joy and Ecstasy of Marital Love

Chapter 1:

- The desire is there for kisses on the mouth.
- Fragrant oils are used.
- They are together.
- The husband may invite his wife into a time of sexual encounter.
- The wife acknowledges the beauty of her body.
- The husband acknowledges the beauty of his wife's body.
- Ornaments and beads of gold and silver are placed on the wife.
- The husband may lay all night between his wife's breasts.
- The wife acknowledges her husband as handsome.

Chapter 2:

- The husband acknowledges that his wife is the most beautiful woman of all.
- Embracing and fondling are part of the lovemaking.
- The husband requests to see his wife's nude form.
- The husband requests to hear his wife's sweet voice.

Chapter 3:

- The wife seeks her husband.
- The wife holds on to her husband and will not let go.
- The wedding is a joyous occasion.

Chapter 4:

- The husband describes the beauty of each part of his wife's body starting at the head and working down to the breasts.
- The passion of love makes the husband's heart beat faster.
- The wife's love is better than wine.
- The wife's lips drip honey.
- Honey and milk are under the wife's tongue.
- The wife invites her husband to eat choice fruits from her.

Chapter 5:

- The husband eats and drinks deeply from his wife.
- When one wants to make love, the other should not make excuses.

Chapter 6:

- There is a mutual delight in each other.

Chapter 7:

- The husband describes his wife's beauty starting with her feet, then her hips, her navel, her belly, her breasts, her neck, and her head.

- The husband touches each part, especially enjoying his wife's breasts and her mouth.

Chapter 8:

- They enjoy fondling and caressing and loving one another.

APPENDIX L

THE UN-STUCK WORKSHEET
(INSURING PROPER FOUNDATIONS)

Underlying principle: Insure that the basic avenues for receiving God's Grace are open and being used!

When you (or your client) are not experiencing healing as you know you should be, discover which avenues for receiving God's grace are being used and which aren't.

I...	Yes	No

1. Am hearing God's voice and receiving Divine vision concerning this problem, journaling it out and doing what God is instructing me to do.   Y N

2. Bind demons and apply the "Law of the Spirit of Life in Christ Jesus" when attacked with negatives. (i.e., "Satan, I bind you in Jesus name." "Jesus, I release Your power to handle this situation.")   Y N

I ...	**Yes**	**No**

3. Seek, receive and interpret revelation from God through my dreams concerning this problem.   Y   N

4. Am healing this heart problem by addressing it using the language of the heart (i.e., emotion, flow, pictures).   Y   N

5. Have completed a "Contributing Strands Worksheet" concerning this problem.   Y   N

6. Have prayed through the seven prayers concerning this problem (i.e., "Prayers That Heal the Heart").   Y   N

7. Have completed a "Biblical Meditation Worksheet" concerning this problem.   Y   N

8. Have completed an "Impassioned Repentance Worksheet" concerning this problem.   Y   N

9. Have established divinely ordained fences of protection in the area of this problem.   Y   N

10. Have received counsel from those to whom I submit concerning this problem, and am acting upon it.   Y   N

11. Have confessed this sin to my spiritual counselor and made myself accountable in this area.   Y   N

12. Am functioning in my divinely ordained ministry, and am ministering God's life to others.   Y   N

If you have applied these 12 foundational experiences of Christianity, and are still struggling with unresolved heart issues, then you should seek out a spiritual counselor for additional help.

APPENDIX M

MINISTERING "PRAYERS THAT HEAL THE HEART" IN CHINA

Following is a praise report newsletter sent out by Dr. Gary Greig. Dr. Greig has served as a professor at Regent University, as well as Educational Advisor of The Apostolic Council for Educational Accountability. Dr. Greig taught and then conducted a spiritual ministry workshop where he practiced the principles of the Prayers That Heal The Heart Seminar Guide during his week in China. He left the seminar guide with the Chinese for translation purposes. Following is the tremendous report of the miracles which took place.

Thank you SO MUCH for praying for us as a family and for my ministry and teaching trip to Taiwan 3/29-4/9. The Lord moved powerfully and I am grateful to be a part of what He is doing there.

When I stepped off the plane into the airport terminal in Taipei, Taiwan, I felt a mantle of authority from the Lord come on me—authority to heal the sick, to cast out demons, and MOST IMPORTANTLY to train the leaders in the churches to do the same.

None of the outpouring of God would have happened without your prayers. Thank you so much!

Love and blessings,

Gary, Catherine, Jon, and Rivkah

3/31 Fri-4/3 Mon—TAINAN (SOUTHWESTERN TAIWAN), RHEMA CHURCH, PASTOR PHILIP YEN

I taught the Biblical Foundations of Inner Healing, and the goal of my teaching and ministry was not just to minister to them but to TRAIN THEM to pray healing prayer for others.

FRIDAY NIGHT 3/31

About 12-15 people—including pastors from other churches—from among the 60 or 70 that attended the conference were healed of chronic back pain, neck and shoulder pain, and congestion of lungs and sinuses, when they renounced being dedicated to the idols at birth and asked the Lord to forgive the idolatry of their family and ancestors. An older woman responded to a word God gave me for someone with weak painful knees, especially in the right knee. When prayer team members and I prayed with her, the Lord completely healed the pain in her knees within a couple of minutes of prayer.

SATURDAY, 4/1

In the ministry time, about 8 women were dramatically and quickly healed of back-neck-shoulder pain and lung or sinus congestion, when they confessed idolatry in their past and their family's past and renounced being dedicated to the idols at birth. These conditions are caused by spirits of infirmity and spirits of divination and idolatry that entered the people when they were dedicated to the idols in the temples as babies. Even 2nd or 3rd generation Christians needed to renounce their ancestors' dedication to the idols as babies and their ancestors' idolatry in order to get free of these spirits and to get healed of the back-neck-shoulder conditions. When we commanded the spirits of idolatry, divination, and infirmity to leave those we were praying for, the spirits in one woman made her scream as they left and threw her to the ground—but praise the Lord, they left, and she was completely healed!

The Lord also healed people who had a spirit of infirmity affecting the right side of their body (I ministered to about 8-10 people whose right side was affected this way)—the right side of their face, right ear, right shoulder and arm, and their right leg—either manifesting pain or numbness throughout their right side. The right hand or right side is an image represents STRENGTH in Scripture (Psalm 18:35, 20:6, 110:1, 138:7, etc.). Many were healed of this condition when they confessed giving their strength—the best of their food, money, gifts—to the idols (The Lord led me to Deuteronomy 32:36-38 to explain this). Others were healed when they confessed bitterness and unforgiveness toward family members or co-workers.

Simon, a leader in the Tainan church, had numbness in the right side of his face, pain in his right forehead and right ear, and numbness in his right shoulder and arm. The Holy Spirit showed me it was a spirit of infirmity that had entered him 7 years ago through his anger at co-workers. When he forgave them for what they did to him, the numbness left his entire right side except for around his right eye. Then the Lord told me that he need to confess "the angry look of his eye at his coworkers." As soon as he confessed his anger, the spirit left his right eye, and he was completely healed!

Pastor Mike of a Baptist church north of Tainan agreed to let me and a prayer team pray over him in front of the conference to demonstrate inner healing prayer. He said he felt emotionally "locked up." When we asked Jesus to take him back to the source and origin of these feelings, Jesus brought memories to mind of his father losing him in a crowded market when he was a young boy and a memory of being publicly humiliated by his grandfather and forced to bow to the family idols. When we asked Jesus to come into each memory, Jesus took him by the hand and brought him back to his parents. In the second memory, Jesus pushed the idol away and put Himself in its place, so that Mike was bowing to Jesus. Jesus also spoke powerful words of truth to Mike in these memories. PRAISE THE LORD, ALL THE INNER WOUNDS LOCKING MIKE UP WERE HEALED and Mike felt A PHYSICAL RELEASE IN HIS BODY from the Holy Spirit and EMOTIONAL RELEASE TOO!

SUNDAY 4/2

The Lord told me to preach on the "prayer of faith" of James 5:14-18 and how, based on the example of Elijah in 1 Kings 17-18, it means hearing from the Lord what He says to pray and praying that in for the sick person till there is healing.

During group prayer ministry and individual prayer ministry, several people were healed of back-shoulder-neck pain and congestion conditions after I led them in a group prayer renouncing and confessing idolatry in their lives and their ancestors lives. One older woman who had 50% loss of vision in both eyes and saw everything in a fuzzy haze was completely healed and saw everything perfectly clear after a couple of minutes of prayer (like in Mark 8:22-26). Another woman's hearing in her left ear, which had been damaged by radiation therapy for cancer, was completely healed and could hear again normally out of that ear. Several people with swollen joints in their hands were healed of the pain and swelling. A medical doctor and his wife received complete healing only after they gave their burdens to the Lord and gave the Lord anxiety and fear about their children. An older woman who was diagnosed with a tumor in her breast, that was probably cancerous, asked for prayer. The Lord told me to have her confess rebellion against authority in her life and her parents' lives, and after she did, she felt the tumor begin to shrink under the power of the Holy Spirit. PRAISE THE LORD!

MONDAY 4/3

We had the people break into pairs to pray inner healing prayer for one another according to the biblical principles we had been teaching and modeling through the conference. The Lord was touching and healing deep wounds in many as they prayed in pairs.

Through inner healing it was easy for most people to get free of demonic spirits. One woman, though, who was a recent convert was praying with her partner through a painful memory, when the spirits in her manifested and caused her to be thrown from her chair and slide across the floor shouting in Chinese, "Jesus I hate you, Jesus I hate you!" We took her into a back room and continued to minister to her. The demons continued to manifest, and as we commanded them to be quiet, it became clear that there were still footholds in her life empowering the demons and that the demons were making noise and confusion to keep us from hearing the Lord and finding out the footholds so this woman could get free of them. I had to step out of the room before I could hear the Lord say, "She needs to renounce being dedicated to the idols

313

at birth and ask Me to forgive her sin and her family's sin of idolatry." When she did this the spirits grip on her was broken and she came out of the back room virtually normal again. PRAISE THE LORD!

The Lord touched and healed many others through the prayer teams' ministry. One man with an irregularly functioning right valve in his heart felt the Holy Spirit heal the valve as we prayed over him. God was so eager to heal and deliver people, it was stunning! GOD IS SO GOOD!

4/4 TUESDAY-4/8 SATURDAY—TAICHUNG (MID-WESTERN TAIWAN), DAYBREAK CHRISTIAN WORSHIP CENTER, APOSTOLIC LEADER PAUL CHU, PASTORS BARNABAS and LYDIA

I taught the Biblical Foundations of Strategic Prayer and Spiritual Warfare, and the goal of my teaching and ministry was not just to pray for them but to TRAIN THEM to pray strategically for their neighborhoods and cities. Between 100 and 150 Intercession leaders came from churches all over Taiwan for this conference.

4/4 TUESDAY

During the ministry time the Lord healed about 18 people of neck-shoulder-back pain that most had had all their lives after they renounced being dedicated to the idols at birth and confessed the sin of idolatry in their past and their ancestors lives. About 6 or 7 people, who responded to a word from the Lord, were healed of chronic pain in their heels. 3 people were healed of problems with the nose and sinuses.

4/5 WEDNESDAY

We were led by the Taiwan National Prayer Network leader, Joy Chiung Lin, on a prayer-walk around the earliest temple in Taiwan, the 17 century temple to the goddess

Matsu, called "the Queen of Heaven" over Taiwan. When the National Prayer Network prayer-walked two other buildings in Northeast Taiwan and Northwest Taiwan that were dedicated as places of worshiping the idols, one building sank about 12 inches into the ground and became unusable, and the other building was destroyed by a Typhoon. So we will see what happens to this temple!

During the ministry sessions, the Lord healed several people of pain in the joints of their hands, several others of stomach infections and one of an ulcer. About 3 or 4 people were healed of conditions on the right side of their bodies which were caused by spirits of infirmity. One young woman was healed of chronic pain in her right shoulder, her right arm, and a bone fracture in her right foot when she confessed idolatry in her family line. Another woman was healed of numbness on the right side of her body, when she forgave her two brothers for speaking abusively to her. At first, when the Lord showed us she need to forgive her brothers, she could not think of anything to forgive them for. Then the Lord gave me a vision of her brothers speaking abusively to her. She wept as she forgave them for several minutes, and afterward was completely healed!

The needs of the people were so deep. The Lord told me that someone there felt like a tight metal band around their head, and a young man responded and told us his mother had beaten him in his head constantly. He received some healing, but needed much more deep level healing.

4/6 THURSDAY

The Lord told us to loose His anointing of revelation and hearing God's voice on the people praying in pairs for one another after the teaching. As we went and prayed over each pair, many experienced higher levels of revelation from the Lord as they prayed for each other. Taiwanese are very conservative culturally, so it was surprising to see several break out under the power of the Spirit into laughter, weeping, and moaning as the Holy Spirit touched and anointed them.

We prayed with pastors and leaders in private sessions for inner healing. Several had dramatic deliverance experiences of demons leaving them, as the Lord healed the past wounds in their hearts to which the demons were attached in their lives.

4/7 FRIDAY

The needs of the people were so great that they asked us to commit the evening session to just praying for anyone who wanted ministry. I was amazed to see that 100-150 people stayed into the wee hours of the next morning just to receive prayer from me and the other pastors praying with me. We prayed for 8 hours straight from 8:30 p.m. to 4:30 am the next morning. I barely had time to shower and get to the airport that morning!

God was so good, His healing presence was strong through the night and early morning. Two people were healed of carpal tunnel pain in their lower arms. One of them, Joyce, an accountant had had the pain for over a year. One woman was healed of jaundice and a related liver problem.

We prayed with a Lutheran pastor and his wife who came up for prayer. She was exhausted. It seemed that every pastor's wife I saw was working constantly and exhausted. The Lord told us to pray for her that she would rest in His presence daily at least 1/2 hour, and that she would have the determination to say "no" to other things and people to do so.

A woman who is a school teacher came up for prayer for an irregular heart beat (upwards of 170 beats per minute at times) and for a life-long feeling of loneliness. Jesus took her back to a memory of she and her mother daily walking through a cemetery, where her mother told her as a little girl that she needed to take care of her mother because her mother was fearful. Parents are supposed to take care of their children, not the reverse! When this woman forgave her mother for putting a false responsibility on her, Jesus' radiant presence came into the memory and healed all the pain in this woman's heart that was controlling her and manifesting as loneliness. The Lord also powerfully healed her heart!

Another young woman, who was an export trade representative for a Taiwanese company, said she constantly fought fearfulness and a desire to run from God. When we asked the Lord to take her to the source and origin—the root—of these strongholds, he brought to her the memory that she was kidnapped as a baby. When she forgave the kidnapers, and we asked Jesus to come into the memory, she saw Jesus take her as a baby away from the kidnapers and hold her tightly, protecting her. The Lord freed her from the spirit of fear and the spirit of alienation by healing her memory of this trauma through which these demons entered her life. PRAISE THE LORD!

A young man with an infected right knee that was swollen and painful asked us to pray for him. He had had the infection for 7 days, so we asked him what else was happening in his life 7 days ago. He couldn't think of anything right away, but he finally mentioned that though he was a Christian, he had worshiped his ancestors with his family 7 days ago, which was a national holiday to worship and honor family ancestral spirits. We explained to him that he had violated the first commandment, "You shall have no other gods before Me" (Exodus 20:2-3). When he confessed this to the Lord and we prayed for his knee, the swelling was reduced about 30-40% and all the pain of the infection left his knee!

Many people waited all night to be prayed for, the needs were so deep and pressing.

The Lord told me that the needs in the U.S. Church are just as deep, but the needs are hidden by us and from us. God help us get them out into His light so that He can set us free and heal us, especially the leaders (John 3:19-21)!

THANK YOU SO MUCH FOR YOUR PRAYERS!! We could not have seen such an outpouring from God without your prayers for us.

BIBLIOGRAPHY

Additional related resources by Mark & Patti Virkler

Communion with God

Dialogue with God

Counseled by God textbook

Counseled by God workbook

Wading Deeper in the River of God

The Great Mystery

Sense Your Spirit

Naturally Supernatural

Biblical Research Concerning Dreams and Visions workbook

Biblical Research Concerning Dreams and Visions Teacher's Guide

Developing Heart Faith

Spirit Born Creativity

How Do You Know?

Divine Authority, Divine Power, Divine Energy

These and many other materials can be ordered from the Communion with God Ministries website, located at:

www.cwgministries.org

Mark Virkler is available to conduct seminars on this and other topics, and can be reached via e-mail at:

mark@cwgministries.org

or by phone:

800-466-6961 • 716-652-6990

Additional resources by others

Restoring the Foundations by Chester and Betsy Kylstra

Ministry Tools for Restoring the Foundations by Chester and Betsy Kylstra

The Transformation of the Inner Man by John and Paula Sandford

Healing Through Deliverance Volumes 1 & 2 by Peter Horrobin

Can a Christian Have a Demon? by Don Basham

Theophostic Counseling by Ed M. Smith (This book is not available on the open market, so contact him at phostic@eagleweb.net or telephone 888-467-3757.)

Breaking Unhealthy Soul Ties by Bill and Sue Banks

Pigs in the Parlor by Frank and Ida Mae Hammond

Blessing or Curse by Derek Prince

Dreams, Wisdom Within by Herman Riffel

Emotionally Free by Rita Bennett

Healing for Damaged Emotions by David Seamands

Healing of Memories by David Seamands

Three Crucial Questions about Spiritual Warfare by Clinton E. Arnold

If you enjoyed this book,
check out these other **Bridge-Logos** books
by Mark and Patti Virkler

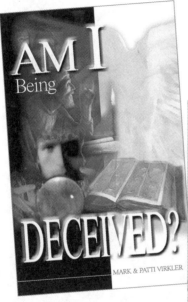

Am I Being Deceived?

Dialogue with God